ROON

18

ROONEY
TEENAGE KICKS

This book is dedicated to Daniel Burdett.

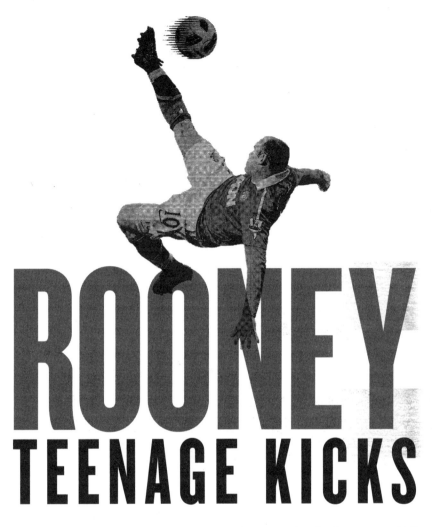

ROONEY
TEENAGE KICKS

The street footballer who ruled the world

BY WAYNE BARTON

Reach Sport

Reach **Sport**

www.reachsport.com

Published in Great Britain and Ireland in 2022 by
Reach Sport, a Reach PLC business,
5 St Paul's Square, Liverpool, L3 9SJ.

www.reachsport.com
@Reach_Sport

Reach Sport is a part of Reach PLC.
One Canada Square, Canary Wharf, London, E15 5AP.

Hardback ISBN: 9781914197338
eBook ISBN: 9781914197345

Photographic acknowledgements:
Alamy, Mirrorpix, Liverpool Echo.
Every effort has been made to trace the copyright.
Any oversight will be rectified in future editions.

Design and production by Reach Sport.
Edited by: Simon Monk
Cover design: Chris Collins
Production: Adam Oldfield

Printed and bound by CPI Group (UK) Ltd,
Croydon, CR0 4YY.

CONTENTS

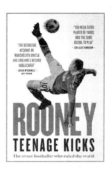

*Wayne pictured alongside Everton idol Duncan Ferguson and brothers
John (left) and Graham in 1997, and below with mother Jeanette*

Chapter One

ONCE
A BLUE

R emember the name. So said Clive Tyldesley on October 19th, 2002, when 16-year-old Wayne Rooney cemented his place in history with a 30-yard thunderbolt past one of the best goalkeepers in the country, ending the long unbeaten run of the reigning English league champions.

In fact, many people around the country were already aware of the name. He was English football's, and Everton's, worst-kept secret.

Wayne Mark Rooney was born on October 24th, 1985, to parents Jeanette and Wayne senior. Two years later, a brother, Graham, followed. And three years after that, in December 1990, John was born to make it three Rooney boys. The Rooneys were proud and Jeanette, in particular, was a mother who ensured everything was kept. School records going back to the infants school, Stonebridge Lane. Then the primary school of Our Lady and St Swithin's, and finally the secondary school of De La Salle.

By the time he was moving into 'big' school, the local football community in Croxteth was already abuzz about the talent of the eldest Rooney boy.

There are a couple of places that lay claim to being the spiritual home of football. You think of Brazil, and the mind transports you to dusty streets and joyous games. You think of hard surfaces and balls fashioned from materials other than balloon and leather. It's a romantic thought because the imagery Brazilian football projects is sheer happiness, often drenched in brilliant yellows and orange.

The early stages of football in England, and particularly the north west, is closer in comparison than distance. Yes, the British version is dour grey, but the principle of the game being something that even the poorest children can enjoy is shared. It helps to cultivate that idea of it being a universal sport rather than something for the elite.

First, you need a football. The ball acts as a social magnet. You can use a driveway or two conveniently placed concrete garden poles to create a goal. Or big stones. Trees. Jumpers for goalposts. If you're lucky you might have a playing field or a five-a-side pitch. Luckier still, there might be some goals and a marked pitch. It was a rare treat indeed to find a goal with netting.

You might be encouraged to play at a young age. You'll be sent on trials to youth clubs, social clubs, pub teams. Hopefully you'll get picked for your school team. Maybe your county team. And, on the rare occasions that professional clubs hold open trials for young kids, local pitches will be over-subscribed with children anxious to impress.

This was an ordinary system throughout most of the United Kingdom.

Wayne Rooney went through this system.

But he was no ordinary player.

Wayne played whenever and wherever he could as a young boy. His first taste of organised football came as a nine-year-old, playing for Copplehouse Colts under-11s – a team based up the road from Croxteth in Fazakerley.

At one of these games, scouts from Liverpool and Everton were present. Both Merseyside clubs were in something of a decline since the halcyon days of the 1980s. Liverpool were stuttering following their imperious period of domination. Everton's decline from their title-winning sides of 1985 and 1987 was even more pronounced, with a battle against relegation in 1994 that was only turned around in dramatic fashion on the final day.

Wayne Rooney was born into an Everton-supporting family. In the grand scheme of the football pyramid, he was pretty lucky. In the closer context, he was not, because even with Everton's greatest days coming so recently, they still did not have the historical success of their closest rivals. These things matter more when you're older but not when you're eight or nine. When you are a child then Saturdays are about going to the game with family. Those players will be your heroes. Duncan Ferguson was Wayne Rooney's hero because the powerful Scottish striker scored goals and made his team a serious threat to any opponent. Shortly after his arrival, Ferguson scored the winning goal in a game against the champions, Manchester United.

It was around that time that Rooney was playing for Copplehouse. The watching Liverpool scout was impressed enough to ask Wayne's father if the boy could go for a trial. Allegiances are a funny thing. They can be compromised so long as the loyalty you're displaying is for the betterment of another. Liverpool were still one of the best clubs in the country and were renowned for bringing through young players at their Melwood complex. Robbie Fowler was one of the finest young strikers in the league,

Steve McManaman one of the best young English wingers. It was an opportunity that could not reasonably be missed, so Wayne senior agreed – and yet *had to* send his son wearing his Everton kit to the trial.

The youngster was invited back the following week. "In the meantime, my dad received a phone call from Bob Pendleton, the Everton scout who had seen me play for Copplehouse," Rooney recalled in his book *My Story So Far*. "Everton also wanted me to attend a trial – but it was the same evening as my second Liverpool trial. Despite that, I went to Bellefield rather than Liverpool. That was that. Once Everton had appeared interested there was no choice to be had. Dad came with me on the bus, secretly hoping to meet Joe Royle, the then Everton manager.

"I loved everything about it: the people, the coaches and the atmosphere. There were loads of other kids, like me, who had turned up in their Everton shirts. Liverpool had probably been just as good to me and I felt my trial with them had gone well. But, being all emotional about Everton, I decided they were so much better and I felt more at home with them. The club asked my dad there and then if I would sign schoolboy forms. Of course, we said yes. Had Liverpool asked me to sign first, then I'm not sure I would have signed for them. I think their system was to ask you along to several trials before deciding. Or perhaps they simply weren't sure about me."

Pendleton, on the other hand, was sure. He was a regular watching the Copplehouse juniors on Long Lane in Aintree.

"Copplehouse had done nothing in the first half of the season but when he signed for them, Jesus…" Pendleton told the *Belfast Telegraph* in 2015. "Jimmy Greaves passed the ball into the back of the net and so did Wayne. The scores would be about 7-0 and nine times out of 10 he scored four or five of them. He got the reputation as being a beast in front of goal. There was a vibe going round Liverpool about him. Different lads used to say, 'Have you got Rooney yet, Bob?'"

Pendleton elaborated in an interview with the BBC in 2017: "I was there every week for more than 35 years. On one particular Sunday, I had to amble over to Copplehouse Boys, who Wayne was playing for at under-11s – two years early. He lashed a goal in from 20 yards and dribbled for fun, passing the ball into the net. So small yet so strong, he'd demand the ball back if he ever needed to pass it.

"I've followed Everton since 1948 week in, week out, and ended up scouting for the club. Of all those years, this day would be one of the most important. A chat with Wayne's parents revealed they were Evertonians. His dad had great humour and, naturally, was elated. We agreed young Wayne would come into Bellefield on the Thursday. Wayne had already been in to train with Liverpool, and I heard they were going to try and speak to him on the Tuesday, two days before his visit to Everton. So we moved the Bellefield trip forward 48 hours.

"You can take kids to Bellefield and they go stiff with nerves. Not Wayne, he was unmoved. He was picking up stray balls and slamming them into the net. I spoke to Ray Hall – who was in charge of the club's youth set-up – and said: 'You have to sign him.' I was fearful Liverpool would try again and I was so determined to get this done. Joe Royle was called into the office. I can see it now. Wayne, again unmoved, was sliding down his chair almost under the table.

"'Sit up straight,' muttered his dad, who was thrilled to speak to Joe. All credit to Ray for trusting me. Yet in that office, on that key night, Wayne was the same as he always was at that age. Shy, and distracted by anything shaped like a ball. But, let's be clear, that shyness evaporated when he walked onto any pitch."

Everton's offer was a place at their Centre of Excellence for the following season, where Wayne would train three times a week, on Mondays, Wednesdays and Fridays after school with games on a Sunday morning.

The feeling of excitement was heightened by Everton's victory in the FA Cup a few weeks after Rooney had been invited to join. Everton suddenly once more looked to have a team befitting of the club's size and their win over Manchester United in the final was followed by the acquisition of one of the best players at Old Trafford. The signing of Andrei Kanchelskis was a power move and there was every reason to believe that Everton could show that their FA Cup success was just the start of a successful period.

Rooney had impressed playing two age levels up but he was placed into his own age category at the start of his time in the Centre of Excellence. It was obvious from the first minute that Everton had something special on their hands. His first game was actually for the under-11s – and he scored a hat-trick in a win over St Helens. When he moved into his own age the quality was evident. A hat-trick against Bury, six goals against Chester, nine goals against Preston. Hat-tricks against Leeds and Nottingham Forest.

Manchester United took their under-10 side to Bellefield in the autumn. Rooney had scored 31 goals in eight games but had something extra-special for this occasion.

"Something happened in that game I'll never forget," Everton youth coach Ray Hall said in 2009. "It was the first sign of appreciating we had something different. There were about 150-200 parents on one side of the field and the coaches from Manchester United and Everton on the other side. Eight against eight. The ball comes across about head height. I looked at Wayne thinking he would head it, but he made a bicycle kick that went straight into the goal. There was a complete silence because no-one had seen anything like that before from a nine-year-old. One person clapped and then everybody started to applaud. The United coach looked to me as if to say 'What have we just seen?'"

Rooney's talent was extraordinary. Physically, he was a little smaller than the boys his own age. After what he did against United, he was given a couple of games in the under-11s – but whereas the overhead kick had been one of six in a 12-2 win, his two goals against Liverpool at the higher age level came in a 6-2 loss. The following week he got revenge with two goals against the same rivals in a 4-3 win, but with some concern that it might be too much, too soon, he was moved back into his own age group.

At such a young age, Everton were confident he would grow, and wanted to test his talent. In addition to the three games for the under-11s, Wayne struck 107 times in 26 games in his first year, and was duly pushed into the under-12s for the following season rather than the under-11s.

At first-team level, Everton had finished a creditable sixth in the league, while Duncan Ferguson had been convicted of assault for an incident that had happened when he was playing for Glasgow Rangers, and in October 1995 he was sentenced to three months' imprisonment. Rooney, devastated for his hero, wrote to him a few times while he was in jail, and was thrilled to receive a response.

Wayne's talent had encouraged the club to take brothers Graham and John into their academy, while Wayne was delighted to be a ball boy for the senior games for a couple of years. He had already upset Neville Southall on his very first outing as a ball boy when the goalkeeper barked at him to 'Fucking hurry up'; and antagonised the legendary stopper further still when he was named mascot for the Merseyside derby at Anfield in 1996. The mascots were allowed to take shots at the goalkeeper in the warm-up and Rooney practised all week for the big one-on-one.

Watching these processions as a spectator can be a heartwarming affair, as you laugh with sympathy while the youngster's kick usually isn't strong enough to even reach the six-yard box, much less test the goalkeeper. Already capable of scoring from range, twice Rooney chipped Southall successfully – one time scoring, one time hitting the crossbar.

"Playing with him as a kid was brilliant," says Scott Brown, a forward who came through the Everton youth structure with Rooney. "He was technically on another level. He could get the ball and score from anywhere. I signed for Everton when I was nine. I was a year above Wayne. Right from the start I remember there being talk about this kid in the age group below and he was breaking all kinds of records. Within a year he was with us in our group.

"As a lad he was brilliant. A raw kid, he was funny, a bit naughty. He was always playing football on the streets with his mates in Croxteth. It was a rough area and I remember him coming in with cuts and bruises from fighting. But he had so much ability, and he could look after himself – his cousin was into boxing, so he would go along with him, and when he was on a football pitch with older lads he wasn't afraid. When he was younger he was very skinny and small. The shirts were baggy. But as soon as he came up against a centre-half he was straight into them to let them know he was there. He loved the physical competition."

Rooney adjusted to the higher level with some comfort. There was never any question about his ability – Everton pondered pushing him an extra year in front. But at the age of 13, he began to have issues with a new coach at the club. Now he was being instructed to defend and didn't want to do it; after answering back to the coach, Wayne was dropped. "I was unhappy for most of the season because of him," Rooney later admitted. "I was convinced he didn't like me."

The problem became so extreme that Wayne confessed to his mother he didn't want to play anymore. Wayne senior spoke to the coach and, instead of siding with his son, told the youngster that he had to listen because it was for his own good if he wanted to make it as a professional. After that strong advice, Wayne decided to stick at it.

"It looked as if Wayne might go to another club," Scott Brown recalls. "All the big clubs were looking at him. The club must have convinced him to stay. I remember it all being in the build-up to a game we played against Blackburn – he scored a hat-trick in the first 10 minutes or something and after the game we were wondering what all the fuss was about."

Rooney felt that it was during this time he started to develop a bad temper. He would argue on the pitch and if he was given any physical treatment, his retaliation was often over the top. However, Rooney's potential was now seemingly so special that it was worth the club putting in the extra hours.

"At the time you just think this is Wayne, our mate who's scoring loads of goals and we're winning every game, so it was class," Brown says. "You're enjoying the experience and not thinking that you're playing with someone who could be the best in England. So many times he could score goals that were so good that we'd be asking him how he did it. He'd shrug and say he didn't know. He became prolific. He was scoring so many goals. I remember Ray Hall asking him, 'What do you see when you're in the box?' Wayne answered that it seemed like everything slowed down for him, and the goal became two times bigger. That was his answer for scoring so many goals."

When there was the need for a positive role model, it came in the form of Colin Harvey. Harvey was a club legend, nicknamed 'the White Pele' by Everton supporters – from 1963 to 1974, he played over 300 times for the club, and then later managed them for a three-year spell before returning as youth team coach. Harvey was one of a dying breed of coaches still schooled in the old-school physicality of the game.

"There were people who didn't like Colin Harvey and those who loved him," says Brown. "Wayne and I loved him. He was hard, sometimes brutal, but he was just getting us ready for what football was like. As a coach he taught us many life lessons. And because we were both Evertonians, and Colin is a god at the club, we worshipped what he said."

Rooney's acceleration through the ranks continued. When he was 14, he was playing with the under-16s. "I remember the first time I encountered him, when I was 16 and playing for Crewe," remembers Mark Roberts. "We were playing at Bellefield. I usually played against a lad called Michael Symes but on this occasion there was this small 14-year-old in a shirt that looked too big for him." Roberts was on his guard immediately.

"He was obviously there for a reason, because the coaches believed he was good enough. And he was. Despite his size he was there to compete, but what was most impressive was the instinct to score. He was there and then he was gone. We won 2-1 but I remember coming off the pitch worried that I was going to get criticised. It was the kid I was marking who scored and he was much younger. Then our coach told me I shouldn't be too upset – Rooney had been called up to the England youth set-up, and he was seen as something very special."

Crewe had their own renowned set-up, but even they could not compete with the legendary production coming out of Old Trafford – which was prolific at the best of times but at its peak in the 1990s. The Class of 92 had graduated to become the most successful team in the country with the likes of David Beckham and Ryan Giggs starring. United were traditional standard-bearers of quality at youth level.

Phil Marsh was a striker in the United youth team, and a year younger than Rooney. "I remember playing against him for the under-14s and under-15s and I can remember the buzz around him," Marsh says. "His physicality was immense. He was running past players as if they weren't there. He was good with both feet, his touch was good and you could see that he should already be playing two or three years above this level. You're at United which is meant to be the benchmark but there are players around the country who get a lot of rave reviews.

"So you hear that Wayne scores a hat-trick yet again and because you're at United, you're thinking, that's the benchmark. That's the level I need to reach every week. We need to make sure our performances and progression are matching what is being talked about elsewhere. Wayne was that much more physically developed, he was bigger, he was broader, he was stronger. Technically he was excellent. With all due respect it already felt as if he shouldn't be at a club like Everton because he was so good."

From the age of 14, Rooney had a growth spurt. His physical strength took a considerable step forward. In November 2000 he was called up to play for the England under-15 team in the Victory Shield against Wales live on Sky Sports; he came on for the last 30 minutes and was named man-of-the-match. At that level he played a handful of times over the next few months, scoring against Scotland and Canada.

"His style didn't change but his confidence grew as his body did," Brown says. "When he was 15 and 16 he grew so much that it was like he turned into a man. We had the summer off and he went into training every day. On the first day of pre-season he was so much bigger and stronger. And he had the confidence to go up against anybody. We started training with the first team and he was going up against them like they were the kids. We're talking about David Weir, Joseph Yobo, Alan Stubbs, Alessandro Pistone. Some of the top players in the country, so much experience. He was bullying them."

The 2001/02 season was significant for Wayne's progression. Although he was not bound by contract to Everton, there had been an incident where Wolves had expressed an interest, and Wayne senior had to go on record to explain exactly what happened. It seemed to expedite the agreement of a 'pre-contract' which was unusual in itself – an announcement was made at half-time during Everton's home game with Derby County in December 2001.

A crowd of almost 40,000 at Goodison watched as the youngster put pen to paper. It was likely that some of the players on the pitch that afternoon had been watching Rooney in the mornings that season. "We played at Bellefield and when the buzz around him was gathering momentum, we noticed more of the first-team players coming to watch us before their game later in the day," Brown says. "There were definitely more as Wayne's reputation grew because they knew how special he was. It was incredible for us all.

"From the age of 15, when we started playing in the Youth Cup, he seemed to move to another level. He stole the show. It seemed like this was his platform to show everybody what he was all about, and he just seemed to grow. He carried us all the way to the final. We just had to give him the ball and it would be game over. He was head and shoulders above everyone."

Rooney was in his last year at school. De La Salle agreed to Everton's request to allow him three days a week off school so he could train full-time. The club's intention was even greater than that – they wanted him fast-tracked into the first team.

Walter Smith was now manager of the club, and his assistant was Archie Knox; Knox had been Alex Ferguson's assistant manager at Aberdeen and Manchester United. He had observed the very early years of the FA Youth Cup-winning side of 1992 and felt sure that Rooney was of that calibre.

"I've only seen two players in my entire life that at 14 years of age you would put money on to be top players – Rooney and Giggs," Knox said in his autobiography *The School of Hard Knox*. "All the rest, even Scholes, Butt, Beckham, the Nevilles, you wouldn't have known for sure. We tried to get permission from the FA to play Rooney in Everton's first team when he was 15. He was that good. He could easily have coped in the Premier League at that age. We didn't get the permission."

At the turn of the year, Smith's tenure was close to the end with the first team struggling. There was no time for the gamble of putting a schoolboy into the team, even with a goalscoring problem that saw the Toffees slip to five consecutive defeats, four of them without scoring. The senior side could well have done with the explosive impact of Wayne Rooney – it was inevitable, and it was imminent.

Chapter Two

HELLO

Before Wayne Rooney, there were plenty of others making their way through the Everton production line and into the first team. Before Wayne Rooney, there was Nick Chadwick. Chadwick and Scott Brown were Everton's goal-getters in the doomed FA Youth Cup campaign of 2000/01. Chadwick scored in the third round tie with Nottingham Forest that ended 1-1; both scored in the replay. The following year he was scoring plenty of goals in the reserves, and so if Walter Smith was going to call on any rookie, it would have most likely been him.

"I was doing quite well as a young player," Chadwick says. "I'd been there since I was 11. I was scoring a few goals and progressing well and started to get some fan mail. I got a letter from someone in Zimbabwe when I was 13 or 14. He wrote to say how brilliant it was that I was scoring goals for Everton's youth team. He went on to say he'd heard all about this phenomenal talent called Wayne Rooney who was 10! That was the first time I'd ever heard his name. It was bizarre. At the time I was concentrating on my own journey. It was competitive and your ambition is to keep your name on the lips of people.

"The first time I saw him up close was when he was coming in as a 15-year-old, probably on his school holidays, and training around the first team. I went to every one of the Youth Cup games. He was playing up a couple of years and had this incredible impact. It was the first time within the club that the attention got really serious. There was also a lot of attention from outside the club."

The physical strength Rooney had developed in the summer of 2001 helped him stand out. He had a robustness rarely seen in 15-year-olds that made it difficult for centre-halves two or three years older to handle. He had made appearances in Everton's FA Youth Cup team since the age of 14 but this growth made a significant difference. In January, Rooney struck both of his team's goals in the fourth-round tie with West Brom. Two more were scored against Manchester City in the next round.

On February 16th, Everton's academy team headed to Crewe to take on the under-19s. Rooney would renew acquaintances with Mark Roberts. "He had grown, noticeably," Roberts says, "and not just as a lad but in presence. We were the home team and he came and acted like this was his pitch. He was in a fiery mood. Flying into tackles. He went in late on me and was booked. At that level, referees rarely took that sort of action, so it was clear they were trying to calm him down. But it was the authority with which he conducted himself that stood out. The way he seemed to be bossing lads who were two years older. Telling his own teammates what they needed to be doing.

"I hadn't seen anything like it. He came into another tackle on me and his studs got my shin pads. The referee was reluctant to send him off but the Everton coaching staff made the decision. They weren't happy with him. They made him do laps of the whole thing until the game ended."

Scott Brown remembers the incident well. "We were tiny in comparison to some of the lads when we were playing up a level," he said. "I remember playing Crewe away, their under-19 side, and Colin Harvey put us both in the game. Wayne went into this tackle on a kid almost knee-high. Colin made him run around the whole complex until the game had finished! He was capable of those mad moments but more often than not he'd score these incredible goals. It was a style that seemed to be there for the first few years of his career."

In the Youth Cup, Rooney continued to lead by example. He scored in a 2-1 win over Nottingham Forest to send his team through to the semi-final against Tottenham Hotspur. A tight first leg was won 2-1 by Everton – for once Rooney was not among the goals, although he was the man of the match. But it was his performance at White Hart Lane which propelled the momentum into overdrive.

On the evening of the return game, a Spurs supporters' event was held on Paxton Road where David Pleat informed fans that Wayne Rooney was rated so highly that Sir Alex Ferguson at Manchester United was keen on him. He warned the home fans that if they were able to make it to White Hart Lane, they may only see the 16-year-old knock them out. Pleat had history for making such proclamations – when he was manager of Luton in 1992, he told reporters that it was the youth team and not the first team at Manchester United that people should be concentrating on. Rooney duly scored twice in the first half to give his team a commanding aggregate lead.

His first goal was exceptional; he received the ball with his back to goal, flicked it over the defender's head and finished with the composure of a veteran. His second was just as good. Just before half-time, Everton were awarded a free-kick almost 40 yards from goal. Rooney, full of confidence, stepped up to take it. The shot ricocheted off the wall back to him. As it was bouncing, Rooney set himself. His half-volley from 35 yards flew into the net and was still rising. It was a remarkable shot.

"That run really helped me to believe in myself," Rooney told the *Evertonian* magazine. "I thought I was invincible... I was absolutely bubbling over with confidence and all the things I tried just seemed to come off."

By now, Walter Smith had been replaced by David Moyes, who soon turned to one of the undoubted success stories of the Smith reign – the youth set-up. "As soon as David came in he wanted a youthful team that supporters could connect with," Chadwick says. "I was a benefactor of that because I'd been scoring goals in the reserve team."

Chadwick's promotion meant there was a space in the reserve team. Rooney made his reserves debut against Sunderland on April 9th, and a week later he scored against Southport in the Liverpool Senior Cup semi-final. It was another stunning strike, this time from a near-impossible angle. He was playing alongside the veteran Kevin Campbell and both were brought off at half-time with their job done.

In the first month of David Moyes' reign, Rooney's statements at lower levels meant that there was a growing demand for him to be given a chance. Next up were Manchester United's reserves on April 18th.

"It was one of our first games at that level," Scott Brown, who had enjoyed his own promotion, recalls. "They had David May and a few who'd played for the first team. Wayne was nutmegging everyone. David May was bouncing off him. They couldn't get anywhere near him. I could hear the United lads talking about Wayne as they came off. I'm sure they were already trying to get the word to Fergie. It was enough to get him on the first-team trip to Southampton, and he was put on the bench. All the fans were egging David Moyes to put him on. He never did, but it was obvious that Wayne couldn't be held back."

Moyes would perhaps have been forgiven for holding back, particularly with the first team game only two days away, but decided to include Rooney on the trip. "Wayne is travelling to Southampton with us – it will be a good experience for him," Moyes said, before adding, "We are trying to look after him and protect him."

Rooney didn't get on. But Moyes told the youngster not to be disheartened – the plan was to bring him on in Everton's next home game, against Blackburn, so that he could not only break Joe Royle's record as the club's youngest ever player but do it in front of his own fans. Instead, Rooney was selected for the England under-17s to play in the European Championship and immediately went to Denmark. "I didn't really want to go as I wanted to make my first-team debut for Everton," Rooney admitted. "It was a shame the two things coincided."

The boy was flying. His form continued for his international team. "Wayne and I played for England all the way through the age groups," Brown says. "The level didn't faze him. He played exactly the same. We went to the championships that summer and he scored this goal against Holland where they seemed terrified of him and he blasted it into the corner. He was fearless. Part of going to those tournaments is experiencing how different teams play but Wayne was just himself."

The tournament ended in bittersweet fashion. England were

dumped out in the semi-finals by a strong Switzerland team but in the third-place play-off Rooney scored a hat-trick against Spain to emphatically confirm how much he deserved the award for best player of the tournament – while his goal against Holland was arguably the best goal, too.

It was not quite time for the summer break. Rooney was back, four days after that hat-trick, to play in his team's Youth Cup final first leg against Aston Villa. 15,000 turned up at Goodison to see the Rooney spectacle and he didn't disappoint; scoring after 25 minutes and then revealing a message on the vest under his shirt: 'Once a Blue, Always a Blue'.

It seemed as if too many of the Everton youngsters presumed Rooney alone could carry them to victory – they were given a harsh lesson when Villa responded with four goals to claim an unassailable advantage ahead of the second leg.

This disappointment was only temporary. Still only 16, Rooney returned for the following season in the first-team plans, and he had prepared accordingly.

"Wayne came back for the next season and he looked like he belonged in the first team, so it wasn't a surprise that he started playing," recalls Brown. "When you're watching a lad who you've played alongside, come through and play for the club you both love, it's mad. I was made up for him and I had nothing but admiration. I'd have loved it to be me, obviously, but he had just moved to a completely different level and I was buzzing for him."

While there was a tremendous level of excitement around the club, that situation came at a cost. "I scored in a couple of games and felt like I was progressing really well," says Nick Chadwick. "I look back now about getting injured and how Wayne came in and there was no way back for me from that. I didn't have his talent. But at the time I just thought it was brilliant we had a manager giving us all a chance, we were all buzzing to be seen as part of an Everton team who were moving in the right direction. My approach at the time was that it would last forever and we'd all be part of the squad, Wayne would come in and we'd be part of that success together. It was so unrealistic to believe two academy lads could lead the line for Everton, but at the time it's just not in your psyche."

Rooney's adjustment to training with the first team on a permanent basis was smooth. His natural ability, and naive immaturity, had many warming to him.

"He started training with us regularly," says Chadwick. "I'm not sure how much he did on a daily basis with the young players because he moved into the group of youngsters who were with the senior players. Me, Leon Osman, Tony Hibbert, Kevin McLeod and Peter Clarke. The rest of us had to earn our stripes, coming through the young pros' dressing room for a year or two before getting in the first-team dressing room. Wayne almost immediately went straight into that set-up. The senior players recognised what a very special talent he was… me, Tony and the others had to go through the process of being tea boys to earn the respect of those experienced players, who were brilliant, by the way. Wayne bypassed that with the reputation of being a superstar.

"He was shy. He was only 16. But I didn't sense any real nervousness. He had that Scouse cocksure type of attitude and confidence, he wasn't fazed by it and knew he belonged there. At the same time he was still one of us, one of the youngsters who wanted to belong. But he was still immature, still a boy. He'd go off with his mates and come into training telling us tales of the things he'd got up to the night before. You realised it was still a boy there. We were thinking about diets, professionalism and being on time. We had the weight of responsibility that came from going through a process that Wayne had effectively skipped. So he was happy-go-lucky, because he wasn't used to the environment."

Rooney was included in the senior pre-season schedule. In his first friendly for the first team he scored in a 3-1 win at SC Bruck, shrugging off two defenders to slot in. That appearance had come as a substitute – the following day, he started against SC Weiz, and scored a stunning hat-trick. Another treble followed a week later against Queen's Park. It was his all-round performance that was most impressive, setting up two goals and looking not only as though he belonged at that level but like he could well be the main man.

The pre-season was rounded off with a fortuitous goal off his shoulder against Hibernian; this was Everton's strongest test so far. A reminder of his immaturity came when he was booked after a scuffle in the 63rd minute and had to be withdrawn a minute after. It was not a red flag that would stop David Moyes from handing Rooney his official debut, however. Two days before the first game of the season, Moyes informed Rooney that he would be starting against Spurs on the Saturday, as Duncan Ferguson was injured. On the morning of the game the nervous teenager ate beans on toast before being driven to the stadium by his dad. After years of watching their idols walk out onto the pitch, the unthinkable was about to happen.

Rooney played as the number 10 behind Kevin Campbell, though he was wearing number 18 – the shirt recently vacated by Paul Gascoigne. His performance was promising if unspectacular; with 10 minutes to go to half-time, the youngster laid the ball on for Mark Pembridge to score. Spurs, though, were unwilling to lay down and play along with Rooney's fantasy and, following some close attention at set pieces, Moyes substituted the 16-year-old midway through the second half. Rooney earned a standing ovation, and though he was two weeks too late to beat Royle's record, it was obvious that he wasn't in the team just as a novelty. The game ended 2-2.

After the match, Rooney did not go to the players' lounge – he was still so new to the process that he didn't know what to do, so instead he met up with his dad and got a lift home, via the pub, as per Wayne senior's post-match routine. A few hours after making his Premier League debut, he was on the street outside his house kicking a ball with his friends.

Rooney was on the bench for the following game with Sunderland but came on towards the end; this was the pattern deployed by Moyes as Rooney played from the start in the home game against Birmingham but was again a late sub at Manchester City and Southampton. Those last two away games had been defeats, the positivity at the start of Moyes' reign had subsided and having engineered a momentum boost by introducing young players, the manager now had to build something of substance. So Rooney was named on the bench for the visit of Middlesbrough but when the first half ended 1-1, the youngster was brought on to provide some inspiration.

He was booked after three minutes for clashing with Boro keeper Mark Schwarzer but went on to have a few positive contributions – one run down the entire right side of the pitch brought the crowd to its feet, and in truth, it was in reinvigorating the Goodison support that Rooney had his most tangible effect. Fourteen minutes from the end, Kevin Campbell grabbed his second goal of the game to decide the points, and afterwards, Moyes was keen to play down the influence of the substitute.

"He helped it a lot but we had to let one or two know at half-time they had to do better," he said. "Wayne just loves to play football. He wants the ball all the time. But I'm not going to have the Wayne Rooney show. He is actually quite a shy boy. He wants to play, enjoys his football – as long as we don't expect too much too soon.

"He's very quick and strong for his age. The problem for Wayne is understanding that you're not against 16-year-olds and can beat eight men and score. These are top-quality players. But I'm certainly not going to knock that attitude out of him. I want him to do that but I also want him to understand the game, which will only come with time. The other lads are all looking after him and I've told them to make sure he's tucked up in bed nice and early."

The acclimation to playing professional football before he was actually a professional was a difficult process. "He got used to it very quickly though," Nick Chadwick says. "It felt like the entire football club took him under their wing. The senior players were quick to protect him. The naivety helped him, 100 per cent. He was just playing football. That's what the people connected to. They could relate. It was just a Scouser off the street playing for Everton. The fact that he'd play with the Everton first team in a morning and then do exactly the same with his mates at night on the streets of Croxteth. I know David Moyes was always on at him to stop doing it. The penny began to drop, the more people told him you didn't expect to see Premier League footballers hanging around the streets of Croxteth at 9pm the night before a big league game. He was just a lad, just a teenager, kicking a ball around, getting into mischief and playing for Everton."

Rooney's impact on the win against Middlesbrough had been more coincidental than instrumental but this was another battle Moyes was having to fight publicly. Rooney started at Villa Park in the next league game and he was exceptional, providing energy and urgency. Defensively, his colleagues were not at the same level, and Villa took a two-goal lead. Thomas Gravesen inspired a comeback, laying on two equalisers – Rooney was then taken off, and Everton collapsed late on as Dion Dublin scored the winner.

"It says much about their predicament that Everton's hopes already rest upon the shoulders of 16-year-old Wayne Rooney," read the match report in the *Express*.

But Rooney, like Moyes, was in need of something to justify his own hype. That came in the form of becoming Everton's youngest ever goalscorer on October 1st, in a League Cup tie at Wrexham. He came on in the 63rd minute; with eight minutes to go he was sent through by a Ferguson flick and showed predatory instinct to slip the ball between the goalkeeper's legs. He celebrated in a stationary position, arms aloft; the self-confident pose of a player who knew it had been inevitable that he would score.

There was still time for another goal – Lee Carsley's raking through ball found Rooney in space on the right. The forward feinted to go inside and fired a shot into the far corner, again managing to get it through the keeper's legs.

Of course, the goals only poured fuel on the fire. Legendary Toffees boss Howard Kendall was more than a little excited after the game. "It's very dangerous to talk about a new era because of one player," he said. "What I do know is that Colin Harvey rates him very highly. He reminds him of Kenny Dalglish – and he doesn't give praise lightly."

It was back to the bench for Rooney as Everton approached their two toughest games of the season. First, a trip to Old Trafford. At 0-0 with 15 minutes to go, Rooney was introduced and gave a decent account of himself, causing some discomfort to the United defence before three late goals took the game away from the Toffees.

Next it was Arsenal. The Gunners were Premier League champions, unbeaten all season – in fact, their run in all league games was 30 matches, with an unbeaten run in away games stretching 17 months to the day. Freddie Ljungberg gave the visitors an early lead but Tomasz Radzinski levelled soon after. With nine minutes remaining, Rooney replaced Radzinski. A creditable draw loomed until Gravesen hit a searching pass out to the left. Rooney killed it with his right foot, catching Lauren off-balance. Kevin Campbell made a run across Sol Campbell, creating a small pocket of space. Rooney advanced and nudged the ball forward.

What happened next stunned the world of football – but to a couple of people in the stands, it was no surprise. From fully 30 yards, Rooney wrapped his foot around the ball and generated a stunning amount of power. David Seaman was at full stretch and could do nothing; the accuracy of the strike was so breathtakingly precise that the ball cannoned down off the crossbar and over the line.

"I was used to seeing Wayne score goals from absolutely nothing," says Scott Brown. "That he'd come up with something brilliant and he could be miles away from goal. I'd seen him do it a hundred times. Brings the ball down. Touch, touch, bang. Top bin. Oh my god. As if he's just done that. This is Arsenal. They're the champions. They've been unbeaten for ages. That's David Seaman. You're watching it happen like a movie. I'm not surprised that I've seen Wayne do it, but it's just mad that he can do it on the biggest stage."

The final whistle went; Everton had won the game, Arsenal's unbeaten record had ended, but the match would be forever remembered for a moment where Wayne Rooney announced himself to the world. There were still five days to go until he was 17.

A generational moment, a generational talent and generational comparisons. David Moyes had attempted to keep a lid on the

Wayne celebrates his first league goal for Everton, an incredible 25-yard effort that cannoned in off the bar to end Arsenal's 30-game unbeaten run

hype but any attempt to do so now would be futile. Immediately, thoughts turned to stars of the past and the impressions they had made breaking through. Maybe Ryan Giggs had something comparable in terms of expectation on his immediate introduction to the first team but even his youth team record hadn't come littered with hundreds of goals in a couple of years. You could probably go back as far as George Best for the last time a teenager was breaking into a top-flight team with a genuine expectation that he could already be among the best in the league.

Best's exploits were tales of legend. But there are Rooney tales for almost every Best one. George taking the ball from kick-off and running to score in a youth team game? Wayne scoring from an overhead kick against a Man United junior side. George chipping his hero Harry Gregg in training? Wayne did the same to Neville Southall when he was just a ball boy. George showing a fearlessness in trying tricks on the established senior United professionals? Wayne did just the same against the likes of Alan Stubbs and Joseph Yobo. Of course, there were differences. George was an elegant slip of a boy, while Rooney was more of a battering ram. But by far the most compelling comparison was the fact that it was only the stage which determined how good they were, and how quickly it became apparent that both of them had the ability and confidence to do the most outrageous things on the biggest platform. At 16 they were both ready to excel in the first team for one of the biggest clubs in the country.

At the precise moment Wayne Rooney was scoring his blockbuster goal, it was evident that he would become just as big a problem for Everton to get a grip on as it would be for their opponents.

Chapter Three

BIG TIME

Wayne Rooney celebrated his goal against Arsenal by having the traditional kickabout with his mates at home. He watched the highlights that evening, at the same time as most of the country were seeing his heroics for the first time. He was made up to hear Arsene Wenger, the Arsenal manager, describe him as 'a better all-round player than Michael Owen' and add: "He is the biggest England talent I've seen since I arrived six years ago."

And yet the first seeds of discontent came from his own manager, as David Moyes tried in vain to temper the hysteria. "I don't believe anyone really expects Wayne Rooney to be in the first team," he said, indicating that the forward would be back on the bench the following week. "He's not mature enough mentally for that."

Moyes was irked by a line of questioning he'd not prepared for – Rooney's future. It was suggested, with his 17th birthday imminent – and thus, that first professional contract – that the player might either seek a better deal than the one he'd committed himself to less than a year earlier, or even look elsewhere. That rumour was motivated by the story that Rooney was set to sign with the agent Paul Stretford, and provoked Moyes to tell journalists in a subtle on-but-off-the-record fashion that he would walk out of his job if Rooney was allowed to leave.

But Rooney's 17th birthday arrived, and the player was now officially a professional for the club he loved; he gave a feature interview to journalists to mark the occasion.

"I am really enjoying my football," Rooney said. "I will sign my contract with Everton as soon as possible. The problem is that my current agent has not agreed to terminate our agreement even though it runs out in December. Everyone knows that me and my family are Everton-mad. Scoring my first Premiership goal against Arsenal was absolutely wonderful – a moment I will never forget."

Moyes, as well as handling the expectations of the boy, was now implicated in how it raised expectations for his team. He had walked into this situation and had to be commended for putting such a precocious talent into the side. But now he had scared Manchester United and slew Arsenal. It would surely be unrealistic for one young boy to transform a team who had been battling relegation into one capable of beating any side in the land, so it was therefore understandable that Moyes demonstrated caution.

He could be grateful for the way Rooney's own heroes had taken to him, helping establish a strong bond with the squad at Bellefield.

"There was something significant about that goal against Arsenal," Nick Chadwick says. "That was a statement that said Wayne was arriving. That goal was a regular thing to see him try in training.

"We'd been in the doldrums, and all of a sudden there was an enthusiasm around the place. The manager was very clever with the way he put us in, one or two at a time, then take them out for a little bit. It was sensible integration. Because Wayne was such a special talent, the senior players recognised there was no stopping it. It must have been really hard for the manager to deal with. I'm sure he must have made a few phone calls to Sir Alex to ask how he'd dealt with the attention that Ryan Giggs and that group of players got.

"Wayne would probably admit that as a teenager he didn't really know how to behave in this kind of professional environment. He was doing these incredible things in the Premier League, but he was still just a lad. It must have been difficult for the manager. Once or twice he took the stern line with Wayne and maybe that didn't end well. But then you'd have a senior player like Duncan Ferguson, someone who Wayne had idolised, taking him aside and having a few quiet words and it would have much more of an impact.

"That rawness was a positive quality – there was a charm to it. It was a positive thing that he still played like he was on the street. That was a unique part of his game. It was a special goal against Arsenal and a defining moment for the Premier League, never mind Everton. I was in the stands watching it. I was genuinely delighted for him. We knew how much the club meant to him and his family. It brought a lot of excitement to have young lads developed by the club coming into the team."

Rooney himself admitted to episodes of immaturity. He became involved in the first-team dressing room pranks – one, for example, placing a bucket of cold water on the top of a door and balancing it so it would fall on some unlucky random victim. In Rooney's case, he did it to Moyes, and couldn't confess.

Complications arose through Wayne's comfort. He noted Alan Stubbs complaining and felt empowered to do the same. He complained about being brought off or not starting. He even complained about the intensity of a Friday training session – prompting a back-and-forth where Moyes said 'When did you become a coach?' to which Rooney replied 'When did you become a manager?'

Rooney then complained about the quality of crosses from Alan Irvine, Moyes' assistant, in a training drill. Irvine threatened Rooney that he would be back in the youth team talking like that. Rooney's retort? "No I won't."

This was immaturity rather than unprofessionalism; Rooney was imitating the bad habits and getting carried away with his own impact. The major difficulty for Moyes was that Wayne's explosion had presented a complication.

"It seemed like Wayne was the main man at the club," says Scott Brown, "and this was before he'd even played for the first team. I think it was quite hard for David Moyes, because he was such a special player, and everyone wanted him to be involved. And he was ready, and David had to make a judgement call. I remember Wayne being frustrated that he was being held back and he was still only 16. It felt like that was the start of what made things difficult between them.

"The goal against Arsenal changed everything, because when you're with him and you're seeing him and everyone is talking… you still don't know. You know he's going to be good. Hopefully great. But then you see him do something that you know he's capable of, and he does it as effortlessly on the biggest stage as he does in youth team games, and you know everything has changed. You're not looking at him as Wayne, your mate. Suddenly he's Wayne Rooney, possibly a superstar.

"The attention grew. It got mad. But it didn't change him. You could see that from the way he went out on the streets with his mate for a kick-about after scoring against Arsenal. When he was training with the first team he was still getting changed in the youth team dressing room. I remember us asking him about the goal and he was just like, 'It's just one of them, innit.' Just like he'd scored it at Bellefield."

Others in the dressing room were able to see it differently – that Rooney was still only just 17. And so in their eyes, the manager was still the main man. "I remember thinking how difficult it was," Chadwick says. "I thought David was managing the club with discipline and that did cause conflict. But he was doing well, the team was doing better, and so more players bought into it. It was a fantastic environment for the young players to develop. But there was so much attention given to Wayne, so many rumours about whether he might leave, that it would have been difficult for any manager. Wayne pushed the boundaries at times. The manager would push back. But it felt more like a parental thing – Wayne not liking what he was being told so he would push back a bit. It wasn't a huge war or clash between them, not in my eyes."

Rooney was disgruntled to be back on the bench at West Ham, but he was brought on again with around half an hour to go with the scores level. Within three minutes he had Everton's best chance so far; and two minutes later, with the hosts dealing with their new headache, Lee Carsley scored the game's only goal. Once more he was the player people were talking about afterwards. "He plays with no fear and stretched us," Hammers boss Glenn Roeder said. "He's like a breath of fresh air and you have to wonder how good he is going to be."

The latest exciting cameo came alongside news about Rooney's professional contract, which was set to be worth around £8,000 per week over five years once his new agents could sit down with Everton in December.

A month after being named the BBC Young Sports Personality of 2002, Wayne signed his first professional contract

Another late substitute appearance with the scores level came at Elland Road on November 3rd; it was another match turned in Everton's favour, and this time it was Rooney with the goal. Just five minutes after coming on, he received the ball in the middle of Leeds' half, and skilfully dodged Eirik Bakke before approaching the experienced international Lucas Radebe. Rooney dropped his shoulder and fashioned enough space to get his shot away early. So early that Paul Robinson's reaction looked late and helpless. The precision, again, was perfect.

The 0-100 style of his impact was inviting comment. Former Spurs and England manager (and now manager of Leeds) Terry Venables was asked to discuss the comparison between Rooney and Paul Gascoigne. "Gazza was very strong and that is important in a young player," said Venables. "Rooney already looks strong and he's full of confidence. He has got that Gazza physique and a Dalglish thing in the way he runs with the ball. He has got his own style though – outstanding players do.

"I don't want to be hyping him up too much. Everton are trying to take their time with the boy, which makes sense. David Moyes looks like he is going to be patient and get it right. It is important to keep players away from the hype."

Moyes, meanwhile, was satisfied to see Rooney score from close range. "I want to see him scoring more inside the box," he said. "That is where good players need to be. It is easy keeping him out of the spotlight, and you can be sure I will look after him."

It was difficult to ignore the positive momentum that goal had on the team. Everton kept winning, with Rooney on the bench if needed; wins against Charlton and Blackburn made it five on the spin, which was the club's best ever run in the Premier League, and the form continued with another 1-0 win over West Brom at Goodison. This time, Rooney's time on the pitch was very brief

– introduced just three minutes before the end of the game – but still memorable. Brought on to run the clock down, Rooney faced up to Baggies defender Darren Moore and stood over the ball, hands on hips, arrogantly teasing the experienced centre-half. Everton saw the game through, but Moore was displeased. "He was trying to be a bit too clever for his boots," said the defender. "I wouldn't advise him to do it again or he'll learn the hard way."

The line between youthful charm and obnoxiousness was thin for some. Rooney was awarded the BBC Young Sports Personality of the Year in early December, but the broadcaster and Everton received complaints that Rooney 'chewed gum, did not express his thanks, and had the top button of his shirt undone'; a club spokesman commented that Rooney had been told not to speak.

By this time, Everton's record run was over. It came to an end at Newcastle, while humbling back-to-back defeats to Chelsea gave Moyes a reality check about the standards his team would have to reach even with a boy wonder in their ranks. With optimism required, Rooney was given a start against Blackburn in mid-December, and it had the desired effect. Goodison was still bouncing from the frenetic early pace which had seen Andrew Cole score for the visitors and Lee Carsley level before Rooney's moment of class in the 25th minute. He controlled a lofted pass with his head, cleverly nudging it away from Martin Taylor before accelerating into the box and finishing with the clinical composure you'd expect of someone twice his age. It was not as astounding as what he had done against Arsenal, but it was just as remarkable in its own way.

It was another match-winning goal for Rooney and inevitably it was suggested he should start in Everton's next game – which just happened to be at Anfield. Moyes insisted that he had 'no qualms about throwing Wayne in', but still only used him as a substitute.

Rooney admitted he was upset – and that anger reflected in his play when he came on, latching on to a pass and thrashing a shot against the bar – the closest either side came to a goal.

He was back on the bench for the trip to St. Andrew's on Boxing Day; prior to the game, Birmingham manager Steve Bruce had described Rooney as 'something we have not seen in this country for a long time', but the same grace did not extend to his players. Rooney came on in the 65th minute and in the 80th he went into a sliding challenge with Steve Vickers. Though Rooney won the ball, Vickers needed stitches; Vickers' team-mate Robbie Savage played antagonist, pleading with referee David Elleray to dismiss the teenager. Elleray obliged, much to the shock of David Moyes.

"I think that at the most it should have been a yellow," Moyes said. "It was a strong challenge between two players. We don't want to see anyone injured, but I don't see it as a sending off." Moyes' moaning fell on deaf ears; the decision was upheld, and Rooney was banned for three games.

He served the suspension, returning as substitute in a defeat at Charlton in early February. In training the following week he was approached by David Moyes who informed him that he had been selected for England. "Is Hibbo in?" Rooney asked, referring to Tony Hibbert, in the belief that his manager was referring to the under-21 squad. "No, you're in the full England squad," he was told.

England manager Sven-Goran Eriksson had selected a youthful squad for a friendly game against Australia at Upton Park later that month. Rooney – with just six league starts to his name – was the headline pick. "I have spoken to Wayne one-on-one," Eriksson said. "We talked generally... about things other than tactics and football. We talked about life and about being young and being famous, which is not always very easy to handle. He seemed to be a bright boy. If you are 17 and going to be the youngest player to ever play for England, then that creates a lot of interest. You cannot avoid that. The plan is that he will start the second half. He may be nervous, but I know he can handle it. Wayne has been very good in training. You can see he is a big talent. When you see him out there you cannot guess he is 17. He is much more mature."

England were 2-0 down at half-time. Eriksson changed his entire team, which meant an international debut for Rooney, and another record broken – he was now the youngest England player of all time, beating James Prinsep's 124-year record by 142 days. Rooney also showed the most promise, having a couple of shots and creating openings as well as starting the move for England's consolation goal – scored by Francis Jeffers.

"If we are looking for plusses, it was so exciting to see Wayne Rooney – what a threat the boy poses," Liverpool legend Alan Hansen told the BBC. "I saw him playing against Liverpool earlier this season and he was blistering. Every time he gets the ball you think something is going to happen. I wouldn't have any qualms about putting this kid on the bench if England were playing in a big game, and if they were struggling, I would throw him on for the last 20 minutes. Rooney would be the one of the younger brigade I would take first into the next full squad."

Still, he hadn't scored a goal for almost two months, and that carried on into over three, before Everton's trip to Arsenal. Rooney was given a start and impressed with his harassment of the home defence, finally getting a reward in the 57th minute when he ran at a terrified Pascal Cygan and finished in almost identical style to the goal he'd scored at Leeds. The goal levelled Cygan's earlier effort, though this time Arsenal had the last laugh with a 2-1 win of their own.

It was a timely contribution from Rooney, as it answered two questions; first of all, it was another big-stage statement, and with England due to play an important European Championship qualifier against Turkey, it was not completely irrelevant that he had shown such confidence at Highbury. Second of all was the goal in and of itself, a vindication that his contribution was not just a burst that was already fading.

So he was called into Eriksson's squad for the game against Turkey which was played at the Stadium of Light in Sunderland. At 17 years and 160 days, Rooney became the youngest player ever to start for England. His performance was exceptional. In a pulsating 90 minutes, he was only denied a goal by a Turkish handball that went unpunished, before two moments of inspiration – the first, an audacious ball-juggling routine, the second, a slalom dribble past two men – helped to create chances. Darius Vassell scored a crucial opener, before David Beckham's late penalty added security. It was another star turn from Rooney, though, which earned rave reviews in the press. The *Express* summarised: "Troubled his markers and delivered deft backheels into the path of his team-mates. Intelligent in attack and diligent in defence, the 17-year-old was irresistible from start to finish."

If he was good enough to start for England, David Moyes could hardly hold him back for Everton anymore, and it was, of course, Rooney who was the main topic of conversation as the Toffees prepared to face Newcastle after the international break.

"He can play much better than that," insisted Moyes. "There are things I see him doing every week that he didn't do in the England game. Wayne Rooney is not the finished article. He is a great boy with a great attitude. I just hope people don't build him up too much and he is given a chance to progress. I keep saying it is more important what he is like when he is 23 or 24 than at 17."

Moyes again emphasised the careful approach the club were trying to take. "Wayne handles things well because we try to look after him," he said. "I hope he is unaffected by everything, but we will only really see the proof when he starts playing again.

"We have to allow the boy to have his life. We cannot take his adolescence completely away from him. We cannot make Wayne's life unmanageable because then we probably won't get the best from him. I want him to do the things boys his age normally do, it is just that he has a bigger responsibility."

Rooney fever continued unabated when the forward scored a clever header after 18 minutes, helping his team to a 2-1 win. Moyes would not have cared to admit it but the 17-year-old was proving fundamental to his team's prospects. When Rooney played, so did Everton, and four of his five league goals had come in wins. The point was repeated by another last-minute winner, this time against Aston Villa, in late April. It was his eighth goal of the campaign, a wonderful accurate left-footer from outside the area.

"It wasn't about the quantity of goals," says Nick Chadwick. "His influence on the team was phenomenal in that first year. The lift he gave the other players. He almost became the talisman overnight, stepping into the shoes of Duncan Ferguson. I think Everton fans and the club itself craved that. The fact he was an Evertonian, that he was so young, that he was so raw. That he played like he was on the street. The connection was perfect. There was very much a feeling that we could all be part of something great. Wayne was the catalyst for that."

The seventh-placed finish for Everton was a strong indication that things were moving in the right direction; but the club, and David Moyes, were to experience the fallout of 'second season syndrome'.

Chapter Four

OUTGROWN

Certainly, it would be fair to say the negative issues between Wayne Rooney and David Moyes never completely went away. Those battles would continue through the 2003/04 season, and at times it seemed as though a week could not pass without some issue or another for the Everton manager to deal with.

He seemed to have taken a leaf right out of the Sir Alex Ferguson handbook by claiming Rooney had ended the season with a medial ligament strain, even though he'd played the entirety of Everton's last two league games. There was doubt about the legitimacy of the injury, considering Moyes had gone on record in April to say he didn't want Rooney being picked for international friendlies. The immediate bone of contention was a post-season friendly in South Africa; it was agreed Rooney would remain in England and join up with the national squad for the friendly with Serbia and qualifier with Slovakia; an uneasy compromise for Moyes, who still didn't want Rooney to play in the Serbia game.

"If you look at Wayne's performances last season he did much better as a substitute than in the games he started," the Everton boss said. "His body was developing. He had just come out of school and he was not used to full-time training. But it will have stood him in really good stead and hopefully he'll be magnificent for an hour in games."

Rooney came on as a substitute against Serbia and started against Slovakia; for the first time, it looked as though he may have been exposed to too much, too soon, as he lacked the sort of composure he'd shown during his first campaign. It was an underwhelming way to sign off for the summer.

On the day pre-season training resumed, former Everton midfielder Duncan McKenzie was quoted as saying Everton 'had to get into the Champions League before Wayne does' if they wanted to keep him. "You come to a point when you must not allow your support for a club as a boy to cloud your entire career," said McKenzie. "I'd be gobsmacked if there wasn't a massive bid for him in the next two years." There were subsequent rumours that Real Madrid had been interested for around a year.

In the short term, Everton's games with non-English opposition would have to be restricted to pre-season friendlies, such as the one they played at Ibrox in late July. In the first half, Rooney tripped unchallenged and twisted his ankle. It was feared he had damaged ligaments, and a cautious Moyes instructed the physiotherapist to take his car and drive Rooney back to Liverpool. In a farcical episode, Rooney remembered asking the physio to put on a Barry White CD; back home, Moyes accused the youngster of breaking the CD player in his car. "If it had got broken, I hadn't done it on purpose," Rooney recalled in his book *My Story So Far*.

Rooney had been interviewed for a new book out that summer concentrating on his first year as a professional, where he spoke about the Real Madrid speculation. "I took no notice," he said, after describing playing for his boyhood club as 'one of the best feelings in life'. "I am 100 per cent focused on playing for Everton and, hopefully, it will stay like that for a long time to come. I know it's part and parcel of football life being linked with other clubs, but you have to remain focused on what you are doing."

For Moyes, that focus meant taking a long term perspective while still trying to get the season off to the best possible start. So Rooney was back in the squad for the opening weekend's game at Arsenal. He was clearly unfit, but with an extra week's recuperation he was back in the starting line-up against Fulham. The first moment of genuine quality came in the third game of the season, against Charlton Athletic at the Valley. Everton were trailing with 20 minutes remaining when Rooney received a ball in the box – his touch was superb, his turn was sharp, and his finish into the roof of the net was emphatic to earn his team a point.

It was a rare moment of positivity at the club in the opening months of the campaign. Moyes *was* hoping to assert a greater authority but it was coming at a cost. Observing that Rooney had a close relationship with Duncan Ferguson and a respect that seemed to supersede that of the rapport between Rooney and Moyes, the manager told the youngster that he felt Ferguson might be a bad influence on him. Rooney admitted 'immediately' telling Ferguson. The trivial nature of these points were developing, in Rooney's mind, into a breakdown in communication.

But he was still 17 and relatively inexperienced into how a professional dressing room worked. Something would have to give if his attitude didn't improve. His evening kickabouts were not happening as often now but he was still coming into training with stories of the night before. "I remember before an away game, he came in having had a scrap the night before," Nick Chadwick says. "You wouldn't see this from any other lad and it was tolerated a little more because of what he was doing on the pitch. You couldn't help but laugh. He was switched on. People would say he was stupid, a typical Liverpool lad from the street, but he wasn't. He was very alert. Ambitious. He was desperate to do well."

In mid-September, Moyes fired one of his 'caution' missives: "Right now, I'd say Wayne is a very, very good player but not yet the great one he is equipped to be. He still has a lot to learn. Everything he has now is completely natural. Nobody else can claim a shred of credit for what he is. But there is a responsibility to educate him while preserving all that natural talent. We do specific coaching with him and show him videos of the likes of Alan Shearer or Ruud van Nistelrooy and tell him, 'Here are people who are very good at things we want you to be good at. What can you pick up from them?'"

It was sensible advice. But one can understand why Rooney was preferring to make his own name on international duty than watch tapes of other players back at his club. By the time Moyes was sharing his words of wisdom, Rooney had already been away with England and scored his first international goals; his first, a clever half-volley from the edge of the box against Macedonia, to help turn a tricky tie around. The second came in almost identical fashion days later against Liechtenstein at Old Trafford. So when it came to Sven-Goran Eriksson's decision on whether to play Rooney in the crucial qualifier in Turkey, the England boss was sure to have curried favour with the youngster by talking him up.

"I am not worried about his experience," insisted Eriksson. "I wasn't for the last game against Turkey so why should I be now? He's a tough young man and I don't think he has nerves at all. He

Wayne Rooney celebrates becoming England's youngest ever goalscorer during the Euro 2004 qualifier against Macedonia on September 6th, 2003

is mature enough. I don't think I should be worried if the game is too big for him, he has never failed with his temperament for England."

In reality, Rooney was way down the pecking order of newsworthy items surrounding both the build-up and events of the game. Beforehand, there was a split in the England camp due to Rio Ferdinand's omission; the Manchester United defender had been excluded from international duty after missing a routine drug test, and was facing a lengthy ban. The United contingent, led by Gary Neville, had threatened to strike.

Rooney actually had the best chance of the opening exchanges, lifting a through ball onto the roof of the net, before England were awarded a penalty. David Beckham blazed it over, and the Turkish team angrily remonstrated at half-time. England kept their cool to secure a goalless draw, which sealed qualification to the European Championship in Portugal the following summer.

The mood was much less jovial back at Goodison. A year on, the blend of experience and youth had developed into a more difficult combination. The veteran legs of Duncan Ferguson, Kevin Campbell, Alan Stubbs, David Weir, David Unsworth and Mark Pembridge were now trudging closer towards retirement. Rooney's star had continued to shine but there was an obvious difference between his potential and the players he had broken through with. Nick Chadwick was looking for a loan move. Peter Clarke was to follow the same path. Scott Brown – who had played up front with Wayne in the Youth Cup – was realising their career trajectories were going to be very different.

"He just got better as his confidence grew and he realised he could do the things in first-team games just as easily as he did at younger levels," Brown says. "I started to think, I love him and I love Everton. But as much as we wanted to be a Manchester

United, we weren't, and that was the sort of stage he belonged on, so that he'd be having those Arsenal moments in the spotlight every week. His overall play just clicked into another gear and you could see that he would be the perfect fit for a team like that. He was so good that you knew that next to those players he would have his proper place where he could be great.

"I was hoping to get games for the reserves. He was not only thinking of getting into the Everton first team – he was expecting to be playing. In my mind, he went on to become the best English player in history, and to become that he almost needed to have that mindset from the very start."

David Moyes was no longer in a position to take it slow; Rooney's time was now, but more pertinently, Everton needed his lift and quality. Moyes had to embrace the youth and the accelerated idea of building a team around Rooney. And Moyes was completely invested in the idea of building his team around Wayne Rooney. If dealing with him was a problem, it was a problem he was happy to have. Rooney was extraordinary, but dealing with a prodigy was no extraordinary issue; it was part and parcel of what Moyes would have expected to navigate as a manager. Rooney had talent, but so did Moyes; he was the manager, he had earned the job and had performed well in it, so he deserved respect.

Still, perhaps the most understandable explanation for why it was never an easy relationship was because of Moyes' own relative inexperience at the top level, and to be given such a gift so early on. His reaction to the excitement over Rooney's performance against Turkey, for example, would not have been what the player wanted to hear. "So far Wayne's form has not been too good," he said. "With maybe the exception of the game at Charlton, Wayne has been below the standards he has set and he is very aware of that."

There were plenty of clubs willing to take the chance on the teenager. Chelsea were swimming in money after their takeover by Roman Abramovich and had spent the summer of 2003 acquiring Glen Johnson, Wayne Bridge, Damien Duff and Joe Cole. Everton chairman Bill Kenwright was keen to stop these stories before they began.

"I am getting a little fed up of saying this, but Wayne is not for sale," he told reporters on October 17th. "David Moyes and I want the same thing and that is Wayne Rooney in the blue shirt of Everton. People will say, 'Well, how could you turn down £35m?' But the answer is easy. You just do."

Chelsea visited Goodison Park on November 1st, a week after Rooney's 18th birthday. In an interview, he explained the days of playing in the streets were behind him because of how many people wanted to join in. "It is still only the start for me," he admitted. "I'm young. I've still got a lot to learn. I never thought I'd achieve what I have achieved in the last 12 months, but I'm always looking to improve."

The Chelsea game was one of those learning experiences; John Terry and William Gallas were impenetrable as the London blues took a 1-0 win. Rooney toiled with no reward. Afterwards, Moyes suggested the youngster was trying too hard. "Maybe he is trying to do too much himself and he needs to go back to doing the simple things," said the manager. "Younger players go through periods like this."

The words would have carried more weight if Rooney didn't continue to thrill on international duty; but against Denmark at Old Trafford in mid-November, he rattled a thunderous drive in off the crossbar for his third England goal of the campaign. So when he was substituted against Bolton in a disappointing defeat at the end of the month, he reacted angrily – the first indication that he was becoming frustrated with being projected as a reason for Everton's difficult start. The contrast in his performances for club and country was a clear indication that his form was just fine so long as he was surrounded with the right calibre of players.

The following week, Moyes made an even bigger show – replacing Rooney at half-time in a 0-0 draw with Manchester City. Rooney was struggling for his club, but without him, Everton were devoid of that buzz, that potential flash of brilliance. Moyes explained it as a 'tactical decision' and how he was sure the player would 'turn the corner'.

But he was dropped to the bench for the trip to Portsmouth, and Everton fell behind after 15 minutes. In the 24th, Steve Watson went down injured, and so Moyes decided he could wait no longer. With Rooney on the pitch, Everton looked a different team, and immediately levelled through Carsley. Just before half-time, Rooney had the luck he needed. The ball dropped to him in the box, he got his shot away, and Pavel Srnicek couldn't stop it from going in. Liberated, Rooney was everywhere; as if the confidence from the goal had brought him back to life. That youthful energy almost spilled over when he pushed Steve Stone to the ground; he even walked off the pitch, expecting to be sent off, but was called back and informed by referee Uriah Rennie that he'd only been booked.

His impact had been dramatic; Moyes felt justified for playing him from the bench and so for the following game against Leicester, Rooney was again a substitute. When James Scowcroft put the visitors in front in the 58th minute, it was a case of cometh the hour, cometh the boy; Rooney again thrown on tasked with turning it around. In the 71st minute he stroked in an impressive equaliser from 14 yards. Everton went on to win.

The case to restore him to the starting line-up was strong, and so Rooney was named in the eleven for the Boxing Day trip to Old Trafford. Ryan Giggs had been asked for his opinion of the Everton whizzkid and couldn't give higher praise: "It's quite simple: he is different class. The impact he made was incredible. He came on as a late substitute at Old Trafford last October and I was astonished at his quality and his all-round ability. He wasn't intimidated by playing against Manchester United in front of 67,000 fans and impressed everyone on our side."

He certainly made an impression in this game, though was once again unable to influence the result. United won 3-2, and Wayne was taken off in the 70th minute with the score at 3-1 – a few minutes after he was booked for a tackle on Cristiano Ronaldo that could comfortably fit into the category of 'emphatic'. Two days later, he was back on the bench for the visit of Birmingham, and once again he came off it to turn the game in his side's favour; this time, scoring the only goal of the game in the 69th minute.

January came, and with it, the opening of the transfer window. History tells us Wayne Rooney went nowhere, but it could have been very different. Behind the scenes, Manchester United had been expressing their own interest to Everton but had received numerous rejections. This went back to when Rooney was still a schoolboy, and then later when he was on the verge of the first team. "We tried to get Rooney at 14, and tried again at 16," Sir Alex Ferguson admitted in his second autobiography. "Finally we cracked it when he was 17." This could be an error – Rooney was actually 18 by now – but it could also be a slip. Because, as Scott Brown reveals, Rooney was telling his team-mates that he had agreed to go to Old Trafford. "In the January he was talking about signing for United," Brown says. "I can remember him in training telling us all he was going to move."

Meanwhile in late 2021, Ferguson reminisced on United's

official podcast: "We went for [Rooney], and we signed him the weekend after we played Everton…"

It stands to reason that the groundwork had been done to some extent, considering Rooney's sudden determination to go to United – strong enough to inform team-mates – which seemed to materialise out of nowhere. United's interest, however, had been apparent for years. Old Trafford academy coaches Geoff Watson and Jim Ryan had reported to Ferguson whenever Rooney put in a star turn at junior level. At each approach, Rooney had informed any United representative that he loved Everton. He still did, but he was beginning to realise that his boyhood club could not realistically provide the platform on which his potential could be realised. His imperfect relationship with the manager and the staggered nature of his appearances did not correlate with his dream career.

In January 2004 Ferguson was in the market for a striker. His need was urgent, but, unable to convince Everton to let go of their starlet, he instead signed Louis Saha of Fulham. Rooney, thinking that his chance might have gone, entertained the speculation of Real Madrid's interest, even discussing moving to Spain with his parents and fiancée Coleen. "To be honest, my heart was hoping for a move to Old Trafford rather than Spain," Rooney confessed.

Though United had temporarily filled their need, Ferguson's interest in Rooney never died, and when Walter Smith went to Old Trafford to assist the United boss for a short spell in March 2004, he told Ferguson – "Get that Rooney signed." Smith described Rooney as 'the best he'd ever seen'.

Instead of lining up for United, Rooney could only watch from the bench as his potential suitors raced into a 3-0 lead at Goodison Park on February 7th. Louis Saha scored twice in the first half-hour. With the Toffees shellshocked, Moyes turned to Rooney; his performance was inspirational as he dragged his team back into the match. Everton made it 3-3, before suffering the late sucker punch of Ruud van Nistelrooy's dramatic winner.

"That was more like Wayne," Moyes said afterwards, though there was a case for saying that it was just like Everton. The late concession meant it was now six games without a win in all competitions. Moyes could not afford to continue with the cameos – Wayne Rooney was going to have to start. At Southampton, he scored twice in a 3-3 draw; the second, an accomplished finish at the near post in front of the away fans. Three weeks later, his was the only goal of the game against Portsmouth – a game that had emerged as a potential banana skin that threatened to drag Everton into a relegation fight.

Leicester City were the next opponents, and they too were in a scrap at the wrong end of the table. If Everton could avoid defeat, they would probably be safe from the drop. Their chances were made that much more difficult when Duncan Ferguson was sent off four minutes before half-time. As the Scot marched off the pitch, he handed his captain's armband to Rooney, who put it on for the last few minutes of the opening period.

Moyes was furious at half-time and ordered him to 'Get that fucking thing off.' In his first autobiography, Rooney said the incident was one of a few that made him think 'I can't see this working'. Still, he let his football do the talking in the second half, as he scored a crucial goal. The Foxes stole a last-minute equaliser, but Everton could rest easier about their fate.

One more goal followed before the end of the season – a strike at Elland Road similar to the one he scored the previous campaign, albeit a little further out. That goal earned another draw but Everton's league form ended disastrously, losing their last four games to finish in 17th place.

It was clear that Everton were going to have to rebuild, but it was also clear that they simply did not have the budget to bring in the type of players to make them title challengers. In April, it was suggested to Moyes that he would get a handsome amount of money to build a squad if he took advantage of Chelsea's rumoured interest, but he was defiant. "The idea is that we try to build a team around Wayne Rooney," he said. "The aim is not us grooming Wayne to go somewhere else. It is keeping him here so that our future is much brighter." A couple of days later, Moyes tipped Rooney to have a positive contribution for England that summer, saying: "He won't look out of place."

A few weeks later, a furious Bill Kenwright was forced to deny a story that a deal had already been agreed to sell Rooney to Manchester United. "It is always difficult to respond to rubbish," Kenwright blasted. "The whole thing is laughable. No deal has ever been discussed, set up or agreed with Manchester United or, indeed, any other football club on the planet."

Chapter Five

THE WHITE PELÉ

There was never any doubt about Wayne Rooney's inclusion in the England squad for the 2004 European Championship. He started both of the friendlies before the squad announcement, meaning he had established a position as strike partner to Michael Owen.

In the build-up, England coach Steve McClaren suggested that Rooney could emulate Owen's impact at the 1998 World Cup. "It's possible," McClaren said. "He certainly has the ability. He has made that impact in the games he has played. The emergence of Rooney has been timely and given Owen a little more support."

At the start of the season, Owen had been asked to give his opinion on his new team-mate, and said: "Whether it is a partnership for the future or for now I am sure it would work. I remember before the Slovakia match, everybody wanted to know if Wayne was going to be the best in the world. Then after the game everyone asked me if we had been expecting too much, as if it was a big surprise that he didn't beat the world on his own that day. I don't know what everyone was expecting. If everyone lets him, he will develop into a very good player."

Owen scored England's goal and Rooney was, according to the *Express*, 'worryingly fleeting (and) peripheral' against Japan in the first warm-up. But four days later, England faced Iceland, and it was the younger player's time to make a statement. He scored a smart effort in the 27th minute but eight minutes before half-time he struck a more memorable impression, beautifully curling a 25-yard strike into the top corner.

Perhaps even more impressive than the goals was the fluid nature of England's play in the first half, with Beckham, Scholes and Gerrard combining with Rooney to play some seriously impressive exhibition football befitting of the 'Golden Generation' tag which had been bestowed upon this group of players. Owen was more of a traditional striker, a forward to run on to through balls rather than be involved in the play. He had suffered a difficult season, too, with a persistent hamstring problem appearing to have an impact on the electric pace he'd displayed in his earlier years.

Elsewhere in the squad, Sven-Goran Eriksson was blessed. Even with Rio Ferdinand missing, he could count on a central defence of John Terry and Sol Campbell. Full-backs hardly come more dependable than Gary Neville and Ashley Cole. And in midfield, Eriksson had a quandary that would have been the envy of any international manager. David Beckham, Paul Scholes, Frank Lampard and Steven Gerrard were an obvious starting four. Nicky Butt – England's best player at the World Cup two years earlier – sat in reserve with Owen Hargreaves and Joe Cole. Eriksson's solution to fit the quality he had into the team was to play a flat midfield four with Scholes from the left. Gerrard and Lampard had never showed a true sign of a fluid partnership but Eriksson was gambling on it becoming effective enough to sacrifice Scholes' influence in that area.

It seemed as though the England manager had the right blend. Against France, in the opening game of the competition, the Three Lions were fantastic. They were fully deserving of their first-half lead, given to them from a Lampard header. Rooney had demonstrated a fine level of temperament with a disciplined showing in the first period. With a quarter of the game remaining, Owen was substituted for Darius Vassell, giving a little extra liberation to the Everton striker.

And what a way he used it. In the 73rd minute, Beckham hooked a clearance high to the left hand side of the pitch. Rooney charged it down in competition with Lilian Thuram, who was making his 100th appearance for France.

What happened next was breathtaking. Anticipating Thuram's movement, Rooney flicked out a leg to pull the ball back over the defender's head. Thuram was long enough in the game not to be completely caught out. But he was not ready for Rooney to have the confidence or physicality to brush him aside. The skill had occurred inside England's own half; the body movement had opened up a 60-yard dash to goal. Rooney had the legs on Thuram, but the Manchester United defender Mikael Silvestre was covering from the centre, waiting until the last moment to commit. Rooney drew him in. In the box, Rooney shifted the ball away from Silvestre, who poleaxed the England forward, denying him what would have been one of the greatest goals in the competition's history. Beckham took the spot-kick, but Fabien Barthez denied him.

Rooney was brought off for Heskey, who gave away a free-kick in injury time. Zinedine Zidane scored from it. Somehow, there was still time for a complete capitulation, when Gerrard's back-pass sold goalkeeper David James short, and Thierry Henry was brought down by the stopper. Zidane made it a brace of injury-time set-pieces to turn the game on its head.

With so much blame to go around, Rooney's incredible moment was almost forgotten – but four days later, England played Switzerland, and the Everton striker demanded centre stage.

Just 23 minutes were on the clock when Michael Owen clipped a cross towards the back post; it seemed destined for Scholes, but Rooney leapt high to get there first, to the surprise of the Swiss goalkeeper. In scoring, Rooney had become the youngest goalscorer in the history of the European Championship. But he wasn't done there. Vassell laid the ball off to Rooney in the 75th minute. Two Swiss defenders tried to close him down, but he got his shot away early; it struck the post, then the head of goalkeeper Stiel, and went in. A more modern dubious goals committee might have awarded an own goal, but at the time, the strike was credited to Rooney.

Before the match, Stiel had made a bold proclamation that Rooney wouldn't get anything past him. Rooney had read those comments and revelled in getting the goals. With seven minutes to go, and on a hat-trick, the Everton star was withdrawn.

"I'm made up," he said after the game. "I came into the dressing room and there was a spontaneous round of applause. The second goal was probably the most important one of my career. It was great to break a record, but I went out there for the team." That much was true – although it was suggested Rooney had been taken off as he'd been booked. He defended himself. "The ball was there to be won. I went in for a 50-50 challenge and I was a bit late. I was going into a tackle and I give 110 per cent. What do people want me to do? I am going to carry on and do what I do best."

Eriksson had to be cautious, with the last group game against

Croatia now a virtual knockout match. Winner would take all. In the days building up to the game, Rooney's contribution was talked up by his team-mates.

"Wayne is magic. He is the new kid on the block," said Steven Gerrard. "He has surprised me more than any other player in the competition. I knew he was a fantastic talent but he has been unbelievable. If he gets better there is a chance he will be player of the tournament. I could go on all day about Wayne because he is a big, big talent."

The England manager likened Rooney to legends of the game. "I have worked with young players like Rui Costa, Paulo Sousa and Roberto Baggio at 18, but Wayne Rooney is something special. He is fantastic, but he is not there yet," he said. He followed the praise with a comment that was likely to go down like a lead balloon on Merseyside: "If I were a club manager I would be straight on the telephone to his agent now trying to buy him."

England faced Croatia at Estádio da Luz in Lisbon. The Stadium of Light, to give it its English name, had been reopened after the previous stadium was demolished. The arena had been most famous in the UK for George Best's arrival as a global superstar, when he single-handedly tore apart Benfica in 1966. The rebuilt arena was opened on October 25th, 2003 – still fresh enough for the new paint smell to linger in the air. It was time for a new British talent to plant his own flag in the fresh Portuguese turf.

England had the advantage on the day. As long as they kept a clean sheet, they would qualify; but those hopes were gone in the fifth minute when Niko Kovac pounced following messy defending. England needed a bit of luck – it came five minutes before half-time. Owen's shot was smothered, and from the rebound, Rooney showed awareness to note that Scholes was arriving at the back post, and the Manchester United man headed home.

Better was to come. This time Scholes returned the favour, though there was a little bit more to do – in first-half injury time, he laid the ball off for Rooney, 25 yards from goal. The striker took aim across goal and it flew into the corner.

Croatia's need to equalise as the second half wore on left them exposed to the counter attack. Rooney exploited this with a one-two with Owen on the halfway line that set him clear. The youngster put Croatia to the sword with the most clinical of finishes. It was a sensational moment. Thirty-eight years on from George Best's miracle night, Rooney had left his own indelible impression on this rectangular space of grass.

Despite again being on for a treble, Rooney was immediately taken off to keep him fresh – both teams scored again, but the Everton striker had been the difference once more.

"I don't remember anyone making such an impact on a tournament since Pele in the 1958 World Cup," Sven-Goran Eriksson said afterwards. "He's absolutely fantastic, not only at scoring goals but he plays football – he's a complete footballer... He deserves all the attention. He has been absolutely incredible, he's ready for anything."

Rooney's team-mates agreed. Beckham concurred with Eriksson's Pele comment, while Gerrard described him as 'the best player in Europe' on current form.

Meanwhile, Michael Owen now seemed much more convinced about the partnership. "Wayne's such an intelligent player that anyone could play with him," he said. "He likes to drop off and link play as well as scoring goals. Our partnership is working well."

Even Pele paid the 18-year-old a glowing tribute: "Wayne Rooney has already emerged as one of the best players at the European Championship."

Being mentioned in the same breath as one of the greatest of all time was a far cry from playing local football. Just two years earlier, Rooney had been starring in the FA Youth Cup. His strike partner of those days, Scott Brown, was watching the madness unfold back on Merseyside. "I was like his biggest fan," Brown says. "He was still one of us and it felt like he was doing it for all of us, all of the lads he had grown up with. That summer was the last time I saw Wayne. He went on to become the superstar we knew he would be from that moment against Arsenal, and that is exactly what he deserved for the talent he had and the person he is."

England had qualified for the quarter-final. Their opponents would be Portugal, who had their own teen sensation up front. Cristiano Ronaldo knew all about Wayne Rooney and had been given a close introduction when the Everton player smashed into a tackle at Old Trafford: "I remember the tackle, how could I forget it? Sometimes when you play against very fast players, you commit fouls to stop them. But I don't want to get into a personal fight with Rooney. He is a wonderful player, and I respect him."

At the business end of an international tournament, England could not afford to rely on a teenager. It was time for that so-called Golden Generation to prove their own worth. In the opening minutes, Michael Owen opened the scoring, and there could have been a fleeting moment where England's pain of previous tournaments was exorcised through the sheer force of Wayne Rooney. A moment where it seemed England could ride the crest of this particular wave all the way to the final. In fact, if you were an England diehard, you might even argue that moment of dreaming was almost essential in order to summon the bad luck which all-too-often befell the country at international tournaments. That moment arrived in the 27th minute when Rooney went into an innocuous challenge with Jorge Andrade. His boot came off;

when he tried to put it back on, he realised that he couldn't, as the pain was so intense. He knew immediately his game was over. Rooney was replaced by Vassell and rushed to hospital.

He had his foot put in plaster, and was back in the hotel all before the game had even finished. Rooney watched as Portugal subjected England to their familiar heartbreak of a penalty shoot-out exit. His replacement, Vassell, was one of the unlucky ones to miss from the spot.

England were out, but Rooney's injury had not only protected him from the avalanche of criticism, it effectively canonised him. It was both a blessing and a curse; an opportunity to say if only he hadn't been injured, England would have won, while at the same time providing a harder spotlight for a talented bunch of players who were now perceived to be over-reliant on the boy wonder.

Chapter Six

THE BIG STAGE

O nce the dust had settled on Euro 2004 – Wayne Rooney finishing as joint top scorer with Ruud van Nistelrooy, and Portugal eventually suffering agony of their own with a final defeat to Greece – most could concur with Sven-Goran Eriksson's earlier judgement about the sizeable nature of Rooney's impact. Eriksson's other notable comment about the player – that clubs would be keen to acquire him – would also ring true.

Wayne had suffered a broken metatarsal against Portugal, and so would miss a decent portion of the new season. It did not stop speculation about his future. For the past three years, transfer windows had been introduced, so clubs could only make signings either in the off-season or in January. Everton's best hope of holding on to Rooney was in other clubs not wanting to take the chance before his injury had healed. Prospective suitors knew that delaying their own move might mean missing the boat.

Just about every major club in Europe were linked. Manchester

United, Chelsea, Real Madrid, Arsenal, Barcelona. Everton were banking on Rooney's fanaticism for the club and David Moyes openly pleaded for Rooney to make a public statement. "I expected it to be difficult, but not this tough," he admitted. "All the uncertainty could be ended by just one or two words from Wayne on his new deal. But so far that hasn't happened so it's making people wonder what is going on. Tell me why I should give up on the best young player in Europe. I will fight to the very end to keep him. My job as Everton boss is to fight the corner for every Evertonian.

"If Wayne was still standing on the terraces and there was a great player considering his future with Everton, he would expect the manager to do everything in his power to keep that player. Well, that's what I'm going to do. It would be special for me if I could make Wayne captain of Everton. It would be wonderful if I can give him that honour."

Moyes' comments were accompanied by a statement of defence: "Sometimes it seems when Sir Alex Ferguson rests Cristiano Ronaldo, everyone agrees it's the right thing to do. But when I don't start with Wayne I get slaughtered. People seem to forget he is still only 18. He is not the finished article. He has a lot to learn as a player, a professional and as a man – and he accepts all that. He has turned into one of the best young players in the world at Everton. So whatever is happening here can't be wrong."

The issue for Moyes was that the international championships had suggested a different idea – that Rooney's struggles in the Everton team were due to the players around him not being of sufficient quality so that his own could flourish. Moyes could promise Rooney the earth but he knew that his power was limited to making the teenager the most prominent player at the club. He would be asking Rooney to sacrifice the momentum and potential big stage, for a future that was vague.

In late July the newspapers were full of speculation about the offer of a £50,000 five-year contract from the Toffees that wasn't going to be good enough. "I think it's incredibly sad that we are contemplating selling Wayne Rooney," said Everton director Paul Gregg. "I wish we could persuade Wayne to stay – he is a big ambassador for Everton and it's sad that other forces make decisions for us. This is a home-bred talent who has not had the chance to mature with Everton. We feel we've not had the full benefit of his talent."

Rooney was most heavily linked with a move to Manchester United, but the Old Trafford club had not made their move. Sir Alex Ferguson had sought to do his business early that summer and had signed Alan Smith to bolster his attacking options. With Van Nistelrooy proving to be prolific in Portugal, plus Diego Forlan and Louis Saha, United were well-stocked in that department.

Of the other options, Chelsea had just acquired Jose Mourinho as manager, and he was desperate to sign Didier Drogba. Meanwhile Real Madrid signed Michael Owen from Liverpool for just £8m. Arsenal were entering a period of relative austerity and felt that with Robin van Persie, José Antonio Reyes and Jérémie Aliadière, they had more than enough in reserve if they couldn't call upon Thierry Henry and Dennis Bergkamp.

Moyes and Everton could remain hopeful, so long as they could get to September and the end of the summer transfer window. Their own transfer ambitions were modest. Tim Cahill came in from Millwall for £2m, and Marcus Bent arrived for £450,000 from Ipswich, but Tomasz Radzinski moved to Fulham, so it could not be said that there was a significant strengthening at Goodison Park.

Everton's start to the season was mixed. The opening day 4-1 defeat to Arsenal showed just how far the club still were from competing and though that was followed with a win at Crystal

Palace, it was hardly a strong enough endorsement that the club would not be involved at the wrong end of the table again. And Wayne Rooney, who was coming from a moment in his career where his impact had been comparable to one of the greatest of all time, was better than that.

Perhaps Everton's only hope of retaining the player would have been if his own stock fell; but that was not likely to happen whilst he was out injured. Particularly if, in his absence, his team were losing games. As it happened, though, off-pitch events moved things in this direction. Wayne's precocious age did not protect him from the age-old tabloid process of knocking someone when they were on top of the world. He was forced to own up after tabloid reports that he had frequented a brothel when he was younger. To his credit, Rooney confessed of his own volition and sought to repair his relationship.

At the same time, the halo in the public image had slipped. This Jack the Lad, loveable bruiser from the working class north-west was now seen in a considerably different light. He instantaneously dropped from 1-2 favourite to win the BBC Sports Personality of the Year to 69-1 rank outsider, with Ladbrokes' Balthazar Fabricius saying: "Wayne Rooney can only be described as friendless."

Fabricius was wrong; Newcastle seemed to sense an opportunity. With the end of the transfer window approaching, and Everton's need for money well-publicised, Sir Bobby Robson made a speculative move to bring him to Tyneside. The day the scandal broke, Newcastle lodged a £20m offer. Everton immediately rejected it, though Newcastle were keen to let them know the offer still stood.

"The club has made a £20m offer for Rooney and it has been rejected, but the chairman has left the bid on the table," said Robson. "Rooney is not just another striker. He is potentially the most exciting player in Europe. We should be applauding the chairman. He is trying to bring the best young striker in the country to Newcastle. Manchester United can't buy Wayne Rooney. They are the biggest club in the land but they cannot afford him. How do I know? Because I know Alex Ferguson."

However, United matched Newcastle's offer later the same day – only to receive the same response. The race was on.

In the background, Rooney had perceived his relationship with Moyes as irretrievable. He told Moyes he wanted to leave, but when quizzed on the reason why, he initially said that it was because the newspaper criticism had made him want to leave the city. The following day, that story was published in the *Liverpool Echo* and Rooney, believing Moyes must have leaked the story, confronted the manager at training. "You're a fucking joke," Rooney admitted blasting. "I don't want to play for you ever again."

Rooney also felt let down by Everton's stance. The club's new chief executive Trevor Birch had flown out to Portugal during Euro 2004 to discuss the possibility of moving to Chelsea with Paul Stretford, who was now Rooney's agent. Chelsea didn't make an offer – but when Wayne arrived back home, Moyes asked Rooney if he would go to Liverpool. The first firm offer, though, came from Robson, which prompted Ferguson into life.

It also spurred Rooney into action. Moyes was resigned to losing him but was keen to ensure he didn't lose face with the supporters.

"I felt I was good enough to go into the Manchester United team so I was ready to move," Rooney told *Amazon Prime* in 2020. "I was ready to move the year before but that didn't happen. I went in to David Moyes and told him this is the situation and Everton needed the money. I think deep down he knew so he said, 'If you want to leave, you'll have to put a transfer request in.' So I went out into the canteen, wrote a transfer request out on a piece of paper and said, 'Here you go.' When I got in the Everton first team, I knew I was the best player. That's not being cocky… plus we had a very bad team at the time. I knew before long I would have to move on if I wanted to win trophies."

With United's interest public, Rooney decided he wanted to move to Old Trafford over St James' Park. His issue was that Newcastle seemed keener and increased their own offer. It was enough to convince Everton to allow negotiations to begin, even though they were still holding out for more money than the £25m that was on the table, and even though Rooney himself had his heart set on moving to Manchester, he entered into a conversation with Newcastle.

"Once I knew [United] did want to sign me, it was the only club [for me] as I wanted to work with Sir Alex Ferguson and play with Ryan Giggs, Paul Scholes, Roy Keane, Rio Ferdinand," Rooney told the official Manchester United podcast in 2020. "It was 40 minutes from my home and it was a perfect fit. United wanted to wait a year, but then Newcastle came into talks with Everton and with myself. I'd gone too far then. I couldn't stay another year at Everton, so I was prepared to go to Newcastle for that year.

"What I wanted if I went there was, after a year, if Manchester United come in, you have to let me go. Newcastle were agreeing to that but with Man United, I went back to them and said, if you don't do it now, I'll go to Newcastle with a clause in place. Man United obviously didn't want me to go there so I came here. It was basically whatever Newcastle paid for me, Man United would have paid a year later."

United raised their offer. Everton accepted. The move was on.

Among the Everton squad, the talk of Rooney's imminent move was spinning their head as much as his. "There was this period where other clubs were making offers and he was involved in those negotiations," says Nick Chadwick. "It was very quickly obvious that he wasn't going to be at Everton for very long. It was unbelievable considering how recently he'd made his debut. But the top clubs wanted him and they were willing to pay a hell of a lot of money.

"Everton couldn't afford to turn down a ridiculous offer. David would have been frustrated, he would have ambitions to build a team around Wayne. From an Everton perspective it was sad. I do remember thinking how amazing it was that a lad who'd come through our academy was moving for that amount of money.

"It was bittersweet. If Everton had had the stature of United he'd never have gone. But they didn't, and United were winning titles. Wayne deserved to be on the world stage and Everton weren't able to provide it. I'm sure there was a genuine sadness or conflict even for him because it was clear to see he loved Everton. He knew he had to think of his career."

While talks were ongoing, there were still a couple of games left to play in August. United were at Blackburn, Everton were at home to West Brom, and then, two days later, Everton were ironically going to Old Trafford.

Everton owner Bill Kenwright admitted it was 'inevitable' Rooney was leaving, but stressed the deal was not complete. Everton won against West Brom, but the coverage of the game was dictated by the events surrounding it. On the walls of Gwladys Street Primary School, directly across from the souvenir store at Goodison Park, the words 'Rooney die' were etched in white spray paint. Chants of 'there's only one greedy bastard' filled the air from the Goodison crowd who once chanted his name.

After the match, Moyes gave an impassioned speech. "I'm so disappointed because how often in life do you get to work with a genius like Wayne Rooney?" he said. "And I have enjoyed it. I have a great relationship with Wayne. This is a real blow to us. I had been in regular discussions with Wayne's advisers and we were getting closer on the new contract. But I just didn't expect an offer to come in from any club. Our contract had such a good price with it. The club really pushed the boat out and up to a couple of weeks ago I felt that Wayne would definitely be an Everton player.

"I have to respect Wayne's wishes but I hoped this wouldn't happen. I am just disappointed. Anyone who thinks this club wants to sell Wayne is off their head.

"My advice to him has been to stay. The club gave him the opportunity – he might not have got that at Manchester United. But it seems that since the European Championship we have been firefighting. We had no word back from Wayne or his advisers to say that he was going to stay. They've given us the word now."

Everton defender Alan Stubbs was keen to defend his soon-to-be former team-mate. "We heard what was being shouted and I suppose that is a natural reaction," he said. "I can understand that, but Wayne is a great lad. He's a diamond. As footballers, you sometimes only get one chance and you have to grab it. That chance has come for Wayne."

The greedy chants were repeated at Old Trafford. United supporters responded with 'Rooney, Rooney'. The game ended 0-0 – both sides clearly missing the spark of inspiration that a fit Wayne Rooney would surely provide.

Later that day it was confirmed that he would be providing it for Manchester United, as he completed the transfer which made him the most expensive teenager in world football.

"I am very excited," Sir Alex Ferguson said. "I think we have the best young player this country has seen in the past 30 years. Everyone is delighted."

Rooney issued a short statement: "It was a tough decision to leave Everton, but I'm excited to be joining a club as big as Manchester United. I feel this can only improve my career, playing with top players in top competitions."

Alex Ferguson welcomes his new recruit to Old Trafford on September 1st, 2004

Ferguson and Rooney elaborated at the press conference the following day. "It is more difficult for the players these days because of the way that television has increased their profiles. There is tremendous pressure on them," Ferguson said. "But we have a good reputation for handling players. Wayne will get the same protection as the others but the dressing room provides a security. Players like Keane, Giggs, Paul Scholes and the Nevilles are all mature, stable professionals and that is the best protection for him.

"Wayne is a phenomenal talent and one we couldn't afford to miss out on. But he is a young lad and he understands that we are not asking him to climb the mountain tomorrow. The important thing is that he is a major player for us in five years' time."

Rooney spoke openly about how it was the stage which had enticed him. "It was a difficult decision because I've supported Everton all my life," he said. "I understand that the fans are upset... if Everton could offer Champions League football then things might have been different. But I wanted to move on for my career. I know I can win medals and become a better player with United. Euro 2004 really made my mind up about wanting to play for a bigger club. I knew I could play with the top players in the big tournaments. And I wanted to do it week-in, week-out. When you hear the other players talk about who they are facing in the Champions League it's only natural.

"I've been into the dressing room and people like Roy Keane and Ryan Giggs were sitting there. If I need any advice I hope I can just turn to them. But no one has to tell me how to behave on or off the pitch because I'm well aware of the responsibilities."

Rooney could claim he had matured, but there was a sense that the player acknowledged his prior immaturity a little too late, and was not yet old enough to attribute the dissolution of his relationship with Moyes in a more appropriate fashion. He was, however, old enough to acknowledge that he could not get away with some of the stunts he did at Everton. There would be no buckets of water on the top of doors to drop on the boss here; no questioning Sir Alex Ferguson's managerial credentials. No football on the street.

The major difference, of course, was that Wayne Rooney had walked into a dressing room of winners led by a man who suffered no fools. You could not afford to get on the wrong side of him. Rooney would later claim that he walked into Old Trafford full of confidence but in his first few weeks, while still recovering from his injury, it took him a short time to become settled.

"I was coming back from my injuries when Wayne signed," remembers Phil Marsh, who was a young player at United at the time. "There was a very short time where we had some rehabilitation together. In the first few days he seemed a little bit nervous. It's probably the only time I saw that from him – that he seemed a little bit overawed by the size of the club and the fact that he was now in a first-team dressing room of all-stars."

The mood was different at Old Trafford to the one Rooney was used to, even at international level. "We didn't talk about transfers. United were always connected to the best players in the world," says Roy Carroll. "At other clubs you would talk. I remember when I was at West Ham and there was speculation about Carlos Tevez signing, all the players would talk about it. At United you're just concentrating on what's around you.

"I remember the wonder goal he scored against Arsenal… there was a lot of talk about him, so you want to be able to see them live to see for yourself. When he came to Old Trafford he was different class. Sir Alex knew a player. When he was going in for Wayne it was the talk of the country. His enthusiasm and energy was so wonderful, he just wanted to play and no player in the world wants to defend against a player like that."

Rooney couldn't wait to play for his new club. He had hoped to be involved against Liverpool in mid-September, but wasn't quite ready for that or the trip to Spurs the following week. It was rumoured he would be on the bench for the Champions League game with Fenerbahce at Old Trafford. United had suffered an inconsistent start to the season, winning just once in the first five games and being left with a nine-point deficit to league leaders Arsenal.

Without question, the Manchester United Wayne Rooney thought he was joining was the relentless powerhouse he had grown up with. The club who had won eight league titles while he had been alive. While he was scoring overhead kicks against the junior United side, the senior team were winning the European Cup. Rooney could believe he was following in the footsteps of Eric Cantona and Dwight Yorke as a striker to serve as the final piece of a jigsaw. Had he known the rebuilding process at United was quite so intensive he might well have been tempted to spend another year with the club he supported. There was plenty of quality at the club but also a high number of players who were transitional in their purpose. In the moment, though, there was still the hope that they would form part of another great United team.

To two of the players who could most definitely not be described as transitional, Gary Neville and Roy Keane, Rooney's arrival was the perfect fillip at the perfect time. Neville described Rooney as being 'at the right club' now while Keane was even more effusive, saying: "That is what Manchester United is all about – exciting players who the fans want to see and who get them up and out of their seats."

In the press conference ahead of the Fenerbahce game, Ferguson was keen to talk up the chances of his team this season, now that he had two of the most highly-rated teenagers in world football in his squad.

"I can't think of another club in the world who have two young players of such potential," Ferguson said. "Cristiano is 19 and Wayne is 19 next month and the prospect of seeing them play together excites everyone here. But I'm not so excited now as I'm hoping to be next May. Ronaldo is improving all the time and we're all looking forward to Rooney's debut. In training players like Wayne will catch your eye and you know you are looking at something special. But the real examination comes when they step out on to the football pitch – and I'm sure he will come through it with flying colours.

"Looking at him as an 18-year-old lad, I don't see where the coaching comes into it. He has a natural instinct for the game; a natural ability to play anywhere on the field. You don't expect to see such maturity in someone of his age. He's quick, two-footed, aggressive, strong, good in the air, can pass, has got good vision and can shoot off both feet. There is not an 18-year-old anywhere who has his potential and you just hope he can eventually put it all together and become the complete player."

Old Trafford would have to wait to see Rooney and Ronaldo together but an hour before kick-off, the United supporters received the news they were waiting for – their new signing would be making his debut. Fenerbahce were champions of Turkey and had started the season well. A run through United's team showed the quality at the club and the areas still to be improved – Carroll, Neville, Ferdinand, Heinze, Silvestre, Bellion, Djemba-Djemba, Kleberson, Giggs, Rooney, Van Nistelrooy.

As they walked out for the first half, television cameras were waiting to focus in on the new boy. Rooney was instantly notice-able for striding on to the Old Trafford pitch with his red shirt torn down the middle. United's Nike shirts did not have collars; the material around the neck stretched, but Rooney had been uncomfortable – something he attributed to working out over the summer and developing his neck muscles – and tore it. It added to the impression of a lad who had been plucked from the streets to play for the biggest club in the land. The feeling of a spectacle was tangible.

This was, by a considerable distance, Rooney's biggest game at club level. Having gingerly acclimatised himself with his new team-mates, now was the moment to see if he could play alongside them. In the end, it barely seemed to matter. All that could be remembered from the evening was Rooney rampaging with the ball, taking on the Turkish team almost all by himself.

In the opening minutes he gave an indication of his ambition when he teased experienced goalkeeper Rustu Recber out of his goal and clipped a shot just over. There was a frenetic buzz whenever the ball was played in to Rooney; almost a sense from the crowd that they knew they were watching history unfold. It was one of the old guard who struck first – Ryan Giggs' early header allowed the hosts to play with a little more freedom. That would explain Ruud van Nistelrooy dropping deep to instigate an attack in the 17th minute. Rooney made a diagonal dash from right to left behind the defence. The Dutchman's through ball was good. Old Trafford was at fever pitch as Rooney charged towards the box and emphatically powered home a left-foot effort high into the goal.

Ten minutes later, Giggs received the ball and passed it like a baton to Rooney. Some 30 yards from goal, with two markers close by, the forward shifted his feet and allowed the ball to run. It was majesty and trickery, coaxing the closest defender to attempt a tackle that was never going to get close. The home crowd roared with anticipation. Just outside the area, Rooney let fly with one of those arrowed efforts that had been so successful against Leeds in an Everton shirt. Against Croatia in an England shirt. And now against Fenerbahce in a torn United shirt. Recber flung himself towards it, but planted his face to the turf in despair, knowing his attempt was as futile as trying to stop fate itself.

Rooney's date with destiny was not quite over. He came back out for the second half – wearing a new shirt, *sans* tear – desperate to grab the hat-trick that had eluded him at the European Championship. An early left-footed half volley from 25 yards stung the goalkeeper's wrists. Nine minutes into the second period, United were awarded a free-kick just inside the 'D'. Ryan Giggs took the ball. Rooney grabbed it from him and said 'I'm taking it, I want my hat-trick'. Giggs was impressed by his confidence, and with good reason. Rooney's strike was impeccable, Beckham-esque, curled over the wall and into the unguarded area. At that moment it was barely even about the game – more the moment.

Powered by adrenalin, Rooney lasted the entire game, despite being out injured for almost 100 days. There was one final contribution – with the score 5-2, Rooney glanced a header into the path of Bellion, who made it six.

"It was a privilege to be on the pitch watching it all unfold," says Carroll. "He was everywhere. You watch the game back and you can see him playing like a kid in the park, chasing the ball everywhere. The goals on top of that, it was an incredible achievement to score a hat-trick. It was a big statement. He was buzzing. We were all buzzing for him."

In the stands observing the performance was Rene Meulensteen; Meulensteen was highly regarded within the club for his work with young players on their technical ability. He knew all about how extraordinary Rooney was – and how extraordinary what he had just accomplished was.

"I remember being at Carrington one Saturday morning," he says. "I was watching one of our young teams play and I was in conversation with some of our scouts. One was talking about this kid at Everton. How he was powerful, direct, a scorer of goals. The week after, he made his first-team debut for them. Credit should go to Sir Alex for being brave enough to make the statement of signing Wayne when he did. To bring him to Manchester United and to say he was ready, that he had all the attributes to go. He had everything that was required to be in the United team that he was building.

"Wayne was already so naturally ready for a player at such a young age… he was so powerful and explosive. He was picking the ball up and running at players and shooting from all angles. It was very difficult to defend against him. Senior players could give him the ball and he could make things happen. The goals he scored were obviously very exciting, but just as exciting was the anticipation of what he could do."

The reaction to one of the landmark nights in Manchester United history was as you might expect. Ferguson was a man renowned for cautious judgements on youngsters, but also had a good sense of when to let the praise flow. This was one such time. "Considering it was Wayne's first game it was magnificent," he said. "Anyone can see what potential the boy has – and don't forget he's only a young boy."

Van Nistelrooy had scored himself so could feel it was job done as far as this new partnership was concerned. "We were all delighted for him," he said. "It was a fantastic debut. Considering it was our first game together, we linked up well. He is only 18 and he knew all eyes were on him and yet he went out and just did his own thing. That is character and is fantastic. He can become a legend here if he carries on like that."

Rooney's impact had already been likened to that of Pele. It was only natural that a George Best comparison would follow, if not for what he did in Portugal, but for the fact he made such a seminal impression in the European Cup. Best was astounded by Rooney's performance. "You have to say that is as good as anything you have ever seen," said the United legend. "The lovely thing about him is his temperament – he loves the big stage and the sky is the limit. He can handle himself, he has two good feet, he's good in the air, he's got it all. You go through all the greats at United and you have to put him in there."

The scale of the achievement helped Rooney dispel those early nerves. He knew that he belonged; that he could thrive; that he could help United improve.

"He was a breath of fresh air," says Carroll. "He wasn't fazed by the stage. He gave everything on the training pitch and somehow found even more to give on match days. He was a hungry young player who was desperate to succeed, you could see that from the first day. It's difficult to describe but he fit in absolutely with the characters like Roy, Ryan and Paul who wanted to win everything. You could see it in the five-a-sides. Every little competition, he wanted to win. Ronaldo would usually take the free-kicks but then Wayne came in and they were both great at them. Facing them in training was a nightmare! I thought I would be okay after David Beckham left but then those two came in."

It would not be fair to ask him to score a hat-trick every week. After the euphoria of his debut, Rooney had to find his place on a more consistent basis. His league debut was not quite so memorable, with Middlesbrough coming away from Old Trafford with a draw and Rooney looking every inch an 18-year-old boy who was recovering from a broken foot. Further draws followed after the international break against Birmingham and Sparta Prague.

Perhaps a big occasion could shock the club back into life again – and they didn't come bigger than the game which fell on Wayne's 19th birthday, three and a half weeks after his debut. Arsenal had regained the Premier League title and had gone unbeaten for the full 2003/04 season. When they arrived at Old Trafford, they did so on the back of 49 league games without a loss. What followed was one of the most memorable matches in Premier League history, with Rooney the game's most influential player.

The match was 90 minutes long but the rivalry went back years. The animosity between the clubs seemed to be borne through the competition of the late 90s but it preceded Arsene Wenger at Arsenal and even Sir Alex Ferguson at Manchester United. Both clubs were well-placed to take the crown of English football's premier team after Liverpool's dominance faded – but United had wrestled control away from the Gunners. After he came to England, Wenger built upon a physical structure in Arsenal's defence with a combative midfield that was no stranger to a red card or two. They were *not* a team to be messed with, and they were unafraid of going toe-to-toe with United. Ferguson had eventually bested Wenger in the intense heat of this rivalry between 1996 and 2003, with five titles to two.

This latest regeneration period at Old Trafford had seen United slip to third in 2004 as they struggled to replace the consistent defending of Jaap Stam and Denis Irwin, the goal supply of David Beckham and the suspended Rio Ferdinand. United had fallen beneath the new Chelsea, and now Arsenal were slowly becoming victims of the Stamford Bridge takeover, with Mourinho's Blues racking up 1-0 wins in a manner that would have made George Graham blush.

There was already a sense that games between Arsenal and United were no longer encounters that would decide the destiny of trophies. Instead, there was a growing bitterness between the teams. In September 2003, a goalless draw had been played out at Old Trafford, with Ruud van Nistelrooy in the spotlight. He was deemed by the visitors to have overreacted to a foul by Patrick

Vieira which resulted in the Arsenal skipper being dismissed. When Van Nistelrooy missed an injury-time penalty, Martin Keown gave a pictorial definition to the word 'harangued', jumping on the striker and almost inciting a riot. Four Arsenal players were given suspensions and two United players were fined for improper conduct.

Thirteen months on, the prior game was on the pre-match menu. "They got away with murder," Ferguson said. "What the Arsenal players did was the worst I have witnessed in sport."

If that was melodramatic, Wenger was matching the tone: "Maybe it would be better if you have us put up against a wall and shot us all. I hope that he will calm down."

What followed was an engrossing match. United were intent on showing a physicality so that there could be no chance of them being bullied. The Arsenal players, meanwhile, all seemed to be imitating Wenger's chip on the shoulder vibe. Gary Neville and Jose Antonio Reyes went at one another – Neville using aggression, Reyes using theatrics. Wenger was furious when Ferdinand stepped across Ljungberg's path and the Swede threw himself to the ground. Both Neville brothers were booked for fouls on Reyes, while Ashley Cole was cautioned for a foul on Rooney where he actually caught him twice in order to stop him. Cole was livid when Van Nistelrooy went in on him in response.

The football match that was being played in the background was almost a non-entity. Arsenal were dominating possession but doing nothing with it. United were interested in forcing the play, but were happy to engage in any confrontation the Arsenal players wanted to start. The visitors became distracted by the physicality and believed they were being persecuted. There had been plenty of moments that would, in a regular game, be seen as flashpoints, but that moment in this encounter came in the

72nd minute. Rooney took possession, moved across the box and played a one-two with Ryan Giggs. He turned and shifted the ball past Sol Campbell. The Arsenal defender stood back and held his hands up as if to say he hadn't made contact. He was right. Ashley Cole also remonstrated.

"I agreed with them," said Rooney. "I hadn't been fouled; I'd just gone down because of my momentum as Campbell stopped me."

Referee Mike Riley infuriated the travelling contingent by awarding the penalty. Campbell's action had prevented Rooney from getting the ball; Rooney's anticipation of the contact had been theatrical, while the visitors could claim there was no contact. Van Nistelrooy stepped up to take the kick, repeating the events of the previous game. His finish was cool; his celebration almost an exorcism of those past demons.

With 15 minutes to rescue their unbeaten run, Arsenal were frantic, but losing their composure. Ronaldo ran at Cole and was brought down in the box – this one a more concrete penalty than the first, but Riley probably sensed civil war might well erupt if it was given. In the end, it was academic – United exploited Arsenal's vulnerability in the last minute of injury time. Substitutes Louis Saha and Alan Smith combined to lay on a golden opportunity for the birthday boy to score his first league goal for United. For the second time, Rooney was responsible for Arsenal heartbreak.

Arsenal's players were incensed. The players clashed in the tunnel, with the visitors shouting 'cheat', and the two managers arguing back and forth. Arsenal youngster Cesc Fabregas emerged from the dressing room with a slice of pizza to throw – whether it struck his intended target is unknown, but for the second time in two years Sir Alex Ferguson found himself embroiled in an incident involving identified flying objects (the previous being the kicked boot at David Beckham's head). Rooney later admitted he had enjoyed the idea of the scuffle and intended on striking Lauren, the Arsenal defender, following comments made through the game – but the scrap was separated before it came to that.

"It was a massive game," says Roy Carroll. "Those games were always battles. It was a credit to Wayne that he came into his first experience of one and won the penalty and scored the other goal. From the view I had it looked like Sol Campbell stuck his leg out and brought Wayne down. For me it looked like a penalty. Maybe today with video replays it might not have been. But we were talking about a very fast game, on a very quick pitch, and those kind of matches must have been very difficult to referee. Rooney was man of the match that day, because he was like an animal on fire, desperate for us to win the game."

But Arsenal would not accept that they had been beaten by the better side.

"We feel we have been robbed," a fuming Wenger told reporters. "We were the better team and the difference was made when the referee awarded them the penalty."

Ferguson was at his mischievous best a few days later, claiming the penalty was a just award. "When I saw it on *Match of the Day* later on, I thought it was soft," he said. "But when we analysed it during the week, the view from behind Sol Campbell shows his leg two feet high! The ball was on the ground, so why the hell was his leg up so high? It was either done to intimidate the player or it was just bad defending. He caught his kneecap. If I was his manager, I'd be asking him that question."

Whatever could be levelled at United and Rooney, the one definite conclusion was that the former Everton man had the temperament for his new stage. Once again he found himself asking a familiar question – were his team-mates as capable of raising their own game in order to achieve greatness?

Chapter Seven

ROONEY SE VOLVIO LOCO

L ife was not quite an immediate fairytale for Wayne Rooney at Manchester United, despite the fantastical nature of his debut and how he had blown Arsenal away. There was a practical issue. United obviously needed to play him, but how he would fit into the side was less straightforward.

Against Newcastle in November, he had impressed moonlighting from the left hand side, though his first goal of two came from the right – a wonderful half-volley across goal early on in a 3-1 win. United had lost to Portsmouth and drawn with Manchester City after the win against Arsenal, and were now 11 points behind Chelsea. After winning against the Magpies, Rooney encapsulated the spirit of his new club by insisting they would continue to fight. "No one should ever write this club off as we always stick in there," he said. "I certainly believe there is enough talent in this squad to win the title."

The fight was a little too literal the following midweek – England played Spain in a friendly that was anything but. The match was marred by continual racist abuse towards Ashley Cole and Shaun Wright-Phillips, and Rooney was riled from the word go. He should have been booked for a wild lunge on Joaquin, and then was cautioned for a push on Iker Casillas. There were still more than five minutes to go until the break and Rooney threw himself into another crazy challenge – prompting Sven-Goran Eriksson to bring off his star striker in the 41st minute. Spanish newspaper *Marca* carried the headline *Rooney se volvio loco* – Rooney is going crazy.

"I think it was the first time for England I have seen him lose his temper," Eriksson explained. "But the experience will be good for him. He will learn a lot. I really don't know why he was like that. Sometimes we forget that he is just a boy. I don't think it is a big problem. He knows what he did and what he should have done."

It could not be denied that the Wayne Rooney of Manchester United was already perceived very differently to the one who'd played for Everton. It was as if the young scallywag had evolved into an unlikeable thug, his off-pitch actions amplified by the divisive nature of the badge he now wore on his shirt. He may have been described as friendless, and for a while it seemed as though the only two men prepared to see the positive side of the teenager were the two men who needed him to perform – his respective managers for club and country.

On Boxing Day, United welcomed Bolton to Old Trafford, and a routine win was blighted by an encounter between Rooney and Tal Ben Haim. The United forward reacted angrily to a challenge and threw his hands up in his opponent's face; Ben Haim sensed an opportunity and thrust himself to the ground. It was away from the gaze of the referee, but all the talk after the game was about a retrospective punishment for Rooney.

"Ben Haim went down rather too easily but you can't get away from the fact that Rooney pushed him in the face," Bolton manager Sam Allardyce insisted. "From Sir Alex Ferguson's point of view it was a bit of play-acting from our player, but Rooney would have been sent off if the referee had seen it."

Ferguson did indeed see it differently: "The Bolton player should be embarrassed. It was absolutely nothing." Three days after the game, Rooney was charged with violent conduct and faced a three-match ban. He admitted the charge, though Ferguson was keen to add a further defence of his player. "We've had a meeting with the senior players and Wayne. He will be alright, it's just a lesson. We know he shouldn't raise his hand and I've spoken to him about that. It was silly – every man and his dog could see it wasn't worthy of a violent conduct charge – but he doesn't need all that goes with it.

"The profile he gets in normal life is unusual for a lad of 19, so we have to get him to act like a 30-year-old. Young boys do have an adventure to them that older players don't. Unfortunately you can't put the clock forward for a boy of 19. But he is going to have to accept the responsibility of being the most-talked about player in Britain."

Ferguson was critical of the FA but had accepted the charge quickly to ensure Rooney was available for the first leg of the League Cup semi-final against Chelsea and the league game at Anfield. He helped his team get a creditable draw at Stamford Bridge and then prepared for his hottest atmosphere to date.

Liverpool bore some similarities to Chelsea; they had a new manager from the continent, Rafa Benitez, and seemed more focused on keeping the score as low as possible, making for cagey and physical affairs. United were in need of fortune or inspiration; Rooney provided the latter in the 21st minute. From the inside left position, he surveyed the picture in front of him, and used the space to get his shot away earlier than Jerzy Dudek had anticipated. The effort squirmed through the goalkeeper's hands and into the net. It was one of those which would definitely go down as an error, though Dudek's opposite number had some sympathy for him.

"I don't know if I'd call it a mistake but Dudek should definitely have done better. He would have wanted to push it away," Roy Carroll recalls. "But Wayne would get his shot away early and catch the goalkeeper off guard. I faced it in training all the time – he was very good at it. He took a short back-lift to get the shot away early and it's very difficult for the goalkeeper to react. He loved scoring in front of the Kop."

United held on to the lead, despite Wes Brown's second-half red card, while the following week, Ferguson gave a glowing review of Rooney's contributions so far. "We've always recognised that Wayne is a big-game player," the United boss said. "He's just a natural for the big occasion. You sometimes wonder with young players how are they going to cope in front of 67,000 at Old Trafford. But players like Wayne don't think that way. They think, 'This is the stage I've always wanted to play on'.

"It doesn't faze him, he thrives on it. And with the terrific games we've got coming up in all four competitions it is very healthy for us that he is coming into his best form."

Four competitions were quickly to become two. Chelsea triumphed in the second leg of the League Cup, while AC Milan won both legs of the second round Champions League tie by a goal to nil. There was, at least, progression in the FA Cup. Rooney followed his strike at Anfield with a goal to knock out Exeter City and set up a fourth-round clash with Middlesbrough. With his side already comfortable thanks to a first-half lead, Rooney turned on the style. Gary Neville hit a long ball forward and Boro goal-keeper Mark Schwarzer thought about coming for it. Indecision was fatal – Rooney executed a perfect lofted chip over the goalie and into the net. That was just the starter. Fifteen minutes later, Saha flicked on a ball from Carroll and Rooney allowed the ball to cross his body before striking it flush on the volley into the top corner from eighteen yards.

Steve McClaren, the Boro manager, could only applaud his team's conqueror. "I saw his debut for United when he scored that hat-trick and it served as an instant message that he could be like Cantona – a player who can win games for you and who everybody adores," he said. "This is a club for heroes, they went out on a limb to buy him, and he will be a hero for them – in fact he is already."

He was still one of the prime villains as far as United's next opponents, Arsenal, were concerned. Their February game at Highbury was the return fixture from the 'Battle of the Buffet' although the Gunners had decided Gary Neville was the main antagonist from the last game, and set about confronting him. It made for a pre-match spectacle as Roy Keane went toe-to-toe with Patrick Vieira in the tunnel. The game was explosive from the first to last minute – Keane set the tone, his team-mates never backed down, and Ronaldo was decisive in a 4-2 win. It was Keane, Vieira and Ronaldo dominating the sports pages, but the angry face of Rooney was seen towards the front, after complaints had been lodged following a reported 100 swear words heard on the television broadcast of the match. Rooney was far from the sole culprit, but he had become the face of it.

It set the tone for concerns over his temper for the following month, as United were due to play at Manchester City, and had also been drawn against Everton in the FA Cup – facilitating an earlier-than-expected return to Goodison Park for Rooney. The worries were unfounded. First of all, Rooney scored in a 2-0 win at City, and then handled the inevitable torrent of abuse at his former home well; despite a pre-match verbal exchange with an angry home fan. United again won 2-0 to go through to the next round.

Rooney's former team-mates could see both sides of the coin. "Maybe Wayne made a rod for his own back with the t-shirt in the Youth Cup," Nick Chadwick reasons. "I think it was genuine but as soon as he moved he was always going to get a certain amount of abuse. Football is very tribal and leaving a club often comes with that sort of feeling of betrayal."

Scott Brown had more sympathy for his old strike partner. "Fans are fickle," he says. "He had to go to United and probably had to go at the time he did. Would he have had the career he had if he stayed at Everton? Probably not."

It was Ronaldo who earned most of Sir Alex Ferguson's praise after the game, following another round of aggressive fouls that he had been subjected to. The Portuguese winger had scored in the match; it seemed very much a case that if one of the world class teenagers didn't turn it on, the other one invariably would.

"When you have a couple of players who are so young with different backgrounds it takes time for them to get to know each other," says Roy Carroll. "Ronaldo was coming from a different league and had to get used to the physicality of the Premier League. He had his own attributes that were different to Rooney's. Rooney was brought up in English football. He had those years with Everton. He would be into 50/50 tackles and getting angry. Ronaldo had this tremendous class with the ball at his feet. Obviously after a little time of them getting to know each other it clicked, but it took time."

Rooney receives a hostile reception on his return to Goodison Park after United were paired with Everton in the FA Cup fifth round in February 2005

Ferguson was banking on the combination becoming fluid enough to terrify defences. They were doing a good enough job of it individually, scoring the goals to get United's next two home wins between them – Rooney's brace against Portsmouth, and a Ronaldo goal against Fulham – though aside from that, the league form tailed off as Chelsea's consistency was unmatchable.

All that was left was the chance of FA Cup success, though Rooney once again learned about the devious nature of the tabloids when there were rumours of a bust-up with Coleen in the build-up to United's semi-final with Newcastle. Rooney later claimed damages and an apology for a fabricated story, but that process would take a year. He was subdued as his team nonetheless won 4-1 to qualify for the final against Arsenal in May.

Three days after the semi, United travelled to Everton in the league. It was a severe case of deja-vu for Rooney – first, in the abuse, and second, in the result – the Toffees winning 1-0 through Duncan Ferguson, a replica of the result almost ten years earlier that he had cheered in the stands at Goodison. Towards the end, Neville and Scholes were dismissed. The abuse turned to taunts – Everton were in fourth place, one behind United. They were set to qualify for the Champions League. Was it really worth moving?

On top of that, Rooney had now gone eight games without a goal. His return of 15 goals for United was pretty good, though nine of those had come in just four games. On April 22nd, he admitted to the club's official magazine that he needed to improve. "I would have liked to have scored more goals," he said. "I have had chances where I should have scored or where I have been a bit unlucky. Even if I had 30 this season I would want 40. That's just the way I am. I cost a lot of money and there is always expectation. I came to this club to play in the Champions League and win things. The last thing I won was the Sunday League with

Copplehouse Under-13s. My medal has still got pride of place at home, but I want to win more trophies here."

Over the course of the year Rooney had been compared to Pele, George Best and Eric Cantona, though one could have also likened him to Mark Hughes – an Old Trafford legend who was a scorer of great goals rather than a great goalscorer. It was clear Rooney wanted to be both, but the point was proven in that weekend's game against Newcastle.

The visitors had an early lead and United, with Ronaldo on the bench and Scholes and Van Nistelrooy missing, were struggling for goal power. United's stuttering form was proving so aggravating to the players that they began to consume themselves in arguments over decisions. Rooney was locked in one such discussion with the referee 10 minutes into the second half – Alan Shearer had kicked the ball away, and Rooney wanted him booked. Ferguson was preparing to bring his forward off, sensing another flashpoint, though Rooney was also suffering from a dead leg. Rooney was still remonstrating with the official when Roy Keane hit a hopeful long pass forwards. Magpies defender Peter Ramage headed the ball away – but the clearance dropped favourably for Rooney to run on to, still fully thirty yards from goal.

Such a description makes what happened almost sound simple. It was anything but.

Rooney arrived to meet the ball perfectly. It was almost two feet from the ground when the connection was made; a perfect height to generate enough power. His position was to the left of the goal; the volley was so true that the ball swerved to the right and just under the crossbar. It was a sensational moment to trump even the pair of wonder goals he'd hit against Middlesbrough.

"It was a phenomenal goal, considering Wayne was injured," Ferguson said after seeing Wes Brown score a winner. "I was ready to take him off because of his dead leg, but he is such a terrific talent that he is always likely to do something extraordinary."

One more league goal followed – a clever chip in a rout of Charlton – before all eyes turned to the Millennium Stadium in Cardiff for the FA Cup final. The build-up to the game against Arsenal had been consumed with talk of Manchester United being taken over by the American Glazer family. It was seen as a move of an opportunist who would, in an instant, take hundreds of millions of pounds away from the club by leveraging the takeover against it. Supporters were furious, but powerless. Demonstrations were held at games throughout the month, though planned protests for FA Cup final day were ruined by torrential rain.

As for the game – Rooney was the best player on the pitch by a distance. In the 30th minute he struck a fierce angled shot that Jens Lehmann tipped over. From the corner, Scholes teed up Rooney, who volleyed just over. He was alive. Just before half-time he set off on a marauding run, beating Cole, Vieira and Senderos. Cole came back at him. So did Vieira. He beat them again. Just when it seemed space might open up for Rooney to have a moment that would equal Ryan Giggs' 1999 solo goal, Senderos came back to haul down the England striker on the edge of the box. Rooney – who deserved the chance to take the kick – fired high and wide.

Nobody watching had expected United to be quite so dominant. Rooney and Ronaldo were electric, and Arsenal had no answer. If either of them could have a moment of realising their vast potential, the game would surely be turned in their team's favour. Arsenal's players were as aggressive as they felt United's had been back in October, with Jose Antonio Reyes in particular on a revenge mission.

In the 67th minute, Rooney drifted out to the wide and hit a cross-shot; it caught out Lehmann, but bounced off his near post and away to safety. The Gunners were packing their defence and had them to thank for blocking goalbound shots from Keane and Van Nistelrooy. In injury time, Rooney flashed a shot from range that went over.

Extra-time was almost a non-event, save for Reyes getting a second yellow for a cynical block on Ronaldo. It went all the way to penalties and Arsenal – who had mustered just one shot on target in 120 minutes (and five overall, to United's 20) – got all five of their spot-kicks on target. So did United, with man-of-the-match Rooney netting, but Paul Scholes saw his kick saved, and Sir Alex Ferguson's side found themselves on the end of what BBC commentator John Motson described as a 'mugging'. Going into the league game in October, Arsenal had been projected as the better footballing team. United had proved comprehensively in the following two games that this was not the case, but they had little to show for it, just the hope of better days to come.

Chapter Eight

THE NEW OLD TRAFFORD

Roy Keane and Wayne Rooney shared a Manchester United dressing room for approximately 14 months. It was long enough to leave an impression.

"He was a top, top player," Keane wrote in his second auto-biography. "I knew that from the first training sessions. And we'd played against him; his ability was easy to spot." Towards the end of the 2004/05 season, Keane went on record to herald the future of the club. "It always takes maybe a year or two for players to settle in," he said. "I still think Wayne and Cristiano are learning the game and they are very much individual players. They have a lot to learn regarding team play but they are outstanding players and that is the stuff we are working on with them every day."

Rooney had enjoyed an interesting introduction to life with Keane in the team hotel before the November trip to Newcastle in 2004. Keane was watching rugby league on television but went to the toilet and when he returned, Rooney had put *The X Factor* on – Keane left to watch the remainder of the game in his room after asking who had the remote.

It was a minor incident but indicative of the generation gap Keane was feeling; the likes of Rooney, Ronaldo and Ferdinand were happy to play video games, and Keane was probably even older than his 34 years. His playing personality was shaped by men like Brian Clough, Stuart Pearce, Bryan Robson, Steve Bruce, Eric Cantona, Mark Hughes and, as much as neither of them would like to admit it, Sir Alex Ferguson.

The dissolution of that particular relationship came in November 2005. To say it had been an indifferent opening to the season would be generous. Chelsea made a runaway start that was looking impossible to catch as early as October. It was going to be even more difficult for United without Keane, who had injured his foot in a goalless draw at Anfield in September. In the coming weeks, United lost at home to Blackburn, drew at home to Spurs and then suffered an embarrassing capitulation to Middlesbrough.

United's players would take it in turns to do post-match punditry for the club's in-house television station, MUTV. Keane was scheduled to appear after the Middlesbrough game but the decision was taken not to air the recording as the captain allegedly criticised a number of team-mates. Keane himself downplayed the severity of it. "I was annoyed, but I wasn't edgy about it," he said. "The idea that I was ranting and raving – no, it was quite calculated. The message was, we weren't good enough and we could do better."

Keane addressed the squad before training, calling a captain's meeting, talking about the need to refocus. When Ferguson noticed they weren't out on the field, he called everyone to watch the video. Keane was irate about being put in that position and argued with Carlos Queiroz and then Ferguson, making a reference to the controversy over a racehorse that had played a part in the Glazer takeover.

On Friday, November 18th, 2005, Keane and Manchester United parted ways after an acrimonious meeting between player and manager at Carrington.

Writing in his *Sunday Times* column in June 2020, Rooney discussed the contents of the video. "I disagree with how it's portrayed," he said. "Roy was supposedly too critical of his teammates but I've watched the video and there's nothing wrong with it. He said that players can't pass the ball 10 yards and they're playing for Manchester United and it's not good enough. Well, he's right."

Rooney went on to say of Keane: "I remember my first United training session thinking, 'I need to impress him.' Not the manager. Him."

When Keane's second book was released, Rooney had been quizzed on the minor references to him in the book, although the *X Factor* anecdote was as rough as it got; Keane clearly had a professional admiration for Rooney, and the feeling was mutual.

"I thought Roy was great," said Rooney – who, by the time of these comments in 2014, had followed in Keane's footsteps to become club captain. "He was hard when he needed to be and he was a nice fella as well. He would speak to you and he wouldn't give anyone any special treatment. Whether you were an older player or younger player, he would let you know what he wants from you. He was a great captain. The thing that surprised me with Roy was his passing in to a forward's feet. He was the best I've ever played with getting the ball into the forwards."

It had only been a year, but sometimes a year is enough – just as Robson passed the generational baton to Keane, he in turn had done so to Rooney. Although Rooney played a different position, the composition of the team had changed, as had the nature of the game. The blood-and-thunder sensibilities that the pair represented were not suited to the chess-style midfield battles that were becoming en vogue in 2005. It was in fact Rooney's tenacity as a forward player that set him apart and made him a nightmare for defenders.

Earlier in the season it seemed as if it might be Rooney's, and not Keane's, mouth that gave his manager the biggest headache. Rooney had a week to forget in September – first, he was involved in a dressing room argument with David Beckham on international duty. England were on the way to a 1-0 defeat against Northern Ireland when Rooney – according to *The Guardian* – called the captain a 'flash bastard'. Beckham had tried to calm his young colleague down after Rooney had elbowed David Healy. Rooney was fortunate to escape with a yellow card, but didn't have the same luck a week later when playing for United in their Champions League group game with Villarreal. The striker was dismissed for sarcastically applauding Kim Nielsen – ironically, the same referee who infamously sent off David Beckham at the 1998 World Cup.

There was no sign of Ferguson being irritated by his young star. In fact, it was quite the opposite – when FIFA president Sepp Blatter made a public remark about how he felt the United boss should 'keep a check' on Rooney's behaviour, Ferguson responded: "FIFA should be concentrating on the big issues – and the temperament of a 19-year-old Manchester United player isn't one of them."

The Roy Keane era had concluded, ironically enough, with a spirited win over Chelsea thanks to a tremendous goal from Darren Fletcher, which ended the champions' 40-match unbeaten run. After the match, Rooney had insisted Mourinho's team were 'catchable', and later in the month, the United manager claimed: "There's no doubt that Rooney and Van Nistelrooy are showing league championship-winning form."

A good partnership was certainly developing. The Dutchman was back after a series of injuries and in good form – and his predatory style suited Rooney's drifting play down to the ground.

Van Nistelrooy had nine goals already, and Rooney five, but they had also scored in four games together.

"He had a good relationship with Ruud," says Roy Carroll. "Rooney would be the player behind, looking to make things happen outside of the box, and Ruud was the penalty area predator. It reminded me a little of how Teddy Sheringham and Andy Cole linked up."

Carroll felt Rooney had taken well to life at the biggest club in the country: "He had an amazing impact in his first year. Playing with him every day, I was able to appreciate how good he was. When you're the goalkeeper you can see the full picture and you truly appreciate the work-rate. He was so committed to helping his team for someone so young and it was incredible to watch. And on top of that he had this ability to score goals that would leave you wondering just how he did it."

Despite the undoubted productivity, it did seem as if the entire club was in a new phase in the post-Roy Keane world. Van Nistelrooy had returned to show his class but there were early signs of an incompatibility. He had been at his best when David Beckham was supplying crosses from the right but that source of assists had been replaced by the more unpredictable Cristiano Ronaldo. It led to some confrontations at Carrington.

Rio Ferdinand remembered one such occasion, talking to BT Sport: "Ronaldo had the ball wide and was doing tricks and Ruud was making the run in the box, Ronaldo didn't pass and Ruud went crazy, screaming. 'He should be in the circus, he shouldn't be on the pitch,' Ruud said, and walked in, off the training pitch, and Ronaldo got upset – 'Why is he talking to me like that?'"

It was also rumoured that Van Nistelrooy had made a cruel remark about Ronaldo's father having passed away earlier in 2005. "Ruud had that kind of ego: he wanted all the passes," Louis

Saha told *FourFourTwo*. "And sometimes, for the development of Cristiano Ronaldo and Wayne Rooney, it was difficult for the manager to deal with. Did Ruud make Ronaldo cry? Yeah, there were stories because I think they ended up in an argument when Cristiano's father had passed away."

Saha's second season at Old Trafford had been plagued by injury, and now he was back fit, it was difficult to get a chance when the front pair was so established. Ferguson was still a big fan of the Frenchman, who was showing signs of being a good fit alongside Ronaldo and Rooney in League Cup games. Coupled with the training ground problems, the United manager observed that he might have to make a change before there was a prominent issue. When Paul Scholes was ruled out for the season in January 2006 due to an eye problem, Ferguson asked his and Gary Neville's advice on what to do with Van Nistelrooy. Scholes said the Dutchman was the disruptive influence. The phasing out began.

As Ferguson was dealing with many moving pieces, Rooney continued to shine. He had grabbed the club's first goal of the season, in the Champions League qualifier against Debrecen, and followed that up with a strike at Everton on the opening day of the league season, much to the frustration of the home fans. He had a special run of form in December; a pair of magical goals in a win over Wigan showcased two different sides to his game. First, he fought like a tiger in the box to retain control of the ball and then finish at the near post. Then, he demonstrated all of his class with a chip over the goalkeeper.

Even when not scoring, he was earning plaudits. "Wayne was absolutely brilliant – I clapped him off the pitch," Gary Neville said after a 4-1 win over Bolton. "He must be a nightmare to play against. Physically you can't handle him and you won't beat him mentally either. And he has the skill. He can play as a centre-forward, drop wide, pass, tackle, shoot – he is brilliant. He is a true Manchester United player."

Bolton boss Sam Allardyce confessed: "Rooney frightened us not only with his skill, but also with his work-rate and his physical attributes. He was brushing off and holding off our players to make sure he kept possession. And some of his touches and skills were absolutely magnificent. He terrified our defence, he unhinged us and that is why we lost 4-1. A lot of other United players played well, but Rooney was the catalyst."

The biggest day of the season came in late February. United had qualified for the League Cup final against Wigan. Rooney was once again the best player for the club in a cup final, though this time, he was not leaving without the trophy. In the first half, he seized on some defensive uncertainty to finish confidently. In the second half, it was the trio of Ronaldo, Rooney and Saha who dazzled, all getting on the scoresheet to give United a comprehensive win and give Sir Alex a glimpse of a rosy future. Saha was starting at the expense of a visibly disgruntled Van Nistelrooy, but his tricky, pacy style made him a perfect complement for Rooney and Ronaldo. There was a new, engaging fluidity about the forward play.

A couple of weeks later – after putting Newcastle to the sword again – Rooney spoke further about life since the move to Old Trafford.

"I'm feeling better and sharper and that is down to myself and the fitness coach who has helped me get into tip-top shape," he said. "Since I joined United I've improved as a player. I'm really enjoying my football and I'm learning all the time. No disrespect to Everton, I'm playing with better players and I'm maturing on the pitch and becoming a better player. I'm also playing for a great manager. I've no regrets about joining United. I love the club. I love the fans. We've won the Carling Cup and that gave me my first medal and now I want more trophies."

Ferguson had spoken about how the League Cup could boost the confidence of this new-look squad. In addition to Ji-Sung Park, he had also signed legendary goalkeeper Edwin van der Sar at the start of the season. In January, he added Nemanja Vidic and Patrice Evra to his defence, and after some early difficulties, the improvement was obvious. The cup final win was the first of eight victories in a row that helped United secure second place in the league ahead of Arsenal. Rooney was showing his increasing importance to the team, with an emphatic goal and performance in the win over Arsenal to help get that runners-up spot, and two goals at Spurs a week later.

As the English press decreed, every rise must come with a fall, and so it came with new reports about his personal life on the morning of the Arsenal game in mid-April. One newspaper carried the story that Rooney had run up a gambling debt of £700,000. He was open about it in his book *My Story So Far*, and denied it was a problem. He cited boredom and it could be argued that it was an understand-able explanation, as absurd as that seems to most people. The man on the street might have tens or even hundreds of pounds of dispos-able income. Rooney had hundreds of thousands and had admitted when he received his first professional pay-packet of £7,000 per week, he wasn't quite sure what to do with it. It remains difficult for most to comprehend, but a story told by Phil Marsh gives a little insight into what normality was like at Carrington.

"When you were coming back from injury you'd have a little free time after lunch and you play ping-pong or something," Marsh explains. "On this occasion another youth team lad and me were playing basketball in the gym. Phil Bardsley, Wayne and Rio were also injured. They came in and joined in. It was a game called 21, you just had to get to that score with free throws. Wayne said he'd beat any of us playing basketball. We were always very competitive so we played winner stays on. Wayne and Phil [Bardsley] ended up against each other and asked what they were playing for. I was expecting them to say £50 or £100. Wayne said 'You're not going to beat me, so bet whatever you want.' Phil says, 'What about your car then?' Wayne had just bought a Chrysler with a personalised plate. Anyway, Phil beat him. The next day, Wayne came into training and threw the car keys at him in the treatment room.

"We were laughing about it – but Phil still had the balls to comment about the registration plate, and Wayne not only ended up giving him the car, but paying to get the plate back off him."

Ferguson was quizzed on the stories after the Arsenal game. His response was blunt and protective. "It's unfortunate the media want to examine every part of him. It was George Best in the 1960s, then Paul Gascoigne and David Beckham – they are searching for someone to fill a headline, so Wayne is manna from heaven for them and it's nonsense. It was a great attacking performance today and Wayne was sensational at times."

What felt like classic breadcrumbing – setting the scene for Rooney's poor character ahead of the anticipated England exit from that summer's World Cup – quickly gave way to an about-face that would have made Saul Goodman blush. Nine minutes from the end of United's defeat at Chelsea (a result which confirmed the Blues as champions) on the last weekend of April, Rooney was challenged by Paulo Ferreira. He was in obvious, immediate discomfort – it transpired he had broken the same foot as at the European Championship two years earlier. Ferguson must have thought the gods of irony were against him, considering his Beckham comment; it was, of course, the same injury suffered by the midfielder ahead of the World Cup four years earlier. He'd been here before. He knew what would come next. The boy who was being profiled to become public enemy number one was now projected as the man on which England's chances rested.

Chapter Nine

BOND

S ven-Goran Eriksson and Sir Alex Ferguson had shared this dance floor before. Ferguson had taken a pre-emptive strike on May 2nd, declaring that Wayne Rooney would not be fit in time for the World Cup. He was hopeful that Eriksson would recall the rush to get David Beckham to the tournament four years earlier, with three weeks less healing time. Though Beckham contributed, he was not the all-action hero who had starred in the crucial qualifier against Greece in October 2001. Knowing the type of player Rooney was – that he, like Beckham, would want to cover every blade of grass – it seemed like the United manager was hoping for some common sense from his England counterpart.

It was eventually agreed that Rooney would travel to Germany, with Ferguson quick to point out he had not been obstructive. "The thing which is most damaging to myself and Manchester United is the suggestions we don't want Wayne to go," he said.

"We have continually supported Wayne with his fight to get to the World Cup but we have to be certain he is physically and mentally fit. The one player I want playing in the World Cup is Wayne Rooney – the experience he would get, the confidence he would get. I want him to be there. I told him that on day one and that's my main drive to do that."

Eriksson confirmed the 'very positive dialogue' with United and spoke of the 'huge lift' Rooney's inclusion would give the squad. He missed the first game of the tournament against Paraguay and was given the last 30 minutes against Trinidad and Tobago. Both matches were won, so England were through to the next round. In the dead rubber group game against Sweden, Rooney started, and his presence gave Joe Cole the space to score a fabulous goal. Rooney was brought off with 20 minutes to go – if anyone thought this game was meaningless, they were given a moment to consider as the 20-year-old punched the dugout and threw his boots on the ground.

In the second round, England faced Ecuador. The game was decided by a Beckham free-kick, but this was the best seen yet of Rooney. "I was surprised at how well he did," Rio Ferdinand told reporters. "He just seemed to get stronger and stronger. We don't want to say he is back to his maximum. It's going to take minutes on the pitch to do that."

The victory took England into a quarter-final with Portugal, who had knocked them out of the last tournament. The problems, though, were already stacking up for Eriksson. Michael Owen had been injured against Sweden. Rooney would have to play in an unfamiliar role as a lone striker. The first half was sterile. Just five minutes into the second period, Beckham went off with an ankle injury. And in the 62nd minute came the major talking point of the evening.

Rooney was pressed by two defenders; with Ricardo Carvalho decidedly more physical than the situation warranted. Rooney shrugged him off, with Carvalho's efforts at wrestling so extreme that he fell to the ground. Rooney tried to regain his balance, but his studs planted into the groin of Carvalho. Referee Horacio Marcelo Elizondo of Argentina blew his whistle. Rooney – and most observers – expected a foul for England. Cristiano Ronaldo was closest to the scene and screamed at Elizondo to show a card to Rooney. Rooney, fuming and confused, pushed his club-mate away; they were separated by players rushing on the scene. Seconds later, Elizondo brandished a red card. Ronaldo was later seen on camera winking in the direction of the Portuguese bench.

With 10 men, England battled all the way to penalties – where, of course, they suffered their customary exit, with Steven Gerrard, Frank Lampard and Jamie Carragher all missing. For once, those who missed would escape the blame. Even Rooney would avoid the sort of ire that Beckham was subjected to in 1998. The role of antagonist in this saga was Cristiano Ronaldo. His intervention was seen as the deepest act of betrayal and this was the narrative played out in the press.

It was suggested there was no way Ronaldo and Rooney could co-exist at United any longer. Liverpool captain Gerrard was naturally eager to fan the flames. "If it was one of my team-mates I'd be absolutely disgusted because there's no need for that," he said. "I think Ronaldo's bang out of order. If I was playing against my team-mates from Liverpool and they were involved in a situation like that, I'd never try to get them sent off."

Sir Alex Ferguson was talking to Rooney over text message and had tried to connect with Ronaldo through his agent, Jorge Mendes. Rooney told the press he 'absolutely categorically… did not intentionally put my foot down on Carvalho'. Ronaldo, meanwhile, was conciliatory, explaining: "There is absolutely no problem between me and Rooney. He wasn't angry with me. He told me to completely ignore what the English press has said, that all they wanted was to create confusion."

Speculation continued – Real Madrid were seen as the likeliest new home for Ronaldo. United did do business with the Spanish club that summer, but only to sell them Ruud van Nistelrooy, for a surprisingly low fee of £10.2m.

Ferguson was adamant Ronaldo would not follow. "Cristiano will be our player next season and for the rest of his contract," he said. "He'll be back to start training again with us. I haven't paid much attention to what Cristiano is supposed to have said about his future. I haven't spoken to him since the World Cup."

Rooney had worked on a book – *My Story So Far* – that was published in August and would include his take on the World Cup. He was keen to tell interviewers that if they were hoping for dirt on his relationship with Ronaldo, they'd be wasting their time.

"Whenever England don't do well in a major tournament people always look for a scapegoat," he said. "Unfortunately this year a lot of people have turned on Cristiano. But I spoke to Cristiano the night of the game and there were no problems. I was disappointed with his involvement in the sending-off but that is in the past now. He was playing for his country, I was playing for mine. A lot has been said about him winking to his bench after I got the red card but he told me that had nothing to do with my sending-off.

"Cristiano is a good friend of mine. In the first half I was trying to get him booked for diving. We are good friends off the pitch and we try to work hard for each other on it."

Rooney admitted Van Nistelrooy's departure was a 'blow' but said he was keen to 'channel my World Cup disappointment into helping United win something this season.' But his preparation for the new campaign was thrown into disarray when he was bizarrely handed a three-match Premier League ban after being sent off in a pre-season tournament in Holland. After challenging it, United were told the suspension would stick – so Rooney would be available for the opening league game against Fulham, but would then have a few weeks off, taking into account the fact he had a two-game international suspension to serve, too.

There was a fair bit riding on that opening day. If you would have taken a straw poll of the supporters heading into Old Trafford, the majority would have said, if it came to it, that they would prefer to sell Ronaldo if it kept Rooney happy. The bigger gamble for Ferguson was trusting that both of them would be able to compensate for the goals lost from Van Nistelrooy. There was a very recent sign of how much they still had left to learn – United had faced doomed Sunderland in April, with the Black Cats on their way to claiming a tag of one of the worst-performing Premier League teams. They went down after playing United, but had held on for a 0-0 draw, with Ronaldo and Rooney misfiring. Ferguson was furious afterwards, telling the pair they'd been 'fucking shite'. There was a more PG summary for the television cameras: "They probably had their worst performances of the season, but we know they will be great players," Ferguson had said, with more than just a smidgeon of awareness that he would be banking on that being the case in just four months' time.

With more than one bold judgment being assessed, the football public watched with bated breath to see if United's young duo would immediately break into fisticuffs the second they got onto the Old Trafford pitch. The first-half fireworks were saved for the football; Ronaldo and Rooney in scintillating form as United put on a spectacular opening-day showing. Eight minutes in, the pair combined to play the ball to Saha. He laid the ball off for Giggs, who crossed for the Frenchman to head in.

Next, the Rooney-Ronaldo combination worked space to find Saha on the left. The drilled cross was intended for Rooney. His marker, Ian Pearce, could only knock the ball into his own net. Soon after, Neville took a quick free-kick – Saha's shot was saved, but Rooney converted the rebound. Just 16 minutes were on the clock.

Three minutes later came the moment the home crowd were dying to see; Rooney shook off a couple of challenges wide on the left, and spotted the run of Ronaldo on the far side. The cross was perfect – the shot matched it – United had a remarkable 4-0 lead before a quarter of the game had gone by.

Never mind the crowd, or Fulham – United's players needed to catch a breath, and they were able to do so at a luxurious pace for the rest of the game, with Rooney adding a second-half goal to round off a 5-1 win.

"I have been saying all summer there isn't a problem between us. People see things their way but they don't know the pair of us," Rooney said afterwards. "We are letting our football do the talking. A lot has been said about the fact we cannot fill Ruud's boots. We're trying to spread the goals throughout the team. It was good myself, Louis Saha and Cristiano Ronaldo all managed to get a goal."

Ferguson described them as 'the best of pals' and described the result as his 'best-ever start' to a new season. His plans to begin the season with a strong run of form in order to keep pace with Chelsea were dealt a blow by the Rooney suspension, but his team were able to keep going, thanks in part to the veterans at the club. Ole Gunnar Solskjaer came off the bench at Charlton after an injury-plagued three years to score his first goal since September

Rooney and Ronaldo doused speculation of a fallout from the 2006 World Cup 'wink gate' by linking to lethal effect in the season opener against Fulham

2003; it was an emotionally charged moment at The Valley. Ryan Giggs then scored the winning goals in victories against Watford and Tottenham.

Rooney returned for the visit of Arsenal but the Gunners stole a late victory at Old Trafford. However, a Solskjaer double against Newcastle ensured United would head into the October international break top of the table.

The October European Championship qualifiers were the stage for Rooney's return for England. By now, Steve McClaren was in charge, and he had made a bold call by dropping David Beckham from his first squads. Even with Rooney, England were unconvincing, drawing at home to Macedonia and losing in Croatia – qualification was not going to be straightforward.

Back at United, more games passed without a Rooney goal, but those games were wins against Wigan, Copenhagen and Liverpool. No-one at Old Trafford was concerned about his contribution.

Carlos Queiroz explained how Rooney had been taking extra training sessions throughout his suspension to get closer to match fitness, and against Wigan, Sir Alex described his performance as 'back to his best'. In the Champions League game against Copenhagen, Rooney had been made captain late in the day, as Rio Ferdinand pulled out before the match. At just 20, he was named skipper ahead of more experienced players, though Ferguson explained why after the match.

"Some players, like Paul Scholes, don't want to be captain, so it was an easy choice," he said. "And Wayne did fantastically, as I expected." The United boss was particularly pleased with the professional 3-0 win over the Danes. It made it three wins out of three in the group stages, after being knocked out at this point in the previous year's competition. "They have grown up," Ferguson said of his team. "They don't want any more embarrassments like last season, and they're playing good football into the bargain."

It seemed as if every Rooney birthday was a milestone; a time of reflection over what had been accomplished so far. His 21st was no different. "I don't want to be remembered as a player who could have won this or done that. I want to be remembered as a winner and I want winners' medals and trophies," Rooney said on the big day. Ferguson described Rooney's impact at the club as 'inspirational', adding: "When we signed him at 18 everyone said, 'What will he be like at 21?' Now he is 21 people say, 'What will he be like at 25?' It was always destined to be that way, because Wayne is truly blessed."

United were blessed to have him. The goals that had been missing since the opening day came back in Rooney's first game as a 21-year-old. At Bolton, he put on a clinic in the art of goalscoring. There was a Michael Carrick pass that was finished decisively at the near post. There was the instinct to latch on to a tackle on Gary Neville, take a touch and fire home from the edge of the area. And, after Ronaldo had made it three with a tap-in, there was the hat-trick goal; a moment of a team perfectly in sync, with Fletcher's first-time pass tracked confidently by the United striker – the ball allowed to bounce before Rooney took the time to make his first touch a goalscoring one.

Further wins against Portsmouth and Blackburn strengthened United's position at the top. Rooney then broke his international drought, scoring against Holland in a friendly in November; and it set him up nicely to hit more goals for his club. A brace at Bramall Lane had Sheffield United manager Neil Warnock declaring Rooney as 'the king… the best player in England and one of the best in the world'.

It was a sentiment clearly shared at Old Trafford – the following week, it was announced that Rooney had signed a new five-year contract which made him, reportedly, the highest paid player in the club's history. In the club's announcement, Rooney could not have made his happiness any clearer. "I love it here and there was no hesitation signing the contract. I want to stay for the rest of my career."

Rooney scored after just six minutes of the Manchester derby and he was joined on the scoresheet by Louis Saha and Cristiano Ronaldo in a 3-1 win. A 1-0 defeat at West Ham before Christmas was followed by convincing wins against Aston Villa, Wigan and Reading, with Ronaldo scoring two goals in each.

Since his return from the World Cup, Ronaldo had clearly taken a step in his physical development. It was as if he'd gone to Germany a boy and returned a man; his first three years had been littered with theatrics which, at times, frustrated even his own supporters. Suddenly United's patience had a pay-off. It could be said that both Ronaldo and Rooney grew now they were no longer in the shadow of a dominating striker and the pair's form was certainly a major reason why United were top of the league table at Christmas. Just before the holidays, Ferguson observed: "Cristiano and Wayne are still only kids but they are the leaders of the new team here now."

The tone was echoed by Wigan boss Paul Jewell after their defeat at Old Trafford on Boxing Day, who said: "Ronaldo is brilliant, and Manchester United are a brilliant team. But Rooney was amazing. We had a three-on-one situation when he got back to clear. The lad does not know the meaning of the phrase 'lost cause'. The difference between being good, very good and world class is desire. He has that in abundance."

Following the Reading win, Ferguson was again praising his youngsters. "Rooney and Ronaldo are helping everyone to realise they have big futures and they are going to be part of that," he said. "They have both signed contracts that will keep them here for a good few years… I'm sure Ronaldo is already in the 'best in the world' bracket. He's only 21 and he will get even better. Players like him, Rooney and Darren Fletcher will get better, no question."

Ferguson couldn't count his chickens just yet, but it was clear to see the improvement from the last few seasons. His team were fluid and rapid and now had a solid structure. Michael Carrick had been signed as a de-facto Roy Keane replacement, though their styles were nothing alike – Carrick was masterful in setting the tempo and moving the ball around in contrast to Keane's unrivalled position as on-pitch manager. Nemanja Vidic and Patrice Evra had helped make the defence much more resolute. It was a platform on which the young forward players could thrill and flourish.

They needed some senior back-up, though, when Louis Saha's injury problems returned. Solskjaer's return from injury was treated as a novel bonus rather than anything to build upon in the long term. Ferguson needed a temporary solution to ease the goal-scoring burden on Rooney and it arrived in the form of legendary Swedish striker Henrik Larsson, who signed on a short-term loan deal. His impact was instant, scoring against Aston Villa on his debut in the FA Cup.

Rooney had spoken about the 'big disappointment' of his career being the FA Cup final defeat of 2005 so he was keen to return to Wembley – particularly as the League Cup defence had ended so embarrassingly down at Southend. It was a humiliation Rooney almost wasn't subjected to. Ferguson had exercised his squad options to give many youngsters their chance. "There were a few of us who played against Crewe and we were pencilled in to play in the next round against Southend," recalls Phil Marsh. "I picked up a knock. One of the other lads did too. So Rooney and Ronaldo got called into the squad. They started – and we lost 1-0. Maybe if we'd have played, we would have won! In all seriousness, it's not a bad pair of players to be replaced by. I can live with that."

In the FA Cup fourth round, United welcomed Portsmouth. This was an opportunity for Ferguson to rotate again – so Ronaldo and Rooney were both given breaks, although Rooney was on the bench just in case. And that just in case moment arrived on the hour with the game goalless. The breakthrough came in the 77th minute when Giggs laid it on a plate for the substitute. But better was to come five minutes later; Rooney's first touch to control a Neville pass was perfectly cushioned with his left foot. It gave him the time and space to consider his next move. What followed had no reasonable chance of succeeding. The 6ft 4in frame of David James was well-placed within his six-yard box. Rooney, from 25 yards, still went for it – an audacious chip across the goalkeeper. It says much about the accuracy that James did not move. The ball sailed over him, clipping the crossbar on its way into the net. "The imagination and audacity to chip that second reminded me of some of Cantona's goals," said Ferguson.

"I was looking for the pass but I couldn't see one, so I decided to chip it and it went in," Rooney said, with some understatement. Thankfully his team-mates were on hand to give the moment the credit it deserved. 'Awesome', said Michael Carrick; Rio Ferdinand gave a more thorough analysis. "It didn't really surprise me," he said. "Wayne is a fantastic footballer. He is a joy to play with, a joy to watch, and that was an exquisite cameo of what he can produce. He is on a learning curve. But when people have been questioning him over his goalscoring, his work-rate and team ethic have never wavered at all and that is testament to him."

Rooney was outstanding against Watford four days later, wonderfully creating a goal for Larsson and then netting with another lofted effort.

Larsson had expected his career to end quietly at Helsingborgs after a successful two-year spell at Barcelona. That time in Spain had concluded with a Champions League win alongside the likes of Xavi, Iniesta, Ronaldinho and a young Lionel Messi. This is necessary background to appreciate the gravity of Larsson's comments in early February. "It's frightening what Wayne and Cristiano can do and they are already up there with the best I've played with," the Swede explained. "Wayne, in particular, has got the vision and can score goals, so as long as you move when you have a player like that around, you are always going to get chances."

United were in a strong position. They had a six-point lead over Chelsea with 13 games remaining. One by one, the games went by. A 4-0 win at Spurs. A 2-0 win over Charlton. The gap remained six points. Then came the emotional boosters. A last-minute win at Fulham thanks to Ronaldo. A last-minute win at Anfield – perhaps the only time in Rooney's career he would have been happy to come off. He suffered a knee injury after a poor challenge by Jamie Carragher, and required eight stitches. He was replaced by John O'Shea, who grabbed United's goal deep into stoppage time.

Rooney ended a run of eight games without a goal when he scored in the FA Cup at Middlesbrough – a 2-2 draw that would go to a replay. Before that, United faced Bolton at home, and hit one of those blistering goal flurries that Fulham had been subjected to on the opening day. Park scored after 14 minutes but it was Rooney's goal two minutes later which has remained the most memorable from this game. And with good cause, too.

From a Bolton corner, Ronaldo took control in his own box and laid the ball off to Rooney. The pair were 30 yards from their own goal and already sowing the seeds of their devastation; Rooney's back-heel was perfect for Ronaldo to race on to. The counter was on. Ronaldo carried the ball 40 yards and waited for the runs of Giggs and Rooney to create space. Rooney's gallop on the left put him in the more favourable position for a pass. Ronaldo's through ball was perfect. Rooney's clipped finish over Jussi Jaaskelainen was too. In a game where United's array of attacking abilities were on show, this was an astonishing showpiece of speed and lethality, a realisation of potential before the eyes of 76,058 supporters. Further goals from Park and Rooney rounded off a 4-1 win.

They grabbed the goals, but Ronaldo grabbed the glory, with Richard Tanner of the *Express* describing the winger as 'arguably now the world's best player'. Two days later, Ronaldo scored as United eliminated Middlesbrough from the FA Cup – James Morrison was sent off in the last minute for a dangerous lunge on the showboating Portuguese star. Morrison's challenge provoked a melee with both benches getting involved. Rooney was angry, pushing and shoving, and could easily have been sent off himself.

For a couple of weeks, the Ronaldo-Rooney show took a breather. It was a time for experience, with Paul Scholes inspirational in a 4-1 win over Blackburn, before a couple of hiccups – a 2-1 defeat in Rome, in the Champions League quarter-final (a game in which Rooney scored his first non-qualifier goal in the competition since his debut hat-trick) and a loss by the same score at Portsmouth that reduced their league advantage to three points.

With the pressure on, and no Larsson – who had returned to his parent club – it was time for Rooney and Ronaldo to step up in the return leg against Roma. It was a remarkable evening at

Old Trafford. Ten minutes was all that it took for United to get an advantage in the tie – Carrick's stunning effort making it level on aggregate. Ten minutes later, Giggs set up Alan Smith for a fine half-volleyed strike and 60 seconds later it was 3-0. Ronaldo, Smith and Giggs combined, and Rooney made a run across goal to the near post and finished off the move. With a commanding lead, United were insatiable, invigorated by a thumping crowd which had been energised by this thrilling spectacle. Ronaldo added more weight to the growing argument about his greatness with two goals, while Carrick added another pearler on the way to a 7-1 win and a genuine statement of arrival.

Following an evening like that was always going to be difficult, and the fact that United's next game was an FA Cup semi-final against Watford only heightened the sense of jeopardy. These concerns were dispelled in the seventh minute when Rooney cut in to unleash a thunderous drive into the roof of the net. Watford levelled, but within two minutes, United had their lead back when Rooney laid the ball on for Ronaldo. When Rooney got his second midway through the second half, it was enough to guarantee a return to the FA Cup final, and an opportunity for those demons of 2005 to be exorcised.

It had almost crept up without notice, but Ferguson had masterminded an incredible run which had opened up a wealth of opportunity. That League Cup win of the prior campaign was not only a springboard in terms of trophies, it was the first of eight consecutive wins. It was the first indication for a couple of years that United, with Rooney and Ronaldo causing the creative mayhem up front, were now able to ride their bike without stabilisers.

With the momentum carried into the following season, suddenly a scenario had opened up which was as favourable as any time since 1999. With an FA Cup final place in the bag, a three-point lead in the league and a Champions League semi-final against AC Milan, it was no longer necessary to talk about the future as potentially great. It was here and it was happening.

That said, expectations were tempered before the visit of the Italians in late April. Six United players were missing against the team who had made the final two years earlier. And yet once the whistle blew, and Ronaldo scored after just five minutes, there was a heightened hope that the blistering performance against Roma could be replicated. There was a heavy dose of reality, then, when Kaka took advantage of poor defending to score twice before half-time.

United's need for inspiration was great. Rooney answered the call in the second half. On the hour mark, he was the beneficiary of a wizardly scooped pass from Scholes, and planted the ball in the net while everyone was still marvelling at the assist. In the last minute, Giggs played a smart ball after running down the right – Rooney was still outside the area and with the angle against him when he took aim with one of those early shots to catch everyone by surprise. It did. Dida couldn't get down quickly enough. Old Trafford erupted. It was going to be a tough trip to Italy, but at least United had a lead to defend.

The energy exerted on the night came at a cost in the weekend game at Everton. The game kicked off at 12:45pm, and Chelsea's home game with Bolton had been arranged for the same time. It was an afternoon of twists and turns; Chelsea had a half-time lead, and United were behind at the break, then five minutes into the second half, Everton grabbed a second, and it seemed as though all of the momentum was with the current champions.

News filtered through of a Bolton equaliser. If United could get their act together, they might strike a significant blow. Inspired by Rooney, they did just that. The former Everton forward had been United's best player in the first half but his team-mates raised their own standard to get on terms – O'Shea netting first, and then Phil Neville, the former United defender, putting in his own net to make it 2-2. With eleven minutes remaining, Rooney's big moment came; he showed composure and calm to beat Hibbert as if they were back on the Bellefield training pitch before sliding the ball into the net. In case he hadn't wound up his former fans enough, he then celebrated by kissing the United badge.

A fourth goal followed to make the result secure, but Rooney's had been the crucial contribution on a pivotal day in the title race. Chelsea's draw was confirmed at the same time as United's win. United now had a five-point lead with three games remaining – one of those was at Stamford Bridge, but if results went their way, the Premier League could already have been decided.

So followed three tough away games in succession – AC Milan, Manchester City and Chelsea. Milan dealt a heavy blow with a professional job at the San Siro, taking a 2-0 lead early on before killing the tie off with a late third. United looked leggy – their squad capable of dealing with domestic competition, but on the stage of the European elite, it was one step too far.

At the City of Manchester Stadium, United came up against a local rival who hadn't scored a home goal since the turn of the year. They seemed more interested in hurting United literally and physically; early on, Michael Ball stamped on Ronaldo disgracefully but escaped punishment. There was a karmic lesson coming soon for the City defender – the next time Ball went in on the United winger, it was in the box, and a penalty was awarded, from which Ronaldo scored. The visitors survived a spot-kick scare of their own when Van der Sar saved from Darius Vassell and United held on for the win. At full-time, Ronaldo removed his shirt to reveal the bruises on his torso from the stamp – it was a clear message that he and this United team could not be bullied.

It was a defiant message ahead of two crucial games with Chelsea. The first, at Stamford Bridge, stood to have a big say in the destination of the title, while the Blues had also qualified for the FA Cup final later in May. The importance of the first game was completely wiped out when the champions failed to win at Arsenal, therefore relinquishing their crown to Manchester United. It was the Old Trafford club's first championship for four years.

It made the league game between the clubs a dead rubber – Ferguson rotating his entire team. One player who would not take the opportunity for a rest was Rooney. He came on at Chelsea and then started in the final game against West Ham, with Ferguson obliged to treat the game with some seriousness considering it implicated Sheffield United's hopes of survival. The Hammers won 1-0 at Old Trafford with a goal from Carlos Tevez, but neither that nor the rain could spoil the championship party.

The season did end with something of a damp squib – Chelsea won a poor cup final, the first at the newly-rebuilt Wembley. United's best moment came in extra-time – Rooney's cross was met by Giggs, whose effort seemed to be carried over the line by Petr Cech. No goal was given – and instead it was Didier Drogba, four minutes from the end of extra-time, who decided the game. Another FA Cup final and another disappointment for Rooney, then, though the consolation of a league winner's medal would have softened the blow.

With 23 goals, it had been Rooney's most productive campaign to date – though it wasn't enough to earn him a third consecutive PFA Young Player of the Award, with Ronaldo winning both that and the main award. There was no danger of his contribution at Old Trafford going unappreciated; Rooney had established himself as the heartbeat of the team in the absence of Roy Keane. Although the word 'young' was most definitely still an apt description, it no longer needed to serve as a qualifier. If the following years would develop a path of divergence between Ronaldo and Rooney, it was only one that could be mapped in retrospect; in the summer of 2007, there was no question about their status as two of the greatest players in the world.

Chapter Ten

GOLDEN BOY

G rowing up has a lot to answer for. Ask any Manchester United supporter and they will tell you that the age of innocence for Wayne Rooney was between the day he signed and sometime in the summer of 2007. Some might extend that all the way until October 2010 but if they do, they will acknowledge 2007 as a turning point to a certain extent.

There was nothing significant that happened. No international tournament, no broken bone. In many ways, it was simply that time had an impact. Rooney had been playing professional football at the top level for five seasons. His game was changing with experience.

Take, for instance, the first goal he scored against Wigan in December 2005. He received the ball from a corner and went on a dribble in the box, taking on the former Everton defender Matt Jackson who he would have cheered as a hero of the 1995 FA Cup final once upon a time. He almost lost the ball, but managed to keep it under his control, and regained his balance to dance past another challenge and fire home at the near post.

Or take either of the first two goals Rooney scored against Fenerbahce on his debut. The Raging Bull of Old Trafford, storming through the Turkish defence, shooting on sight with the liberation of youth. There were moments where he genuinely did appear to be a British heir to the Brazilian Ronaldo – not quite the white Pele, although that would not rhyme quite as well in the chant that United fans had created. He was untamed. Wild. All of the conversation about this fierceness included a variation of the line 'you wouldn't want to take the fire out of him'; this was to mean that the temper within him was a necessary condition to carry that street footballer quality which had thrilled so many.

There is a line in the movie *Rocky III* where the titular character is addressed by his manager, Mickey Goldmill, who feels that the boxer has lost his edge. "The worst thing that happened to you, that can happen to any fighter," he tells him. "You got civilised."

There could be no question about Rooney's ambition. But there was a salient point to be made about experience and how it changes an individual. It was an inevitable consequence of the path Rooney led – both in coming into the game so young, and playing at the top level for three years and challenging for trophies.

Let's use a United comparison to prove a point. Ryan Giggs was an outlier, as he came into the team early and racked up appearances at a similar rate to Rooney. But let's take the end of the first title-winning season as a line in the sand – Rooney was 21-and-a-half and had made 223 first-team appearances. At the end of the 1996/97 season, when David Beckham turned 22, he had played 105 first-team games. At the same time Paul Scholes, seven months older than Beckham, had played 89. In terms of professional experience, by comparison, Rooney was effectively playing David Beckham's treble year or Paul Scholes' 1999/2000 campaign, and any United supporter who saw those seasons could attest to how remarkable the performance of those players was.

They would also attest to the change.

During his first ton, Beckham had been an industrious, almost scrappy, midfielder who had this capability of producing gems of goals. He matured into a refined right-sided marauder, the finest crosser in the world and arguably the greatest set-piece taker on the planet. Scholes, meanwhile, had tried to find his place as a number 10. Sir Alex Ferguson was never sure if he should play behind the striker or in a midfield two. In key games, Nicky Butt was often preferred in the pair with Roy Keane, until Scholes blossomed into a metronomic dictator of play whose execution of spectacular gravity-defying goals seemed as simple as a five-yard pass. In actual fact, it was Ferguson's belief in Scholes as a link-man that resulted in the signing of Juan Sebastian Veron in 2001. You could say it was only Veron's arrival that finally proved Scholes' true place in the side.

The point is that there is a retrospective argument sometimes played out that doesn't always reflect favourably when Rooney's career is discussed. People discuss the Raging Bull years as though something was lost afterwards. And perhaps that is true, for in football it is often necessary that something has to be sacrificed in order for something to be gained. Perhaps, even with all of the extraordinary facets to Manchester United's play over the following two years, what was to come would not have been possible without Rooney's professional maturity.

After 200 games, more than half of them playing for the biggest club in the country, almost every touch you've had of the ball becomes so scrutinised that it is only natural you do it yourself. It's not necessarily a second-guessing; more a moment of awareness to consider: *Is this the right choice? Are we more likely to score a goal or win the game if I do this?*

This was a development of time and not a product of coaching. Manchester United were keen to keep as much of the natural Rooney as possible. In fact, they were just desperate to get him on the pitch at all – in the opening game of the 2007/08 campaign against Reading, he suffered a hairline fracture of his foot and would be missing for a month. It was his first league game wearing a brand new number – United had announced that Rooney would be switching from eight to 10, and used the moment to indulge comparisons with Denis Law, who had worn the shirt with distinction in the 1960s.

Rooney himself described it as a great honour to wear the shirt, while Sir Alex Ferguson added: "There have been some wonderful footballers who have worn the United number 10 shirt – people who capture the imagination of our fans around the world with their skill and their goals. Wayne is the right man to carry on that tradition."

There was no inspiration against Reading. Rooney came off, and United couldn't score with or without him. United's goalscoring issues were compounded when Cristiano Ronaldo was sent off in the next game and would miss three matches.

John F. Kennedy was responsible for introducing a misconception into modern language – that the Chinese term for crisis also means opportunity. The truth is that the second component of the word means, by itself, 'change point', and this is probably a fairer summary of the situation United found themselves in in August 2007.

Coach Rene Meulensteen had returned to the club in January 2007 after a short spell at Brondby and was working on technical

skills development with senior players. He had been at the club
when Rooney arrived and noticed the change in him when he
returned from Denmark. During Ronaldo's suspension, Meulensteen spent some concentrated time with the United number
seven. He was as well-placed as any to summarise the stature of
the respective players at the time.

"I had a spell working with Cristiano when he was out
suspended… he had scored a good number of goals but I felt that
we could add something to his repertoire. There was room for
more," Meulensteen explains. "Cristiano always wanted to score
the perfect goal. Because of that he missed a lot of opportunities.
So almost rewiring the mentality – we talked about the amount of
goals and the variety. The more the better.

"That was something Wayne already understood but it ran
deeper with him. He loved to score any goal but he also loved to
assist. So long as he was involved in a Manchester United win,
that was all that mattered. In that respect you would say he was
advanced in development in comparison but that was something
that came naturally to him.

"Wayne benefitted from the two years of Premier League football
at Everton. He was very versatile – he did have his favourite
position, playing up front, but he was capable of excelling in any
position. What he did was play on his intuition and his natural
instinct and quality. The last thing you want to do as a coach is to
interfere. You don't want him to overthink. You don't want him
to second-guess himself. You can trust his natural intelligence of
playing the game, the way he was so direct, and you can trust in
the level of unpredictability that came with him. You can't coach
that. You don't want to."

The English term for crisis was very much apt when it came
to United's goalscoring issue. Louis Saha was out injured until

September, and so there was pressure on the summer recruits to fill the void. After being left short of players for the latter stages of the Champions League, Ferguson had made a significant splash in the transfer window, signing Anderson and Nani from the Portuguese league and then Owen Hargreaves from Bayern Munich. Finally, on the eve of the league season, the protracted saga of Carlos Tevez's move from West Ham – or Media Sports Investment agency – was completed. The Argentinian was rushed into action following Rooney's injury despite not having a proper pre-season. United's options up front were still threadbare.

The results at the start of the season highlighted the problem. 0-0 against Reading, 1-1 against Portsmouth, 0-1 against Manchester City and, finally, a 1-0 win against Sunderland with a goal from the returning Saha to head into the September international break with a modicum of positivity.

Ferguson's concerns about starting the season poorly were softened by events at Stamford Bridge – it was announced in mid-September that Jose Mourinho had left Chelsea by 'mutual consent' after not winning the league the previous year despite the arrivals of Michael Ballack and Andriy Shevchenko. It just so happened that their next opponents were Manchester United at Old Trafford – by which time, Rooney and Ronaldo were back in the starting line-up. United claimed an important win through Tevez's first goal for the club and Saha's late penalty.

United's next game was against Coventry in the League Cup and before the match Ferguson said Rooney had been annoying him in training: "Wayne has been in my ear wanting to play. He's been saying, 'I want to play, I want to be captain, I want to take the penalties, the corners, the free-kicks, the goal-kicks, the lot'." He didn't – and United suffered an embarrassing 2-0 defeat at Old Trafford.

A narrow win at Birmingham with Ronaldo's first league goal of the season was followed by a Champions League group stage victory over Roma – achieved with Rooney's first strike of the season. The single-goal victories only emphasised the feeling of United's run of results looking more like binary code than the result of fielding the best young attackers in world football with some of the greatest creative minds of their generation.

At half-time against Wigan Athletic in October, Ferguson had headaches at either end of the pitch. United were still not firing up front and in defence players were dropping like flies. Nemanja Vidic had to come off, then John O'Shea, while Patrice Evra was probably wishing he too could be replaced as he tried to deal with the blisteringly quick Antonio Valencia. However, the reshuffle actually worked to United's benefit. Vidic was replaced by Anderson, with O'Shea moving back into the defence before he too was injured. Anderson's industry in midfield was matched by that of Tevez and Rooney up front. All three were involved in the breakthrough 10 minutes into the second half. Rooney came deep to lay the ball off to the advancing Anderson. The Brazilian played a first-time through ball to Tevez, who rounded challenges from a defender and the goalkeeper to fire into the net. The dam had broken. Goals spilled everywhere. Ronaldo benefitted from Giggs and Rooney crosses to make it 2-0 then 3-0. With eight minutes left, Rooney got the goal his own efforts deserved, thanks to a great cross from Danny Simpson.

Next up for United was a trip to Villa Park; a happy hunting ground traditionally for Ferguson's team, though the hosts were enjoying a resurgence of late, with a recent victory over Chelsea to prove their own credentials under Martin O'Neill. They even took the lead with an early goal through Gabby Agbonlahor. With ten minutes to half-time, United turned it up a gear. Nani's cross somehow found its way past an entire cast of home defenders before Rooney crept in at the back post. A minute before the break, Tevez stabbed a pass in to Rooney. From 15 yards out, the England striker turned and fired in to turn the game around. Ferdinand and Giggs added efforts to make it a second game in a row with a four-goal score for the champions.

Ahead of the trip to Dynamo Kiev, all the talk was about the burgeoning relationship between Tevez and Rooney, two forwards who were so alike in style that there was the danger of them being *too* similar. "We've had some fantastic partnerships over the years and most of them took time to develop, apart from Cole and Yorke, who were terrific in their first season together," Sir Alex said. "Wayne is 22 this week, Carlos is only 23 so they are both young players. Both have great attributes – courage, speed, ability to beat men, all the qualities are there. They are two exceptionally good players who pose a real threat to defenders. But it's maturity they lack. Once they get that, you will see greater authority, better timing and judgment. And when that comes, hopefully they'll still be at this club and people will see something really special from them."

It was classic Ferguson – talking of the future to take the pressure off today – but the pair proved their current worth again, with Rooney netting one in another four-goal rout. The 4-2 win (the other goals coming from Ferdinand – again! – and a Ronaldo brace) was more emphatic than the two-goal difference suggested.

There were four more goals against Middlesbrough, with Rooney crowning his birthday week by getting on the scoresheet again. The tone had been set by a spectacular early goal by Nani. Boro equalised, but were forced to extremes to defend their parity – Stewart Downing was harassed into giving the ball away in his own box by Nani, and Rooney was there to accept the gift graciously.

In the second half, the party was under way; Anderson found Tevez, who lobbed the ball in to Rooney. Rooney, tracked by three defenders, showed intelligence beyond his years to back-heel the ball into the vacated space, allowing Tevez to slide into the net.

Ferguson had compared the duo to Cole and Yorke; there was a synchronised telepathy the pair seemed to share that was so familiar. It would be unfair to exclude Ronaldo from that, and the winger was involved in the final goal of the day – his clever flick sent Rooney away. Again, followed by numerous terrified Boro defenders, Rooney was able to pick Tevez or Ronaldo as the beneficiary of his work. Tevez had the slightly more favourable route to goal, so he was the chosen one to convert the opportunity.

So it was four goals in four consecutive games, and more to the point, United were playing the best football supporters had seen since the treble side were in their pomp. Rooney was clearly delighted with his new strike-partner.

"I know now that it is my job to score goals and try to score in every game I play in," he said. "We know how Carlos plays – just in behind the opposition's midfield. That is where I like to play but when Carlos plays I will stay higher up the pitch and be the centre-forward, whereas if Louis Saha plays then I will tuck in a bit more. I enjoy playing both roles and I feel I can change my game to whoever I play with.

"I feel better and sharper with each game. I'm playing like an old fashioned centre-forward – I've started to score easy goals which I've never done before. We're playing brilliant, fast, attacking football and that is the sort of football that I want to be involved in."

The manager was thrilled. "Our third goal summed up the Rooney-Tevez partnership," Ferguson said after the game. "It was an example of great thinking and also courage by Wayne in attempting the back-heel to set up Carlos. They are young players and hopefully we will see the complete partnership. It's amazing that after all the 1-0 wins, it's now a case of fours. Some of our attacking play was very good."

With due respect to the opponents, United were still waiting for a sterner test to see how their new style would hold up – a test in the form of Arsenal, who were on a little resurgence of their own following their dip in previous seasons. The likes of Thierry Henry and Patrick Vieira had left the Gunners and in their place were new stars like Cesc Fabregas, Alex Hleb and Emmanuel Adebayor. They had won eight and drawn two of their opening 10 games, a run which included a thumping 5-0 win over Derby County.

Before the game, Ferguson discussed the young prospects in the United ranks. "In two or three years' time I want to be saying my players are the best in the world because at this moment they are showing those signs," the manager said. "Players such as Rooney, Ronaldo, Nani, Anderson and Tevez are all young and have the best of their careers in front of them. Maturity brings the authority and consistency and also what is important is what they win. Can they go on to win European Championships, are they playing in World Cup finals? These are all things that true greats like Pele, Cruyff and Maradona were judged on. These are the challenges. Any young player with potential must always be judged that way."

What followed was an entertaining 2-2 draw, with Rooney's shot on the stroke of half-time deflecting in off William Gallas to open the scoring. Gallas, though, scored an injury-time equaliser to ensure he would have the last laugh of this particular battle. When it came to the war, however, Gallas would be remembered rather differently.

Against Kiev four days later, the attacking combinations paid dividends again. Tevez and Rooney combined for the Argentinian to score before Rooney and then Ronaldo got goals of their own in another four-goal rout. Before the next game, Rooney picked up an ankle injury tripping over one of the goals at Carrington – he was expected to be out for a month. His recovery, as usual, was swifter than that, though in his absence Tevez and Ronaldo proved more than adequate in goal supply.

For England, however, Rooney's presence was most definitely missed. The national team were defeated by Croatia at Wembley, spelling the end of their qualification hopes for the European Championship and also for the managerial reign of Steve McClaren. It had been a doomed year-and-a-half.

As Rooney waited in the wings for a recall, both he and Tevez gave interviews about their partnership. "It's down to hard work and instinct," Rooney said. "Although we don't speak the same language, it is just something we know from one another's movements where the other one is going to go. It's also about making eye contact and knowing where you want the ball and just nodding, really. You just play the game as you see it. We work on it at the training ground and it can only get better. Me, Carlos and Cristiano are all still young players and have still got much to learn."

Tevez repaid the compliment: "Everyone is now seeing I can play effectively with Rooney. The more we play together the better we'll understand each other and more damage we'll do to teams. Between us, we can hurt any team."

Rooney was back for the December trip to Anfield but it was Tevez who scored the game's only goal – and Ronaldo then got both goals in a 2-1 win over Everton. United headed into Christmas one point behind league leaders Arsenal.

On Boxing Day, United went to the Stadium of Light for a bit of an old boys' reunion with Sunderland. The manager was Roy

Keane, who had used his Old Trafford connections to take several familiar names to help him in the north east. United won 4-0 in a game mostly remembered for a thumping Ronaldo free-kick, but it was Rooney's deadly finish after a fine move that got the show on the road – his first goal for six weeks.

"Strikers do go on a run where they can't score and that's been Wayne lately, but he was close to what you would expect of him against Sunderland," Ferguson said – but the chance of starting a streaky run was lost when Rooney added illness to injury and missed two games with a stomach bug.

He was well enough for a place on the bench for the FA Cup trip to Aston Villa. Ferguson had hoped to get through the game without having to use him, but was feeling a spark was missing. Carlos Tevez was injured after scoring the only goal against Birmingham – a game which saw the Old Trafford crowd criticised by the manager for a perceived lack of noise and encouragement.

Those same criticisms could never be lobbied at United's travelling support, but at Villa Park, the players were not responding. Inspiration needed to come from elsewhere – it duly arrived with 20 minutes remaining, when Rooney stepped off the bench to galvanise his team. He had a shot within a minute; soon after, Ronaldo broke the deadlock, and in the dying moments, Rooney scored to secure the result. In front of new England manager Fabio Capello, the United striker had demonstrated just how important he was.

"Rooney is worth gold," Villa striker John Carew admitted afterwards. "They should call him 'Braveheart' because he is playing with a big heart. He is one of the world's top-10 players. I am sure Fabio will build his team around Rooney."

January was certainly a month where United's goalscoring stars proved their value – Ronaldo grabbed his first ever hat-trick against Newcastle and then the following week, the Rooney-Ronaldo late double act was on the road again, this time at Reading – and this time Rooney's goal the decider. "Two of their players frighten me – Rooney and Ronaldo," Reading boss (and United legend) Steve Coppell had said pre-match. "They are key individuals. That combination, that artistry between the two of them, is what you have got to stop. If they keep those key individuals healthy, then they will win it."

Ronaldo scored two more in the FA Cup win over Spurs, and then struck another double against Portsmouth – one a memorable free-kick from distance. Still in January, this was the winger's 27th goal of the season. "I spend ages watching him practise in training, but I can't work out how he does it," Rooney said of the technique Ronaldo used to strike the ball; almost a straight-on run and strike, generating dip and a vicious swerve. Ronaldo's increased potency had necessitated a slight formation change. "Ronaldo's form means that he's now starting playing upfront, while I'm on the wing," Rooney said. "I don't mind too much, anything for the team, but I'd rather play as a striker."

At first, it was not a deliberate move, more a by-product of the roaming capabilities of the forward players, with certain limitations. Ryan Giggs had matured into a playmaker from an out-and-out touchline winger but still mostly played from the left. Nani could move from side to side. Tevez was not work shy, but was more inclined to keep that energy in his forward position, and was not as keen as Rooney to be involved in the play. All of this meant that when Ronaldo would move from his nominal starting position on the right, it was usually Rooney's demonstration of that greater in-game maturity that came to the fore.

The quirk in United's play had been identified early on by Ferguson and his coaches. They decided to try and harness this strength and maximise the team's potential.

"I remember having a conversation with the front players about their fluidity," says Rene Meulensteen. "I spoke about their ability to play in any area of the front line and how simple movements from the start might cause a lot of confusion in the opponent. For example if Cristiano moved into the forward position, and instead of a straight switch with the player already there, the number 10 moves out wide instead. As long as all of the positions are covered, you are giving the defender a new headache every time because they are up against a player of different qualities and they can't just focus on one. The only thing we needed to do was to understand that when there was a turnover of the ball, the players would have to defend from the position they were in, and therefore they had to understand that position and the responsibilities that came with it."

Rooney was fully engaging with these new responsibilities. "He was very receptive," Meulensteen explains. "He was great to coach. Every day he would come in to training and ask what we were doing that day. I'd talk him through the session and take the piss pretending the entire session was based around him. We'd talk about the team we were playing against and what our emphasis would be. Wayne was keen to know as much as possible. There was no problem with him understanding his responsibilities.

"Wayne was a player from what I call the outside category. You could class him in the bracket of a player like Cristiano, or Ryan, or Dimitar Berbatov. They have so much quality in the attacking side of their game that you almost have to make sure you're making clever concessions to avoid diluting their qualities. For example we might tell Wayne we wanted him to start the press from up front. We'd talk about the qualities of specific players – to put pressure on a defender who wasn't so good on the ball. Or to stop the passing lane into the number six. He was very good at knowing what we wanted and carrying it out."

Rooney was also acutely aware of the role Ronaldo's form played in the change. It was an exceptional accommodation because of the exceptional talent. Everyone at Manchester United could see the Portuguese attacker was developing into something great and so the idea was to facilitate that improvement and see where it took both him and the team. It clearly added to the already star quality of the side, and it seemed Rooney's contribution was not being sacrificed. What is also clear, though, is that these circumstances were reliant on the individual personalities being attributed as they were. That is to say, if Ronaldo was the one having to move around for Rooney to have greater importance, there is no guarantee that it would have been as amicable. In Rooney's book *My Decade In The Premier League*, the chapter on the period is titled *Sacrifice*, and even if the player himself had little to do with the actual wording, it was clear he agreed with the sentiment.

Ferguson seemed conscious of this and was full of pointed praise for Rooney after the game against Portsmouth, even though he had played poorly. "Wayne has a wonderful appetite for the game," he said. "You wish every player of yours had the same desire to play. It's such a joy to see a lad with that natural enthusiasm to play. However, Wayne worked too hard on Wednesday and that cost him the opportunity to get goals. Wayne's doing fine but he didn't need to expend so much energy dropping back into the midfield. All Wayne has to do is make sure he looks after his energy."

Those were words for ears that were not listening, and Ferguson would have been thankful for that, as United chased their next game at Spurs after falling behind. Rooney was booked for diving – it would rule him out of the Manchester derby – but Tevez proved his growing sense of occasion by snatching an injury-time equaliser.

Against City, United commemorated the 50th anniversary of the Munich Air Disaster; their performance was as subdued as the occasion, and City went away with a 2-1 win. The result revealed a quirk – there was a common factor with all of United's defeats this season. Wayne Rooney was not in the team.

As if to prove the point about his influence, Rooney – without the assistance of Ronaldo or Tevez, who were given the day off – delivered arguably his best performance of the season against Arsenal in the FA Cup. He was outstanding, scoring the opening goal by heading in Anderson's flick, and then generally terrorising the visitors' defence. Fletcher, Nani and Fletcher again scored further goals to give a comprehensive gloss to the scoreline, but the thrill of seeing Rooney off the leash was as great a joy as the 4-0 win.

Ferguson gave one of his prophetic predictions after the game, declaring the result could have psychological repercussions for both teams. He was right – the next round of league fixtures saw moments that would prove pivotal. In the early Saturday afternoon fixture, Birmingham and Arsenal played out a 2-2 draw. It was not only eventful due to the scoreline. You could probably trace the perception that Arsenal were easily wound up all the way back to October 2004 and Pizzagate. It was perhaps unfair, but the Gunners didn't always help themselves. There had been incidents when Arsenal lost, such as in November 2006 when Arsene Wenger had reacted so angrily to Alan Pardew celebrating a late winner for West Ham that he actually pushed him.

So the perception of petulance was perpetuated. Wind up Arsenal, and they'll throw the toys out of the pram. Of course, Arsenal saw it differently and felt victimised. They had only themselves to blame in the second half at Old Trafford when Emmanuel Eboue was sent off for a dangerous tackle and then William Gallas and Mathieu Flamini were lucky to escape punishment for hacking at a showboating Nani.

At St. Andrew's, though, they had a point. Striker Eduardo was the victim of a bad Martin Taylor challenge and suffered a broken leg – to incense the visitors even more, they turned around an early deficit only to throw it away by conceding a late penalty. The culprit, Gallas – the Arsenal captain – stormed away, sitting down close to the halfway line while the kick was taken and remaining there for several minutes after the final whistle. It was a spectacle that screamed implosion.

United, meanwhile, had a spring in their step, and were galvanised by another late Tevez equaliser in the Champions League against Lyon. After watching what had happened with Arsenal, United systematically took apart Newcastle at St James' Park, with Rooney once more in inspirational form. He opened the scoring with a smart volley from a Ronaldo cross, and then Ronaldo scored two himself before Ferguson took him off. When there remained Rooney, there remained an insatiable need for goals, and two more came – the hosts grabbed what they thought was a consolation, but almost immediately wished they hadn't have bothered, as that merely woke up United. Sixty seconds later, Rooney curled in a quite stunning effort from the edge of the box. A fifth came in injury time when Rooney remarkably pulled three defenders away to give Saha the space, and then the assist, to get on the scoresheet. Arsenal had a three-point lead, but still had trips to Stamford Bridge and Old Trafford to come. As it would transpire, those would be the only games the Gunners would lose, but they would prove to be crucial.

With the competitions coming thick and fast, attention was diverted away from the Premier League momentarily. There was the good: qualifying for the quarter-finals of the Champions League to face Roma yet again. That came with the bad: the realisation that Rooney would have the summer off after England's failure. "Not qualifying still burns inside of me," Rooney said in March. "It would still be disappointing to watch the European Championship on television, even if we had won the Champions League. Would winning in Moscow make up for the England defeat? I'm not sure."

But then came the ugly – the FA Cup quarter-final with Portsmouth that ended those treble hopes. It was a game remarkable in its own way. Ferguson was taking this one seriously with his first-choice defence and most of the big hitters in attack on the pitch. Ronaldo, Tevez and Rooney all missed chances in the first half. Frustration was already evident when Rooney launched into one of those angry tackles that earned him a yellow card. Chances were missed by the bucketful. Vidic, Tevez, Ronaldo. Carrick had one cleared off the line. Evra hit the post.

Edwin van der Sar had gone off injured at half-time. His replacement, Tomasz Kuszczak, was sent off as Pompey launched a rare counter-attack and Milan Baros got himself into the box to earn the visitors a penalty. With both goalkeepers used, one of the outfield players had to go between the sticks. In training, Rio Ferdinand and Wayne Rooney would often go in goal. John O'Shea had taken the gloves in a game at Spurs the previous year, and had actually done pretty well. But he was not on the pitch today. Rooney – in a further illustration of his work ethic – had been the last man covering and seemed keen to go in, but word was given from the bench for Ferdinand to assume the position.

"The biggest mistake the manager made was not putting me in goal," Rooney quipped to the official club podcast in 2020. "But I think he was worried I wouldn't have saved the penalty and then we're 1-0 down so he needed me to try and score… I remember the boss, it was (for) about two weeks – he didn't speak a word to us. He knew that was the chance of doing the treble again."

Sulley Muntari scored the kick – none of United's megastars could penetrate the Portsmouth goal, which was leading a charmed life. United were indeed out of the competition. Even in defeat, though, they had played with wonderful attacking verve and spirit – it was a reminder of the sort of luck required to make history.

Ferguson's players still had that in mind. The response to the FA Cup exit was strong, though it took a long time to get over the hangover in the next game against Derby County, who had only won one game all season. It took 76 minutes of missed chances until Ronaldo finally scored – the almost-two-game-mini-crisis was over, and normal service was resumed when Ronaldo scored an early double against Bolton the following midweek. Liverpool were brushed aside 3-0 and then Aston Villa were the visitors just when people were wondering if Rooney was in another goalscoring lean patch. The Midlands side found out to their cost that this was not the case.

United were fantastic on the day, with plenty of skills and thrills to keep the Old Trafford crowd lively. Ronaldo's exquisite side-heel finish through four defenders and a goalkeeper from a corner was the highlight of the game but it was breathtaking in another way to see how simple United made their evisceration of Villa look. It was a lesson in movement, selflessness and intelligence. Rooney and Scholes led the charge before Ronaldo crossed for Tevez to make the result comfortable before the break, but after that, it was all about the number 10.

His desperation to get on the scoresheet was evident four minutes in when he exchanged a lightning-quick one-two with Tevez and fired just wide. Three minutes later his goal finally came, and it was exquisite. Giggs played a ball in to Ronaldo and the number seven flicked it outrageously behind the defence. The only person who anticipated the audacity was Rooney, and he held off a challenge and rounded the goalkeeper. Later he got his second goal, when Giggs, Tevez and Ronaldo all helped to create an opening with a brand of one-touch football that evoked gasps and olés from the crowd.

After United had recorded another 4-0 victory, Rooney was in buoyant mood. "I used to love watching Brazil when I was growing up," he said, "and the football we are playing is similar. The movement and passing is brilliant and I love playing for this team. It's just a pleasure to play football like this. It's why you want to be a footballer."

He took a moment to praise Ronaldo after receiving two assists from him. "It's a pleasure to play with him and quite rightly he's labelled the best player in the world," he said. "I only fully appreciated his goal when I saw it again at half-time. It was brilliant. He was probably the only player on the pitch who could have done that."

Just like watching Brazil, then. Nobody could argue with United's style since October. The midfield guile and energy of Carrick, Fletcher, Scholes, Hargreaves and Anderson and the attacking riches of Rooney, Ronaldo and Tevez were hinged together by the industry and creativity of Giggs, Nani and Ji-Sung Park. Somehow, Ferguson had found a way to make 11 (12 including Saha) into six positions not only flow but do so seamlessly. The result – 11 games so far with four or more goals. The Villa game was also the 13th that at least two of Rooney, Ronaldo and Tevez had scored in the same match.

All three scored in the quarter-final tie against Roma to make comfortable work of the Italians. Ronaldo's header in the first leg – scored in the fashion of a steamroller, with the forward not even in the camera frame at the moment Paul Scholes played his cross –

has been replayed arguably more often than any of the seven goals from the prior year.

The trio continued to strike most of the goals – Rooney hit a vital equaliser at Middlesbrough to get a point. Tevez struck another late equaliser at Blackburn. It was gracious of all three of them to allow Hargreaves the opportunity to strike a free-kick against Arsenal, which earned another crucial win.

United were up against Barcelona in the semi-final of the Champions League; the Spaniards, under the guidance of Frank Rijkaard, had a great team who were European champions in 2006. The likes of Xavi and Andres Iniesta were coming into their prime. Wherever you looked there were big names – Puyol, Zambrotta, Thuram, Abidal. Yaya Toure. Henry, Eto'o. Ronaldinho and Lionel Messi. The latter two were at opposite ends of their Barcelona careers, and it was obvious that the Brazilian would be leaving that summer to vacate the number 10 shirt for the Argentinian. Ronaldinho was famously close to a 2003 move to Old Trafford and, in March 2008, had made no secret of where he wanted to go in the summer. "Who would I most like to play alongside? Wayne Rooney," he told reporters. "Rooney is a very strong player and he scores important goals."

That strength, in the first leg at the Nou Camp, was going to be deployed from the right. Owen Hargreaves was going to play right-back behind him. Rooney admitted being disappointed with the news. "It's hard to take at first, but when the game starts I work all over the pitch, tracking back, running the wing, putting tackles in all over the park," he recalled later. This move would ostensibly enable Tevez and Ronaldo to cause havoc on two solid platforms of four players. It was a credit to Rooney that when Ferguson had considered the best way to replace the injured Nemanja Vidic, his professionalism was the asset called upon. The defensive side of the plan worked with comfort, and United should really have taken a lead and an away goal, as Ronaldo missed an early penalty. The game ended goalless.

United's strong league form had put them in a favourable position heading into the final three games. A three-point lead over Chelsea was effectively four with a far superior goal difference – it meant that even a loss at Stamford Bridge, in the next game, wouldn't be a disaster so long as United could win their last two league games of the season against West Ham and Wigan. Ferguson took a calculated gamble to rest Hargreaves, Scholes, Ronaldo and Tevez ahead of the second leg against Barcelona.

However, the United boss soon found himself counting the cost. Vidic had been brought back in but it was too soon, so he was replaced. Chelsea scored just before half-time – United didn't look likely to get back into the game until an errant back-pass gave Rooney a rare chance. He took it, advancing past the defence to finish, but immediately looked in discomfort. An existing hip injury had flared up. He was desperate to continue but was brought off within minutes.

United lost to a late penalty. The cost was potentially greater when Rooney had a scan and rest was advised – there was no way he could play against Barcelona, and it was touch and go whether his season was over. That depended as much on United's own form. So Rooney was in the stands as his team-mates battled Barcelona without him. Paul Scholes scored a sensational goal. United had chances to make it two. With 14 minutes to go, Scholes and Nani were replaced by Fletcher and Giggs. The pragmatic approach came early – too early for the home crowd's liking. There was an anxious energy at Old Trafford similar to the one against these same opponents in 1984 – and a goal for United might well have yielded similar audible results – but in the end the supporters were just as happy to see the game through to full-time.

Although Barcelona had territorial supremacy, United were well-organised and came through without giving away too many significant chances. The game has gone down in history as one that saw United's backs to the wall for 90 minutes – sometimes that is even perpetuated by those associated with the club. It's not entirely accurate, and it was a credit to United's increased maturity that they were able to see through a tightly-contested tie. They were deserved winners. Their prize for this? A European Cup final in Moscow against Chelsea. Owned as they were by the Russian, Roman Abramovich, it felt a little like getting to the final level of a video game only to find the villain is a *super*-villain.

Rooney was in the stands again for the last home league game of the season as West Ham were dismissed by an early Ronaldo double on the way to a 4-1 win. On the final day, the number 10 was back as they made comfortable work of Wigan on a day when tension could have crept in. Ronaldo and Giggs scored the goals on the day. As the players celebrated in the rain in front of the travelling fans, Rooney remembered being at Goodison Park on the final day of the 2003 campaign when United were celebrating. He remembered looking at Giggs and being envious.

In the post-match celebrations in 2008, Rooney observed Giggs once more. "The older lads have been here before," he said. "They know there's more hard work to come. They know we can do all the celebrating we want after Moscow."

Chapter Eleven

SUMMIT

S ir Alex Ferguson leaned heavily on the theme of history in the build-up to Manchester United's Champions League final with Chelsea. He had been in the job long enough to weaponise it; a powerful tool which can only be deployed once you have survived any threat of being burdened by it.

On the evening before the trip to Moscow, Ferguson made his players watch a film of the 1999 final with Bayern Munich, when United had conceded early and then survived a number of scares before scoring two goals in injury time to claim the European Cup in the most dramatic way in history.

"The game is the history of the club," Ferguson told his players after turning the sound down after the final whistle. "It proves that as a team we never give in." He turned the television off – the room was silent. "Remember. No regrets."

Ferguson could have been speaking for himself as much as for his players. He'd been around the block. 1999 was his Holy Grail; restoring United as the European elite, following Sir Matt Busby and winning the biggest trophy in club football. In 2008, it was about a dynasty, a legacy. Getting to Russia was a little victory. Winning the trophy would cement Ferguson's legacy at the same time as his young team were proving their own ability.

Ahead of the final, Rooney spoke of how Chelsea reminded him of Portugal; there was a history of bad memories to exorcise. Of course, Chelsea still had a Portuguese influence at Stamford Bridge following the departure of Jose Mourinho who signed many of his compatriots, most notably Ricardo Carvalho, he of the 2006 World Cup altercation. "The incident with Carvalho was a turning point in my career," Rooney said. "I've spoken to him a couple of times since then; he's a nice guy. He's the hardest defender I've ever played against. He's strong and he's quick and he reads the game very well."

Rooney, though, was not sure where he would figure in the manager's plans. Hours before kick-off, Ferguson called a team meeting to name the side. Vidic was fit – so Brown was at right-back. Hargreaves right midfield. Ronaldo left wing. Rooney up front with Tevez. Ferguson's selection was smart. Much of the build-up had been about the confrontation between Ronaldo and Ashley Cole, the Chelsea left-back. They'd each had success in past duels. Over the course of the last year, Ronaldo had blossomed into much more than just a right-winger. Ferguson understood there was plenty to be gained by putting his strengths against Chelsea's weaknesses. They were well-matched all over the pitch, but the one potential avenue to exploit would be Michael Essien's relative unfamiliarity at right-back.

There was one more Ferguson pep talk before the match. He reminded the players of the hard work of his grandparents and parents. That this was 90 minutes of working hard to win a football match. That they were in a very privileged position.

With teams so familiar and the price for failure so significant, the game was inevitably cagey. United exploited Essien for Ronaldo to tower over him and score in the 26th minute. Frank Lampard took advantage of a deflected shot to net the equaliser just before half-time. Stalemate. It went to extra-time. Rooney had battled admirably but was now feeling the hip injury. In the 101st minute he was replaced by Nani.

In the last moments, a scrap broke out as players complained about time-wasting. Drogba was sent off for a slap on Vidic. The drama had only just begun.

Penalties.

United go first.

Tevez scores. Ballack levels.

Carrick scores. Belletti levels.

Ronaldo – the usual taker – sees his effort saved.

Lampard – Chelsea's usual taker – nets. The Blues have the lead.

Hargreaves and Cole score. Nani – United's fifth taker, and so the spot Rooney would have theoretically taken – scores under intense pressure.

John Terry, the Chelsea skipper, steps up. He knows a successful kick wins the trophy. All eyes are on him. He adjusts his captain's armband to ensure the big 'C' is visible. Prior to the game Terry had rubbished the concern of groundsman Matt Frost, who had expressed his 'total disappointment' about the surface. "The pitch is the same for both sides and if we get the footwear right we will be fine," Terry had said. "We are not worrying about that at all."

As he strode confidently to take the kick, the defender slipped and the ball struck the outside of the post, handing United a reprieve.

Anderson scores. Kalou levels.

Ryan Giggs is making his own history. In the last game against Wigan, he'd scored to earn his 10th league title medal. He'd done it equalling Sir Bobby Charlton's appearance record for the club. Tonight he was breaking that record. He scored.

Next was Nicolas Anelka, the former Arsenal, Liverpool and Manchester City striker who missed only Leeds United from his CV to have a full house of clubs who detest United. And yet he endeared himself to millions of Red Devils fans around the world when his kick was saved by Van der Sar – Manchester United were European champions.

The celebrations went on into the early hours. Ferguson interrupted them to make a speech. "Next season, we have to do it again."

***

Ferguson was left with a similar dilemma to 1999. His team had proven themselves to be the best in the country and on the continent. Back then, he had been accused of standing still, with Roy Keane being one outspoken critic about a talented squad not maximising its own potential in the two years which followed that triumph.

The landscape was a *little* different in 2008. This time he had the best player in the world. The best player in the world had forward partners who were the envy of any team. The composition of the squad was almost perfect. Almost *too* perfect. There was an overflow. An embarrassment of riches and a set-up that was so autonomous that you almost got the impression that Ferguson could have slept for a year and his team would still enjoy a great season, motivated by the fear of what might happen if he were forced to wake up.

So how to add to it? Well, Ronaldinho didn't get his wish, but there was an increase in Brazilian influence in the United dressing room. Rodrigo Possebon was a talented midfielder, while hopes were high for twin full-backs Fabio and Rafael Da Silva who turned 18 over the summer. The United boss also had an itch he just had to scratch. He was desperate to sign Tottenham forward Dimitar Berbatov, a tall, languid striker with very different qualities to the forwards United already had. The chase for the Bulgarian would last all summer, but Ferguson eventually got his man.

Just as important, though, was keeping hold of Cristiano Ronaldo. The forward had invited speculation about his future after the final by saying 'only God knows' but also told one different reporter 'I stay'. It was clear as mud, then, and enough for a summer where Real Madrid were constantly linked to a transfer. Ferguson met with his player in July and told newspapers that Ronaldo was not for sale.

The United manager also took the time in pre-season to ensure Wayne Rooney was given due credit; Ferguson admitting he might have held Rooney back. It was put to him on United's tour of South Africa that the forward hadn't been quite as prolific as Ronaldo (42) or Tevez (19), with his 18 goals placing him as United's third top scorer in their double-winning season.

"I have to take a bit of responsibility," the manager said. "Wayne has sacrificed himself and never complained, which says a lot for the lad. He will score goals. But we kept using him in different positions. We need to define his role better. We played him wide and in other positions. Even in the Champions League final he was doing well, then, when Chelsea got control, we had to stem that and play three midfield players. There are lots of occasions when we need to play three midfield players. At home we can play 4-4-2 with the wide players Ronaldo and Nani. Park will be back.

There is competition in that position and that makes it difficult for the style we've always played."

Similar sentiments were echoed a couple of weeks later. "We have to be fairer to Rooney this season," said Ferguson. "He is such a willing performer that you are tempted to listen to him at times. He says he can play centre-half or centre-midfield or in goal. If you ask him to do a job, he never complains."

One might read between the lines and think Ferguson was playing a longer game. Of course those comments can be taken at face value. You might also be tempted to think he was currying favour, understanding Rooney's importance to the team, and laying the groundwork so he could emphasise the significance of it further down the line. Ferguson later admitted he had reached a compromise with Ronaldo – that he could leave a year later if a club offered a world record fee, but not in 2008. Having accepted that Ronaldo was likely to eventually go, it was a sensible approach to butter up the players he would be counting on in the longer term.

He was right, though. There had been a cost. Rooney was capable of playing well and influencing the game anywhere on the pitch. He was a valuable member of the team. But if you were asking him to run down the right flank and be conscious of a certain player, you were significantly reducing his opportunity to do the unexpected in an area where it would leave indelible memories. You would be losing the free spirit who did what he did against Fenerbahce on his debut. The wanderer who scored spectacular volleys against Middlesbrough and Newcastle. It's fair to summarise that United couldn't complain about receiving a raw deal, nor could Ferguson, nor could Ronaldo, and it's again only fair to note that Ferguson did acknowledge the role this had played in Rooney's development.

In the years that followed, the different paths taken by Rooney and Ronaldo often feature a heavy attribution of responsibility to Rooney's diet and dedication. We'll get to that in due course, but it's worth dwelling on the thought that another significant factor was the sacrifice that all parties acknowledge existed. There is no telling how things might have transpired if Ronaldo had been told, for example, to stay in his lane. If United had been more rigid with Rooney playing as a striker. Could Rooney have done what Ronaldo did? It's certainly possible. However, it has to be remembered that things turned out the way they did because two brilliant players worked in tandem for their team, and a world class management structure identified how that potential could be maximised. Rooney was more interested in trophies, Ronaldo driven by personal acclaim. They both got what they wanted.

Sir Alex Ferguson got what he wanted, too. He'd been told by Carlos Queiroz – who had just left his job as assistant manager to become manager of Portugal – that he had done well, because no player of Ronaldo's background and ambition would have stayed in England for as long as five years. Ferguson knew he was being greedy asking for six – but he got it, and Manchester United were treated to another year of Ronaldo and Rooney together. What followed was one of the greatest seasons in Manchester United history. There were going to be new rivals for trophies in 2008/09. Arsenal were hoping to build upon their improvement with the clever signings of Aaron Ramsey and Samir Nasri. Liverpool had improved having signed Fernando Torres, the rapid Atletico Madrid striker, a year earlier. Chelsea had a new manager – Luis Felipe Scolari. Manchester City, meanwhile, had a new owner. Sheikh Mansour of Abu Dhabi assumed control from Thaksin Shinawatra and sanctioned the transfer deadline day capture of Brazilian forward Robinho from Real Madrid.

United started the season in unconvincing fashion, hindered by the absence of Ronaldo, who had ankle surgery and was set to miss the first few weeks. Only one of the first four games was won – Ronaldo's return couldn't come quickly enough. It coincided with a return to winning form for the team and goalscoring form for himself and Rooney. Both were on target in a 2-0 win over Bolton, then Rooney got the European champions off the mark with the first goal in a 3-0 win in Aalborg. Rooney's sensational strike from the edge of the box at Ewood Park secured a 2-0 win – and that hot streak continued into the international break, with two against Kazakhstan and another brace against Belarus.

Back on duty for United, Rooney was in inspirational mood, scoring a great goal against West Brom to make it eight goals in six games for club and country. United won 4-0, with Ronaldo netting and Berbatov getting his first league goal for the club.

"I've probably not had a better week in professional football," Rooney said after the game. "I've played well for England, we won both games, I got four goals and I've scored again for United and we've won – but I know I can get better. Everyone at the club will tell you I work hard, I want to practise, I want to learn. I've said I would like to score more consistently."

The hot run continued – Rooney scoring the third in a routine win over Celtic in Europe, a smart finish from the edge of the box for his 99th club goal. Everything seemed conveniently contrived for the 100th to come in United's next game – at Goodison Park.

"It's always nice to get to 100 goals and if I could do it back at Everton that would be really pleasing," he said. "I'm playing a lot higher up the pitch and attacking defenders a bit more than earlier in the season. The season before last I scored 23 and I went a bit down last year to 18. I'd be disappointed if I didn't top that this season."

The milestone goal didn't come against Everton. Nor in the following games against West Ham, Hull City or Celtic in the return. "It has happened throughout my career that I score in clusters," the striker said before the visit to Arsenal. "Hopefully I can become more consistent in front of goal. It's difficult to conserve energy because I've always thought of myself as an honest player. If I end up towards the left or right and the opposing full-back is running forward then I just couldn't let him run past me. I'd naturally run back and help our defence out. It is just the way I am."

United were in desperate need of goals at the Emirates after going down 2-0 – but Rooney was misfiring, and Ferguson brought him off for Tevez. In the end, the consolation goal scored by the champions came from another substitute – right-back Rafael Da Silva, who scored a fine half-volley from the edge of the box in injury time.

Rafael and his twin brother Fabio had already made an impression on Rooney; the fearlessness of youth and the way they played as if they were on the playground forged a connection that transcended a language barrier.

"Sometimes football *is* the language," says Rafael. "Wayne liked the way we were as players. Before we signed as professionals, we came over from Brazil and trained with the United players. It was our second time over when Albert Morgan, the kitman, told the guy who was looking after us that Wayne had said how much he liked us. I remember it clearly. 'These guys are brilliant, I love the way they play'. We couldn't understand each other. But in football talk we were able to bond. Sport is great for that, but football above all others, it helps you to speak without speaking. We developed a great respect for each other."

Rafael had made an instant impact, with standout performances which had thrust him straight into the first team. Fabio would have to wait for that same chance due to a shoulder injury – but he remembers those early encounters with England's best player.

"I had a good relationship with Wayne but I would admit it's not even close to the connection my brother had with him," says Fabio. "They were so similar – they'd get angry really quickly! It was that aggression that made Wayne really like my brother. He saw a little bit of himself. He had that passion on the training ground and on the pitch. It is a standard unlike other football teams and other players. Here is a guy with millions in the bank and you know he has the hunger to win as if he has nothing. You have to share that attitude if you want to succeed. It really helped me."

Rooney had only just turned 23, but, according to Fabio, "It seemed like he'd been there for even longer than some of the more experienced players. The way he acted, the way he trained and the way he carried himself. He was a big character."

The wait for that century of goals didn't go on for too long – on the last day of November, United travelled across the city to play at the Etihad. It was a day for the number 10 to show his importance, which he not only did in scoring just before half-time, but also in a hardworking display after Ronaldo was sent off with 20 minutes to go. With United defending the 1-0 lead into injury time, City won a corner. Their goalkeeper Joe Hart came up for it. As the visitors attempted to clear their lines, Rooney was desperate for the ball close to the halfway line. Once he received it from Giggs, he was equally desperate to engineer a shooting opportunity. From around 45 yards, he struck – but Hart got back just in time to claw it away.

Goal 100 was followed by 101 in a 2-2 draw with Aalborg; United had already qualified for the next round, and the point saw the European champions top their group. The other goal-scorer on the day was Carlos Tevez, the player to most suffer from loss of game time after the arrival of Berbatov. When he did play, the Argentinian had demonstrated his worth – a week earlier, he'd scored four in a League Cup win over Blackburn – and he remained a popular figure with the fans and plenty of the players.

Speaking almost 10 years later on Sky Sports, Rooney paid Tevez the ultimate compliment. "Tevez would be my preferred partner, we suited each other's games and we worked off each other," he said. "It must have been horrible to play against us because we were always in opponents' faces. People said we couldn't play together, but we hit it off and I really enjoyed it."

The compliment was definitely returned – and not just because Tevez found himself the latest member of the Old Trafford dressing room to be the beneficiary of Rooney's automotive generosity.

"I identified a lot with Rooney," Tevez told ESPN in 2019. "He came from a poor area in Liverpool and always fought for the ball as if it were the last… [At United] even the worst player came with a Ferrari. I was there with an Audi which the club had given me and they all laughed at me. 'Take the Lamborghini,' Rooney told me. I went to find it at his house and he let me keep it for 10 days."

Even at their worst, Rooney and Tevez together were still a constant headache for defenders. At their best, they were a pair of Tasmanian devils with movement and goal threat to give opponents nightmares. Ferguson, however, was not quite so enamoured with Tevez – the forward wasn't universally loved at the club, and the manager was monitoring the mood of the squad. He felt the Argentinian had not reacted positively to the signing of Berbatov and had become more selfish – and decided early into the second year that he would not take up an option to sign him at the end of the campaign.

It was starting to feel as if players were going to have to think selfishly in order to be considered first choice – for Rooney, a statement of his worth was well-timed indeed in December.

Ironically, Tevez had started in the Club World Cup semi-final against Gamba Osaka in Yokohama, and Rooney came on as a late replacement with United two goals up. The local side pulled a goal back while Rooney's arrival on the pitch was still being announced – but within a minute, Rooney made it 3-1. It sparked a mini-capitulation, with Fletcher scoring two minutes later, and then three minutes after that, Rooney made it two for him and five for his team from Giggs' through ball. This time he allowed himself a smile, having previously seemed frustrated at his initial exclusion.

The opponents three days later were LDU Quito of Ecuador. This time Rooney was in from the start. This was a much tighter affair than the semi (a mood heightened by Vidic's dismissal) but the decisive goal was still devastatingly simple – Carrick, Anderson and Ronaldo were involved in the build-up. Ronaldo laid it off to Rooney who struck the ball first time across goal from the angle. It was a perfect strike – enough to earn United the title of world champions. The match-winning goal was merely the seal on a man-of-the-match display.

With Ronaldo having been the dominant name in the prior campaign, it was positive for someone else – and Rooney in particular – to receive the plaudits for his contribution. "For every player it's good to have a moment like that, a moment where you play a big part," says Rafael. "It was good for him and for his confidence."

Earlier in the year, Rooney had acknowledged that his ambitions

Wayne celebrates United's 2008 FIFA Club World Cup triumph having scored the winning goal in the final during his Man-of-the-Match performance

of a major personal award were for the future. "With the likes of Ronaldo, Messi and Aguero, you're speaking of players who deserve to be up for World Footballer of the Year," he said in October. "Hopefully I can get there one day. But I'd rather win a trophy with the team than any personal trophy."

It was fitting, then, that a player who had shown such selflessness for the team had a crucial say on one of the biggest occasions. And after the game, Rooney reflected on his 'perfect' 2008. "If we hadn't won this trophy, it would have been very difficult to go home," he said. "We would have been on a downer. But having won it, we can return full of confidence, and get some momentum going. It's the perfect way to end the year, winning a third trophy to go with the Premier League and Champions League."

Back in England, United were concerning themselves with their domestic championship. They had games in hand over the teams above them, but those teams – most notably Liverpool and Chelsea – had points on the board. With United and Chelsea set to go head-to-head, Liverpool manager Rafa Benitez launched an astonishing broadside at Sir Alex Ferguson, complaining about fixtures, officiating and describing his outburst as 'not playing mind games, just facts'.

If it was an attempt to destabilise the Old Trafford side, it did not work. The champions were in the middle of an incredible run of clean sheets, with seven before the Chelsea game – which ended 3-0 to Ferguson's side, with Rooney getting the second – and clocked in eventually at an impressive 14 in succession. For the second half of that run, Rooney was missing, having injured a hamstring shortly after scoring in the first minute against Wigan.

On his return against Fulham, Rooney scored in a routine 4-0 win in the FA Cup – United also held a seven-point cushion with a game in hand at the top of the table, and had recently won the

League Cup, a game Rooney was desperate to make but could not be rushed back for. They were purring ominously, looking as though they might even eclipse the achievements of the previous season.

Against Inter Milan in the Champions League, Rooney was in impressive form in tandem with Giggs and Scholes, though Vidic and Ronaldo got the goals in a 2-0 win that earned qualification to the quarter-finals. And then the wheels came off. Liverpool won 4-1 at Old Trafford, and United followed that by losing 2-0 at Fulham, as Rooney was sent off for throwing the ball at the referee in the dying moments. It was a second yellow, which meant he'd be missing for only one game, but this added to United's strike problems with Berbatov also out injured. The stage was set for a dramatic introduction to first-team football for young Federico Macheda, who scored an incredible last-minute winner against Aston Villa to restore some positive momentum to United, and then followed it up a week later with a winning goal at Sunderland.

Either side of that trip to the north east, United took on Porto and made hard work of them – Rooney and Tevez scoring in a home draw, with Ronaldo netting a thunderbolt from distance in Portugal to send them into the semi-finals.

They also had another semi-final – this time against Everton in the FA Cup. Ferguson, though, rung the changes – Ronaldo, Rooney, Giggs, Van der Sar, Fletcher, Carrick, Evra and Scholes were all given the day off, though the latter two had to come off the bench. It was not the wisest day for the United boss to shuffle the pack, though he could rightly point out that his team deserved to win, and that they should have had a penalty – in the end, it was the Toffees who won on penalties themselves after a 0-0 draw. United had come even closer to repeating their treble of ten years earlier, only to have a new source of anguish to rue.

Most of those names were back after their rest for the visit of Portsmouth three days later – Rooney scored inside the first ten minutes as United won 2-0 on a night when Liverpool and Chelsea dropped points.

Another morale boosting afternoon followed a few days later when Spurs came to Old Trafford. They were 2-0 up at half-time, prompting Ferguson to unleash all of his star strikers. Rooney, Ronaldo, Tevez and Berbatov were all on the pitch at the same time, and while there was definitely an argument for too many cooks spoiling the broth, it was the perfect ingredient on this occasion. That owed much to Rooney's move to the left – he and Ronaldo were simply devastating in a 14-minute spell where they scored two goals each. United eventually won 5-2 in a game that was as crucial as it was memorable.

It had proved Ferguson a prophet once more, as he had declared of Rooney before the game: "His stamina levels are unquestionable. I'm quite amazed at him sometimes. He has got this desire to be involved all the time. Sometimes that can be costly in the sense that he can burn himself out and then, for maybe 10 minutes, he will drop off in a game. But suddenly he explodes again and away he goes. He's amazing. He never stops. There are very few with that desire and hunger. It is wonderful to see in a young person."

Rooney, clearly aware of the growing clamour among the support to sign Tevez on a permanent basis, made a pointed remark after the game. "Carlos coming on at half-time was a big plus for us," he said. "He gets the crowd up, he chases everything down, he never gave the defenders any time and that gave myself, Cristiano and Berba more space to get on the ball – and thankfully it paid off... I've played on the left a few times this season. It is not the ideal position for me but, if the manager asks me to play there, I will play there."

United's momentum was evident over both legs of the Champions League semi-final against Arsenal. The Gunners were dealt with in comfort, but this didn't make it any less spectacular. The second leg, in particular, was memorable. United built on their first-leg 1-0 lead with an early Park goal, and added to that in the 11th minute with a simply outrageous Ronaldo free-kick from almost 40 yards. It would take something special to beat that to the headlines, but that's precisely what United served up in the second half.

As Arsenal committed men forward, they left themselves vulnerable to the counter. As the ball was cleared, Ronaldo found Park, who spread it wide to Rooney. The striker appeared to slow play down for a moment, encouraging two red Gunners shirts to approach him. This created space for Park and Ronaldo, and Rooney then timed his ball across the box with perfect speed and accuracy – a gift of an invitation for Ronaldo to make it three. The Portuguese's break-neck speed to get into the position to score just 10 seconds after his touch earlier in the move was breathtaking.

If the European Cup was the pinnacle of their achievements together then this was surely the zenith of their combined artistry. This was their respective qualities in tandem on the biggest stage exhibited in exhilarating style. If it was a triumph of individualism and expression, it was also still a product of the training pitch, actioned to perfection.

Rene Meulensteen refers to the positional intelligence the players adopted – or, in the case of Rooney, appeared to come naturally. "This tactic was particularly successful against Arsenal because they only had one way of playing and we knew how to set traps to intercept the ball," he explains. "Once we had that, we set our own break – Wayne would usually be the deepest player and he was able to start off our attacks that were like the Red Arrows. There was never a moment where Wayne would be frustrated by anything that was asked of him. He was always eager to learn how he could make a difference for his team."

It's fair to say that without Rooney's willingness to play the team game, the goal wouldn't have existed. It is only recent history but it has still gone down as a Ronaldo goal, an example of his own greatness to the football public at large. To United supporters, the goal is a reminder of how fantastic the team was. It's also never lost on the fans – or indeed his team-mates – just how crucial Wayne's involvement was in moves just like that.

"Sometimes people *do* forget," Rafael says. "I would add an important point. The people who matter, the people who understand, they don't forget. People who already appreciated Wayne. United supporters. His team-mates. You can include Ji-Sung Park as well. We all knew how crucial they were to that counter-attack. Football is like this – these days more than ever. They look at the goalscorer and he gets the attention. Rooney made a great pass. Without him, without Park, that goal doesn't exist. That's the truth of football – you need those other players. Even a player like Ronaldo can't do it all alone."

The connection was the result of five years playing together. Ronaldo and Rooney were in sync. Lesser players, or lesser men, might have reacted with some petulance. They might have used the excuse to rest on their laurels. It was to Rooney's eternal credit that he not only contributed, he thrived. "Wayne and Cristiano were not similar players but their styles complemented and I would say each completed the other," says Rafael. "I think Rooney did a lot, he almost changed his style because of Ronaldo scoring so many goals. Rooney kept scoring but he dropped back to create more and make more assists.

"He's such an intelligent player. He could play midfield, on the wing, defensive midfield. He could even play right-back, I'm sure! His knowledge and understanding of the game is so great that he would do it and already appreciate everything that it takes to play in that position. I love players like that."

United, of course, were reaping the dividends of having two of the world's best young players who had now matured into two of the greatest without the need for qualification of their age. However, the victory over Arsenal came with a cost when Darren Fletcher was harshly dismissed for a seemingly clean tackle. United had no right to appeal, and the key midfielder would be missing when the European champions met Barcelona in the final in Rome.

The Manchester derby was next up – a crucial game for United in their quest to win the league. Before the match, Rooney gave his assessment of the run-in.

"Once Abramovich went into Chelsea it looked hard to beat them," he said. "But thankfully we stopped them from winning the league for a third year running and we've really kicked on. Some of the football we've played has been brilliant and we can get even better. This team is a lot better than the one I joined in 2004. I was only 18 then; Cristiano was the same age, Fletch was a year older. We had a lot of young players then, but over the last few years we've gained the experience."

He admitted that the ambition was to become the first team to win the Champions League for two years in succession. "We set out to retain the title and be the first team to do it. We're so close now and it would be amazing if we can pull it off," he said.

It was put to Rooney that former England manager Terry Venables had suggested his performances from the left were so impressive that he could emerge as a player like Lionel Messi, who, like Ronaldo had blossomed in a 'false' position starting from the right. "I don't think I've quite got his trickery," Rooney modestly responded. "Messi is one of my favourite players, probably one of the best ever. In some games you get a lot of freedom playing in that position and in other games you just have to defend for the team. I've always said playing up front alongside another striker is my favourite position."

Rooney was on the bench for the derby – and by the time he got on to the pitch, his team were two goals in the lead. The scorers had eventful days. Ronaldo had struck a wonderful free-kick, but was brought off and reacted angrily as he was desperate to finish as the league's top scorer ahead of Nicolas Anelka. Tevez scored a fine goal of his own, prompting Old Trafford to sing 'Fergie, sign him up'; the Argentinian reacted by cupping his hands over his ears. It was all part of the public dance – Tevez's representatives were claiming that he was desperate to stay, while 'sources' from the club claimed the prospective fee to take him on a permanent basis was unrealistic.

Tevez continued to state his case, coming off the bench to score a crucial equaliser at Wigan, with Michael Carrick scoring a late winner that meant the champions only needed one point from their remaining two games to win their third successive title. Next up were Arsenal at Old Trafford, and Rooney had the game's best chance, heading wide in the first half – but Tevez once again grabbed the spotlight, this time dramatically waving farewell to all sides of the stadium as he was substituted late on.

He couldn't take the headlines – those belonged to United as a club, who had achieved what would have felt unthinkable 20 years earlier by drawing level with Liverpool on 18 league titles. "The great challenge now is to try to win it next year because that would be something special," the relentless Ferguson said during the celebrations after the 0-0 draw. "A 19th league title would give us a special place in the club's history."

All eyes turned to Rome. In the build-up, Rooney's name dominated discussions, his role in the team even more pertinent considering the speculation that Ronaldo and Tevez were likely to be on their way in the summer. Ferguson admitted he was likely to persist with Rooney from the left, comparing his incisive performances to how Thierry Henry operated for Barcelona. "That is the sacrifice he is making for the team," the United boss said. "We have other players who would not be able to do it. But Wayne's got the stamina and resilience to keep [helping out the defence] and still cause a threat when he attacks. He's played the role fantastically.

"There are many attributes but the most important is his fantastic hunger and desire. You have to channel that desire, and sometimes, with the anger, it exceeds the emotions. But we hope that the maturity is bringing a real professionalism. But he is such a winner. Every training session, the poor referee gets absolutely murdered. Every ball, every tackle that goes in, it's like a cup final to him."

For this actual cup final, Rooney would indeed play from the left, with Ferguson changing his shape to play Park from the right and pack the midfield with Carrick, Anderson and Giggs. Ronaldo would start through the middle with Tevez and Berbatov on the bench.

Rooney, who had confessed to feeling inspired by the Moscow pre-match team-talk, had a different reaction to Ferguson's address in Rome. Rooney told Jamie Carragher for the latter's book *The Greatest Games*: "[Ferguson] said, 'We are Manchester United and we are not going into the Champions League final to sit back all game. We are going to attack them and do it the right way.' We were all sitting there thinking, 'Oh f***'. Sir Alex went through their side, saying 'let's go at them'. Then you saw the names like Messi, Eto'o and Henry! I was like: 'F***ing 'ell, how much pace do you want in one team?'"

United actually started the final well, and had a number of early chances, but their momentum was shaken when Samuel Eto'o scored in the 10th minute. Barcelona's midfield were dominant and a second goal for the Catalan side followed in the second half when Messi out-jumped Rio Ferdinand to head in; a clear sign that it was just not United's day.

As the dejected Manchester United players prowled the Stadio Olimpico pitch, there was an anti-climactic feel in the area. It wasn't supposed to end like this. Not just the season – this team. The campaign was not quite as smooth as the previous year but those individual moments and the coming together of the team had connected to strike almost the right combination of notes at precisely the right time. United were league champions and League Cup winners. They'd won the Club World Cup. And they were even closer to a clean sweep of everything than they had been the previous season – penalties away from an FA Cup final, and a Darren Fletcher away from at least a more competitive Champions League final. This was one of the most successful seasons in Manchester United history, not that it felt like it on the evening of May 27th, 2009.

Chapter Twelve

MAIN MAN

Wayne Rooney was not able to break the club record with consecutive Champions League wins but equalled an international record that summer when his two goals against Andorra on June 10th took him to eight in World Cup qualifying – the same number as the legendary Tommy Taylor had notched in the 1958 qualifiers, before his untimely death in Munich. He would have appreciated that his goalscoring touch would be required a little more regularly in the coming season. It was clear that Carlos Tevez would not be remaining at United, and he moved to Manchester City as part of their £100m+ summer spend.

United, who technically had Tevez on loan, received no payment, but they did receive a significant fee when they accepted Real Madrid's offer of £80m for Cristiano Ronaldo. It was a world record – breaking the £56m that the Spaniards had paid for Kaka days earlier. The £80m fee looked like a considerable price at the time – it would turn out to be a bargain.

United's supporters were hopeful that money would be reinvested in the team. They were disappointed. Antonio Valencia was signed from Wigan for less than £20m, and the only other senior arrival was the now-veteran and injury-plagued Michael Owen, whose contract had run down at relegated Newcastle. His goal-scoring instincts still made him a good squad option, but United supporters were right to express concern that he could not replace the contribution of Ronaldo or Tevez in either goals or build-up play.

Sir Alex Ferguson knew that his team would have a much-changed dynamic for the coming months. "We are a different team now," he admitted. "We will shape it differently, we will be more compact in midfield. We will have an increasing maturity in players like Darren Fletcher, and Owen Hargreaves will come back from his injury problems. Anderson will improve, Nani will improve. Rooney will improve. I'm sure Dimitar Berbatov will have a terrific season."

Before the new season, Ferguson explained that Rooney would play more centrally. "I don't think the responsibility of getting more goals will affect Wayne," he said. "He has the mental strength for all that. He will be used through the middle this season. And he is maturing. He tends to go on these bursts of goals. Last season I think he hit seven in a row at one point but if he can do that more consistently over the season he will get to 25 and above. In some games, Wayne played wide left and in some matches it worked well. But in others it was not a good position for him. We will change that."

The new system had a successful start. Rooney grabbed the only goal of the opening Premier League game against Birmingham, before scoring twice against Wigan, once against Arsenal and again at Tottenham to make it five from his first five.

Spurs boss Harry Redknapp praised Rooney's early season form: "He was a big star until Ronaldo came along and took over. But now, once again you can see that all their lads will step up. That's why United are what they are, why they have won the Champions League. They always have three or four options when they get the ball and there's always movement."

Next up, it was the Manchester derby. It had been a big summer across the city, and Tevez was not the only top name to move to the blue half of the province. The signings of Emmanuel Adebayor and Kolo Toure were landmark as they arrived from Arsenal – Arsene Wenger now facing up to the reality of seeing his better players poached by richer clubs. It was a signal of intent from City, who also hoovered up talent from other clubs closer to their stature – Gareth Barry from Aston Villa, Roque Santa Cruz from Blackburn, and Joleon Lescott from Everton, strategic moves to strengthen their squad while weakening those around them. The signing of Tevez was the most eye-catching, not least because City paid for billboards in the city that had an image of the player drenched in sky blue with the words 'Welcome to Manchester'.

City had not been established as a top side since the early 1970s and Rooney embraced the challenge, describing it as 'great for everyone in Manchester now there's another team challenging'. He also spoke about his own growing responsibility. "Ronaldo is the best player in the world so questions were always going to be asked," he told *Nuts* magazine. "But I've been under pressure playing first-team football since I was 16 – it really doesn't affect me. It's a good challenge more than anything else. I hope I can be United's main man. This is the most important year of my career."

Rooney was the man for the big occasion, scoring after just

two minutes – but City refused to go away, equalising that goal and then two Darren Fletcher strikes to look as though they'd snatched a point. The stage was set for one striker dubbed as a traitor to steal the show – but it was Owen and not Tevez who scored a dramatic winner deep into injury time. Following the chaotic conclusion, Ferguson beamed that it was a victory against 'the noisy neighbours'.

The following few months were rather flat in comparison. Rooney went on a lean streak, scoring just once in his next eight games. There was a definite sense that the responsibilities were growing – during this spell, Coleen gave birth to their first child, and Rooney was also named England captain for a friendly against Brazil in Qatar. The need for his goals at club level was growing, with United suffering from a defensive injury crisis that meant their watertight back-line was leaking goals at a comparatively regular rate.

As usual, the duck was broken in spectacular fashion – a hat-trick against Portsmouth in late November – and the following week, Rooney scored the fourth in a 4-0 win at West Ham that featured a back-line of Fletcher, Carrick, Brown and Giggs in the last minute. United couldn't survive the knocks unscathed and fell to damaging defeats to Aston Villa and Fulham in December, which left the champions with five defeats from their opening 18 league games.

United travelled to Hull the day after Boxing Day looking to bounce back. They were leading through Rooney's goal when the scorer played an inexplicable backpass to goalkeeper Tomasz Kuszczak. Hull intercepted and won a penalty; per the *Express*, Rooney cast a 'nervous, apologetic glance' across to his manager. The hosts scored the penalty, but Rooney was instrumental as United scored twice more to earn victory. "Giving the ball away for the goal was a bad moment but he was exceptionally good," Ferguson said after the match. "He is a natural winner. He has always had a great attitude. He will be more sick than anybody that he made a mistake but he rectified it in a nice way."

An embarrassing exit to Leeds in the FA Cup in early January left United with three trophies to play for; one of those the League Cup, in which they'd qualified for the semi-final where they'd face City. The first leg was lost 2-1 – before the second, United played against Hull in a quick return, and the East Yorkshire side felt the full force of Rooney's goalscoring power. An early poacher's goal was followed by a very late showing – three more strikes followed in the 82nd, 85th and 93rd minutes, the fourth goal having the visitors on strings as he juggled the ball and then fired into the net.

"The difference is that I am consciously getting in the box more and trying to put myself in scoring situations," Rooney said. "The last time I scored four I was 12 so I'm proud to get four for the first time as a professional."

Ferguson was known for setting targets for Ronaldo and decided the time was right to do the same for Rooney. "We want to encourage Wayne to get 20 goals," he'd said in mid-January. The fourth goal against Hull was his 20th of the campaign. The manager also suggested that he would take the opportunity to rest Rooney when it became available but couldn't afford to do it in the next two games – the second leg with City, and the visit to Arsenal. In both games, Rooney showed exactly why his team could not do without him.

City started with a 2-1 advantage, both goals scored by Tevez in the first game – United then edged ahead on aggregate through strikes from Scholes and Carrick. Tevez then scored again, making it completely level, and presenting the prospect of extra-time –

before Rooney sensationally headed a Giggs cross into the net in injury time to take United to Wembley. It was just reward – Rooney had been the heartbeat of a pulsating second-half performance.

Ferguson, who had declared before the game that there weren't 'many players matching him at the moment', purred at the vindication of his remark. "It was a wonderful performance, a true, world-class display," the boss said. "I thought Wayne was much better today than Saturday and he scored four goals against Hull. His control, his leading of the line and his penetration were all absolutely fantastic."

Team-mate Darren Fletcher was also full of praise for Rooney's performance. "He was up there on his own against City, and I know sometimes it's difficult for him," the Scot said. "But there's no one you would rather have up there on his own because he does the work of two players. His work-rate for the team, the quality he has got, is amazing. He fully deserved to pop up with an unbelievable winner. Good job, too, because extra-time wouldn't have been ideal preparation for a massive game at Arsenal on Sunday."

Ferguson had a mantra going back all the way to his early successful days at United. In the game before a big game, the United manager would stress the importance of a strong performance, as it would stand them in good stead for the matches which followed. So the Hull game was followed by the City game, and that was followed by a trip to Arsenal where his players put on the kind of show that suggested that Ronaldo might not be missed as much as one might think.

Yes, it was the style United showed in a 3-1 win that was impressive, but it was also the way they were able to run through a near carbon copy of the counter-attack goal from the Champions League. There were two first-half highlights – the first, an outrageous piece of skill from Nani that saw him flip between two defenders when it didn't seem there was space for a ball to get between them, much less his body. The criticism of Nani over the years had been too much of this and no end product – but now, it was starting to feel as though the product was finally here, with another exquisite piece of skill and a glorious lofted chip over the keeper into the far corner.

Within five minutes, United struck again. It was a case of deja-vu for the home defence; from an Arsenal corner, the ball was cleared to Park, who laid it off to Rooney. Rooney showed fine awareness to strike a gorgeous ball to Nani, who was 15 yards inside his own half but had the pace to accelerate into the yawning acres in front of him. Suddenly, the figure of Rooney emerged on the scene – intuitively knowing the area where the ball should be played – and raced past two Arsenal defenders who'd had a good 10 yards on him. It was an awesome demonstration of pace and power, and Nani's pass was good – Rooney's finish was accomplished, as if he hadn't broken a sweat. In that moment it was clear to see he simply wanted it more.

The roles had shifted – Nani more of an orthodox winger, Rooney fitting into the 'Ronaldo' role of the other striker – but the style remained. It also answered a question – did the naturally stocky Rooney possess the same sort of athletic prowess as other top players?

Once more, this was a question that was asked outside of Old Trafford, with those within the club already knowing the answer was affirmative. "On the pitch he was a big leader. He was a player who would outrun everyone," explains Fabio Da Silva. "People spoke about his body shape. But you couldn't question his athleticism. That probably impressed me more than anything. He was very competitive. Sometimes it's difficult for players to be so competitive all the time like Wayne was. It can lead to words on the training pitch. For me it was a good thing. It's missed these days – you don't often see it."

United won 3-1, their third coming from another counter led and scored by another of the unsung heroes, Park. Not that you could call Rooney unsung any longer – his goalscoring form was matched by his level of performance. "He was the key man for us because they just couldn't handle him," Ferguson explained, after describing the forward as 'unbelievable'.

United had changed their system to play a 4-3-3 or 4-5-1 in big games, though Rooney's role as a number nine was intriguing. He was proving himself good enough to do that as his goal record attested, but he was far from a goal-hanger, with his natural inclination to help his team a key feature of his play. As a result, there was a new conversation on the table – was Rooney now blossoming because he was being allowed to?

"He grew after Cristiano left and I'm sure everyone at the club would say the same thing," says Fabio. "Cristiano helped everyone and it helped your chances of success. But his numbers and his contribution were so phenomenal that the spotlight was always on him more. Karim Benzema is a good player to use as an example. After Cristiano left Real Madrid, people said that Karim was a different player. He wasn't – he was the same great player. But people didn't notice as much as they should when Ronaldo was there. They didn't see his light. It was similar with Wayne. Many players would struggle under that pressure but he didn't, he was very important for us, and everybody could see his light."

In early February 2010, due to his hot streak, there was a suggestion that Rooney was indeed the best player in the world. It led to speculation that he might be tempted to test himself abroad, with two years left on his contract. "He's very happy at the club,"

Ferguson said. "You couldn't meet a better lad. He is a down-to-earth boy and he won't change."

Later that month, United went to Italy to face AC Milan as the Champions League resumed. The build-up was dominated by arguably the most high-profile English players of the last generation, with Rooney in such tantalising form and David Beckham having signed on loan for the Italian side from LA Galaxy.

Beckham was now a veteran of 34 – it was expected that the striker in his prime years would have a greater influence on proceedings. "Wayne has changed his mentality," said Patrice Evra. "Now he concentrates more on staying around the box. He wants to score and he wants to be a killer. And that is very important for us. He has not lost any desire to still press the ball but now he knows he needs to score a lot of goals because Ronaldo has gone. He understands what the team needs."

Ferguson was clearly wary of repetition in his comments but understood Rooney would be the main topic of the pre-match discussion, not least because they were returning to the scene of such underwhelming performances in 2005 and 2007.

"World class is a misused word but you have to consider Rooney to be one of the best players in the world," Ferguson said. "Manchester United fans build up heroes very quickly and Rooney will be that kind of player. I know he came to us as a young player from Everton, but they will always look upon Rooney as one of their own, developed at their own club. His form has brought him to the high point of his career."

United had a creditable 1-1 scoreline to take back home until Rooney made his mark in ten unforgettable second-half minutes. In the 66th, he met a Valencia cross at the far post with a magnificent looping header. In the 75th, he engineered unfathomable power on a clipped pass by Fletcher, heading into the top corner when others would have tried to control the ball. It was difficult to choose which of the goals was more impressive. United ended with a 3-2 win with a strong second-half performance which had been inspired by Rooney's words and actions.

"I was very frustrated with a lot of things in the first half," he said after the game. "Some people were not doing their jobs right and I let my feelings be known. We learned from that and we won the game."

When Ferguson was once again pressed on just how good Rooney was at the moment, he couldn't hold back. "He was absolutely devastating," he said. "They just couldn't handle him. He's one of the best players in the world now. He is improving all the time and if he continues that trend, he must be considered alongside all those players such as Lionel Messi, Kaka and Cristiano Ronaldo. In the last two months we've seen a development in his game. Confidence has a lot to do with it. His basic ability is as good as any of those players, but he needed to score more goals. Now he is doing that."

Two more goals followed in a comfortable win over West Ham before the League Cup final against Aston Villa. Rooney was nursing a slight knee problem so was on the bench, but was called upon when Michael Owen – who had scored himself – had to come off just before half-time. There was an element of inevitability about the decisive moment – Valencia crossing from the right and Rooney heading into the net.

The first post-Ronaldo cup final had been decided by the man who had so often had to share the spotlight with him – but this was Rooney's moment, and the first real sole statement that he was capable of handling all that came with the lofty proclamations of the past month. "I'm in the best form of my life," he admitted after the game.

Wayne heads home the winner against Aston Villa in the 2010 League Cup final at Wembley, later declaring "I'm in the best form of my life"

In good time for his national team, too – England had qualified for the World Cup in South Africa, and earlier in February, managers of the qualifying countries had been in Sun City where they had almost all to a man spoken glowingly of United's in-form star. Notable quotes came from coaches of England's group rivals, with Slovenia manager Matjaz Kek saying Rooney was alongside Messi and Ronaldo as 'the top three in the world'. Algeria coach Rabah Saadane said: "When I look at Rooney now, I see a player who is at the summit. It is not just the goals he is scoring and the talent he has, but he is also at the top of his maturity as a player – and that is what defines a great player."

The greatest compliment came from Germany manager Joachim Low, who described Rooney as 'unstoppable'. That was put to the player himself, who admitted: "I do feel unstoppable. I feel good. I feel every game I play I am going to score. I hope I can make a difference for England at the World Cup."

It didn't take Rooney long to inflict further nightmares on Milan in the return leg; he'd already gone close twice by the time he headed in Neville's cross in the 13th minute. Within 60 seconds of the second half, it was 2-0 and two for Rooney; Nani's clipped pass behind the defence was met by the cutest of touches by Rooney, who rolled the ball past Abbiati for his 30th goal of the season. Park – who had spent the preceding two-and-a-half hours of the tie following Andrea Pirlo – broke free to net a third on the night. Darren Fletcher's late goal made it four on the night and 7-2 on aggregate. Milan manager Leonardo paid tribute to his team's executor, describing him as 'the complete player'.

"This result is going to send out a great message about us," said Rooney. "Every game will be difficult so we are not bothered who we get in the next round. We've been in good form and we are building up a nice head of steam. But a win like this gives you so much confidence and belief that we can win the competition again this year."

Ferguson had suggested Rooney had the momentum and capability to match Ronaldo's 42 goals from two years earlier. The England forward embraced the comparison and for the first time seemed comfortable to address that he was in similar company without dismissing it. "It would be great to win trophies and get 42 goals as well," he added. "I'm delighted to have reached 30 but those goals are behind me now and hopefully I can get even more. I felt more was expected of me when Ronaldo left. I knew I could do more. I hope in the future I can do even better. I am certainly happy we are still in the competition. Maybe I will ring Cristiano and speak to him about it."

The last comment was a tongue-in-cheek remark referring to Real Madrid's elimination by Lyon; United's chances of a third consecutive Champions League final improving by their absence. The Milan game had been played against a backdrop of growing protests against the United owners, with supporters upset after the relative lack of spending in the summer considering their receipt of a large sum; their feelings were inflamed by Ferguson's statement in January when he declared: "We have got the money. There is no question about that. I just don't see that player who can make a difference for us in terms of value or ability."

With players like Mesut Ozil, David Silva and Sergio Aguero on the market, many United fans felt that Ferguson was making an excuse – they felt the Ronaldo fee was going to service the colossal debt still hanging on the club. Whatever the truth, they could not contest that the club had remained competitive despite losing two of the team's best players – and Rooney was the player most responsible. The performance against Milan evoked memories of his debut, all the more remarkable as he was one front player playing the role of two and still excelling.

Goals 31 and 32 followed in a 3-0 win over Fulham, and 33 was the equaliser in a 2-1 win over Liverpool. United were leading the table and in strong health ahead of a crucial week in which they would face off against Bayern Munich either side of a home game with title contenders Chelsea.

The first leg of the European tie was in Germany, and it brought more continental plaudits, this time from Franz Beckenbauer, who admitted his club 'feared' Rooney. "If he continues scoring like that and playing like that he can win the World Cup for England," Beckenbauer insisted. "Argentina have Lionel Messi, who, along with Rooney, is the best player in the world right now. But Wayne has made the biggest improvement to his game. He has changed the way he plays and, at 24, has added a maturity. Playing as the frontman, he makes it so hard for defenders to mark him and he is able to use the crosses from both wings so well. I've never seen him play better and I have been watching him for a long time now."

Just 66 seconds had been played when Rooney justified that fear by powering in a Nani cross from inside the six-yard box, a shot thumped with all the conviction and belief of the words that had been spoken in the previous eight weeks.

Chapter Thirteen

SUMMER OF DISCONTENT

Manchester United's – and Wayne Rooney's – 2010 took a distinct turn for the worse at around 9.35pm on the evening of March 30th. That Bayern Munich had recovered to win 2-1 with an injury-time winner was a mere minor nuisance compared to the worrying sight of Rooney turning his ankle in the build-up to that late goal. United had made all their changes – and the injury was so severe that the forward had to be taken from the field by the physios. It was confirmed that he had suffered ligament damage which would rule him out for four to six weeks.

Sir Alex Ferguson insisted his squad had plenty in reserve to compensate for the absence in the big games which were to follow. "I'm sure the players are not going to let this upset them in terms of what lies ahead of us," he said. "They know the incentive of winning against Chelsea and against Bayern Munich. Do you honestly think they are worrying whether Wayne Rooney is going to cost them it by not being there? Not at all."

But United's reliance on Rooney was significant. None of their other forwards had the breadth of attributes all in one player – and Dimitar Berbatov, who was tasked with replacing him, was ill-suited to the 4-3-3 formation Ferguson was reluctant to change. United were uninspiring against Chelsea, but still didn't deserve to lose, and especially not in the circumstances which unfolded. The Blues already had a 1-0 lead before Didier Drogba scored from a clear offside position to secure the result. It gave the visitors a two-point advantage in the title race.

"Berbatov failed to make a convincing case for himself, either as Rooney's deputy or a presence capable of leading the attack on his own," Paul Wilson wrote in the *Observer*. "Too much of the game passed him by and too often he was easily knocked off the ball. Neither of those charges can normally be levelled at Rooney."

It seemed that Ferguson agreed, despite his public comments. But then there was a definite case of bluff being called that week – United's medical staff had informed Rooney that he had a good chance of making the return game with Bayern, with Ferguson interjecting and saying he wanted Rooney to wear a protective boot in the meantime. The reason was two-fold – one, for its purpose, and two, to catch out the German team who would be preparing to face another player. Rooney put in a full training session before the game, admitting that even though he could sprint, he couldn't turn or stop. "It's like my brakes have gone," he wrote in his book *My Decade In The Premier League*.

The ruse was successful. Everyone was caught out when Rooney was announced in the starting line-up. For the next couple of hours, Old Trafford seemed to be carried away on a wave of delirious optimism. Darron Gibson scored a fine goal from the edge of the box after three minutes, assisted by Rooney. Nani's back-flick goal four minutes later was even better. In the 41st minute, Nani got his second, with Rooney confessing that in the moment, he felt like he was playing in another 'Roma' game.

But this was not Roma, and there would be no happy ending. Two minutes later, Michael Carrick made a rare error, allowing Olic to score just before the break. It shifted the momentum of the game, with the German side needing just one more to go through on away goals. Then, early in the second period, a hard task was made even more tough when Rafael was targeted by the mischievous visitors to get a second yellow card. He fell into the trap. A limping Rooney was replaced by John O'Shea, so that Rafael's gap could be plugged. Bayern got their goal – a fabulous volley by Robben – and United were out.

Rooney would have to sit out for a proper recovery period. The gamble had backfired. Ferguson went for experience and a more usual shape at Blackburn, with Giggs and Scholes in central midfield and Berbatov and Macheda up front. Macheda had scored a consolation goal against Chelsea so it was hoped he could repeat his previous season's heroics – he could not, and United were frustrated without the dynamism of their talisman.

Ferguson had rightly observed after the Chelsea setback that his team would have to win all of their remaining league games, and even then they still might not be able to overcome the Stamford Bridge side.

They gave it a go, inspired by yet another last-minute winner against Manchester City (to make it three for the season). A win against Spurs followed before Rooney was called back into the side for the last two games – he was unable to add to his 34 goals for the season, and despite United winning those final games, Chelsea's final two home games were won 7-0 and 8-0, giving them a fair claim on a title they won by a single point.

It's easy to argue that with a fit Rooney, United would have been more competitive against Chelsea or that they might have found a way through a stubborn Blackburn defence. It's not an excuse that sits easy with United's players.

"It's hard to say," Fabio Da Silva states. "Of course he was important. You just never know. Yes, it's obvious you have a better chance, but it's still always just a chance and not a guarantee. You only have to look at what happened the year before when Wayne was injured and Federico came in and Welbeck also came on. They were only involved because of the injuries. We weren't winning and we weren't playing well. The boss put Macheda in and the season changed completely."

Fabio's brother, Rafael, concurs. "It's easy to say he didn't play so we didn't win the title," he says. "But like my brother says, sometimes these injuries present a place in the team where someone comes in and helps us win the title. His injury was important and influential. But I think it would be unfair to say we didn't win the title because of it."

Rooney admitted that after such promise, the season's conclusion felt like a 'let down', and it certainly felt as though he took a bad mood into the World Cup. In one of the warm-up games, against local side Platinum Stars, Rooney screamed 'fuck you' in the face of domestic referee Jeff Selogilwe.

That felt like a more ominous sign than the positive noises the England camp were insisting on making. "Rooney is spontaneous, not uneducated," said Three Lions manager Fabio Capello. "He's instinctive and when he goes out on to the pitch he goes out to win. He's someone who gets angry when he's treated to something unfair. I've spoken to him, but he'll be fine for the World Cup, just as he was for the entire qualifying period."

Steven Gerrard, meanwhile, insisted that Rooney was 'in a position to make this World Cup his own, like Pele and Maradona'.

As it transpired, England's World Cup journey was one of the most miserable in living memory. There was a 1-1 draw with USA in the opener and then a 0-0 draw with Algeria. At the end of the game, England's players left the field to jeers, and Rooney broke the fourth wall in addressing one of the cameramen who had approached him on the pitch. "Nice to see your own fans booing you," Rooney said into the camera. "That's what you call supporters."

Before the crunch group game – England needed to win against Slovenia in order to qualify – Capello insisted better was to come. "He is one of the best players in the world," he said. "Sometimes the pressure is so big, even for important players. He's improved in training in the last three days. I hope, I'm sure, he'll play really, really well."

He did – and England won 1-0 thanks to a goal from Jermain Defoe. They had scraped their way through to the second round, but luck was most definitely not on their side against Germany. Capello's side slumped to a 2-0 deficit early on, but staged a pre-half-time comeback through Matt Upson and then Frank Lampard, whose shot crossed the line via the crossbar – but the goal was not awarded. The Germans scored twice in the second half to send England home. This time there were no penalties or red cards, but the rank underachievement of the squad meant it was open season when it came to blame; and Rooney's outburst after the Algeria game, as well as his status as the country's best player, had propelled him into the role of central antagonist.

As always, from a distance, Sir Alex Ferguson was in firefighting mode. "There was such expectation," he told reporters on July 6th. "There was talk he was going to be the player of the tournament. Don't forget, that was the prelude to the whole thing. He was going to be the star, he was going to outshine them all, Messi,

Ronaldo. So that level of expectation comes into it. And he's not got great experience of the World Cup really. You wait, though. In four years' time you will see a different player."

There was a cloud that seemed to hang over Rooney. The United boss was frustrated to see newspaper pictures of his star man smoking and urinating in an alleyway. News of discontent at United would not be made public for more than two months, but it was in fact on the eve of the new league season when Ferguson recalled Rooney informing him that he did not intend to sign a new contract. David Gill then had a meeting with Rooney's agent, Paul Stretford, where Gill was told that they didn't think the club was ambitious enough.

United's transfer activity hadn't been blockbuster – Chris Smalling, a promising young defender, had signed from Fulham, and Javier Hernandez was an unknown quantity of a striker who had arrived that summer from Mexican club Guadalajara.

The disagreements were hardly ideal preparation for a renewed championship push, but while these discussions continued in private, more lurid and more personal stories of Rooney's private life made it into the gossip pages during the September international break. United's first game after it was at Goodison Park, and Ferguson felt it was wise to take him out of the squad so he wasn't subjected to 'terrible abuse'. When he was back in the team, he was in subdued form, and was taken off against Bolton on September 26th with what Ferguson described as an 'ankle problem'.

Before the trip to Sunderland on the first weekend of October, the United boss elaborated: "Wayne has been playing for a few weeks now with his niggling ankle injury. He has kept it to himself and he is not doing himself justice. Wayne being Wayne, he wants to play. But I've got to take the view that this injury has been niggling for quite a while and he has kept on playing with it. Now we have identified that, we have to be dead sure we are doing the right thing. He thinks he's fit because he always thinks he's fit and that's the problem with the lad. He's always too willing to play even with injuries, which is a great trait."

But Rooney was thought fit enough to play for England – which he did, playing in a 0-0 draw with Montenegro in which he was booked for unsporting behaviour. Afterwards, it was put to him that his ineffectual displays were down to his injury concerns. "I've had no ankle problem all season," Rooney snapped at reporters.

It was clear to see there was a disconnect beyond a mere misunderstanding. "The lad has a high profile and the press are always going to seek him out for an interview," Ferguson told Key 103 Radio on the morning of October 16th, hours before a home game with West Brom. "But it is water off a duck's back really. It just passes off. I don't know where all these things come from."

Rooney came off the bench but was unable to inspire a subdued United to get more than a 2-2 draw against West Brom; there was a definite sense of foreboding at Old Trafford over the weekend. The Sunday newspapers suggested the relationship between player and manager was 'beyond repair' and that a 'clean break' was needed; that United were moved to make a statement dismissing it suggested there was no smoke without fire.

"To suggest Wayne will be sold in January is a nonsense," a club spokesman said, saying nothing and saying everything.

Ferguson and Rooney had a meeting the following day where the player confirmed what his agent had told Gill. Rooney went further down the 'lack of ambition' line, suggesting that the club should have tried harder to sign Mesut Ozil before the playmaker moved to Real Madrid. Twenty-four hours later, in his pre-match press conference before the Champions League group game with

Bursaspor, Ferguson gave one of the most memorable interviews of his entire tenure as United manager.

"We would like to present the facts because that is important to present the facts as we understand them," he said. "David Gill had a preliminary talk with his agent at the end of last season and it was to be continued after the World Cup. He told me he was on his way over from Carrington and said, 'I have some bad news for you.' His agent has intimated that he wouldn't be signing a contract and wanted away. It was a shock. I couldn't believe it, as in earlier discussions, he intimated he wanted to stay and sign a long contract, he was happy at the best club in the world and I was terribly disappointed as we couldn't quite understand it.

"I had a meeting with him and he intimated to me that he wanted to leave. We had a discussion and I said, 'The one thing I want from you Wayne is to honour and respect the club's position and its traditions and behave like a proper professional and we'll try and see it through.' Although I did say, there is an offer there if he is prepared to accept it. It's an offer… we've never gone into any financial discussion. But, I know David was prepared to offer him a contract that would be difficult to better elsewhere. That's what we do with top players. We've been facing these problems for quite a while now. Contract issues in the last 10 years have accelerated to become quite phenomenal.

"However, the area which has created a lot of the mystery about it is this issue with his injury. I've never had an argument with Wayne. He got an ankle injury in the Rangers game, he was seen clearly hobbling. He confirmed it himself in an interview with Sky. I spoke to him before the Sunderland game and my planning was, based on the fact he wasn't playing that well, was to leave him out of the Sunderland game, make sure his ankle is properly prepared for the next game and give him a 10-day recovery so he could play for England. My hope was that with playing for England at Wembley he could recapture his form.

"His entry into the mixed zone at Wembley has created that next stage we have had to deal with. He said he wasn't injured. That was disappointing as we know full well he was carrying an injury. We sent him for a scan and that showed a minor defect in terms of the ankle injury, nothing serious, but needed treatment and he has had treatment.

"I feel that we still have to keep the door open to him as he is such a good player. We've done nothing but help him since he came to the club and that is another mystery. We've helped him with his private life and other matters.

"He's not the only one that gets that privilege as we do that with all players. It is part of our job here that we look after our players which creates a tremendous loyalty that has always been the foundation of our club.

"So, we're as bemused as anyone as we can't quite understand why he would want to leave a club that no-one can deny is one of the most successful in British football. We've won more than 40 trophies, reached countless cup finals, have a fantastic history, great stadium, great training arrangements, incredible romance and we don't understand it. I can't answer any question about why he is doing it. You can speculate and it won't matter a dicky bird simply because the player is adamant he wants to leave. We have to deal with the next part of that which we will do as best we can. I can do no more than we have said at the moment because, in my mind, we still have the door open and who knows? There is no offer on the table, because they're not prepared to listen to an offer, but there's always an offer there from Manchester United to negotiate with a player, and that's still there."

It was remarkable. Not just for the situation at hand but for what it represented historically. Long was the list of people who had challenged Ferguson and paid the price with their Old Trafford careers. Paul Ince, Andrei Kanchelskis, Jaap Stam, David Beckham, and even, as Rooney himself had witnessed, Roy Keane. Now there was a significant difference. Rooney was United's star player, at the peak of his powers. What's more, realistically, few clubs could afford him. Barcelona had been linked with an £80m move but hadn't made it.

The strongest speculation linked Rooney with a move to Manchester City, and although Ferguson would surely have let any player rot in the reserves before it came to City getting one over on him, he would also have found the saga difficult to stomach – Rooney's contract expired in 18 months, which would mean if they were to sell, they'd be forced to sell the following summer. More pressing a matter was how United functioned as a team without Rooney. They were unbeaten so far in the league, but it was no coincidence that when he was missing, United generally didn't win, with Rooney absent from the starting line-up in four of the five league draws.

Critically, as much as Ferguson did not want to say so publicly, Rooney had a point when it came to the relative lack of investment. There was no guarantee that if Rooney were sold, the money would be there to reinvest – the Ronaldo episode had proved that, much to the ire of the support. Even if there was, United were still missing the fluidity and class that came from fielding their triumvirate of Ronaldo, Rooney and Tevez. They hadn't replaced the two they had lost – it could not be that they would lose the other.

"It was probably as tough a decision as Ferguson ever faced," former journalist and Ferguson biographer Paddy Barclay explains. "He was going to have to swallow his own principles, or rewrite them radically. He did. Such was his gamble that he appeared at a press conference and bared his heart… it was an extraordinary acting performance by Ferguson because he cast himself as the victim. The little Manchester United were being preyed upon. He knew he couldn't afford to lose that argument. And he didn't."

Ferguson's projection of vulnerability did a number of things – the first, put Rooney in a position to provide clarity. The second was to manipulate the context. Supporters were likely to have agreed on the principle of Rooney's disgruntlement, considering their early-year protests. But that was not what was being presented. Instead, we had a manager telling the world that a player had the temerity to ask to leave a club that had done nothing but help him. It brought into focus the more recent personal controversy, and the protection United had provided.

The day passed without comment from Rooney, but two hours before kick-off, a statement was issued from the player's representatives: "I met with David Gill last week and he did not give me any of the assurances I was seeking about the future squad. I then told him that I would not be signing a new contract. I was interested to hear what Sir Alex had to say yesterday and surprised by some of it. It is absolutely true that my agent and I have had a number of meetings with the club about a new contract. During those meetings in August I asked for assurances about the continued ability of the club to attract the top players in the world.

"I have never had anything but complete respect for Manchester United. For me it's all about winning trophies – as the club has always done under Sir Alex. Because of that I think the questions I was asking were justified. Despite recent difficulties, I know I will always owe Sir Alex Ferguson a huge debt. He is a great manager and mentor who has helped and supported me from the day he signed me from Everton when I was only 18. For Manchester

United's sake I wish he could go on forever because he's a one-off and a genius."

United won 1-0 – but after the game, when Ferguson faced the cameras, he was once again asked to comment on a player who wasn't playing. It was another performance more impressive than the one his team had put on. "We have done everything we possibly can to help him," the boss said. "Since the minute he has come to the club, we've always been a harbour for him. I don't know how many times we have helped him in terms of his private life and other matters. This is a club which bases all its history on the foundation of loyalty and trust between player and manager and club. That has been the case for many years – before Alex Ferguson, since the days of Sir Matt Busby. Wayne has been the beneficiary of that help, just the same as Ryan Giggs and Paul Scholes and all the players – that's what we're there for."

But things were already accelerating behind the scenes. Rooney arrived at Carrington for a meeting with Ferguson and a con-ference call with the owners. In that call, Rooney agreed a new five-year contract which made him one of the highest paid players in the country. After the call, Rooney apologised to Ferguson, who told him he should apologise to the fans.

When Gary Neville confronted Rooney at Carrington later that day, the forward diffused any argument by saying he was staying at the club. Patrice Evra was quoted by the *Express* as saying: "If one player in the team does not trust the others, he should not play in the team. Me, I trust everyone. I know we can win matches and trophies."

Neville remembered Evra joking with Rooney that he must have changed his mind when a group of United supporters wearing balaclavas showed up outside his house. Ferguson claimed there was a division among the players, some who were nonplussed and others who were unhappy. There were some who felt that much had been made out of nothing – Rooney, after all, was very popular with most of his team-mates, and had not explicitly expressed his desire to leave to them.

On Friday morning, United issued a statement confirming the news of the new deal.

"Once it all came out it looked as though there was nowhere to go," Rooney admitted. "But the manager made it clear the door was still open for me to sign. That's when I said to my agent, 'Let's go and sit down and get it resolved'. We spoke to the manager, the Glazers and to David Gill. I am glad that we sorted it out. The talks have confirmed that this is the right club and that I will be successful and continue to win things. There were other things I wanted to air and then I was happy to sign. I am sure the fans have been upset… it has been a difficult, complicated week.

"My message is that I care for the club. I just want it to continue to be successful. Some fans may not take to me again very quickly. It may take time. But I will give 100 per cent and try to rebuild that relationship. I hope we can work together and try to win trophies."

Rooney was keen to stress Ferguson's importance in his decision to stay: "He is one of the reasons I came to the club, to work under him and be successful. He is not the only reason I am staying here but he is a big reason."

Ferguson seemed happy to let bygones be bygones. "Once all that publicity came out, particularly the impact and response from everyone about how big Manchester United is, I think that resonated with Wayne quite a lot," the manager said. "He has apologised to me and the players, and he'll do that with the fans as well, which is important because we've all been hurt by the events of the past few days. I always feel it's a quality in a person when they say they're sorry. I think he has realised the enormity of Manchester United. Sometimes when you're at a club you can't look outside. You seem to think something's better elsewhere."

By all accounts, this was a masterstroke in management from Ferguson, and a necessary statement considering the fact City had spent another £100m in that summer's transfer window, acquiring the likes of David Silva and Yaya Toure. It was a transfer strategy bound to pay off sooner rather than later, so Ferguson's intervention was a timely reminder who the top club in town were.

"I'm not sure whether Sir Alex was hurt by it… he was long enough in football to understand that can be part of running a club," says Rene Meulensteen. "He had told countless players it was time to move on and a couple had said the same to him. I think the thing that hurt Sir Alex more than anything was the fact that Manchester City were the club linked with him. I'm not saying that if Barcelona or AC Milan had come in, the manager would have let him go, but he might have understood the need for a different challenge. But City were the team linked.

"Wayne was 25 – still ready to reach the peak of his career, and with all of these trophies already won. Sir Alex would not have wanted to lose a battle of prestige with Manchester City and he had to do everything to keep Wayne. In training, Wayne was great. He didn't change. He didn't sulk. There was so much experience within the squad that I think those guys were just taking the piss with him. There was never any animosity, everyone got on well and Wayne was the perfect professional."

Neville suggested that after the World Cup, Rooney had 'lost all that spark, that energy' of being one of the 'most bubbly, noisy players in the dressing room'. Meulensteen concedes that the cloud that had been hanging over the player since South Africa might have played a part in his disillusionment. "You could argue that the criticism in 2010 was part and parcel of what comes at that level," he says. "In 2004 you saw the Wayne Rooney of the two years before and two years after. He had freedom and showed that conviction and brilliance. He raised expectations of his own performances and then he joined a club that had those expectations every single week. They were competing for the biggest honours and it comes with the biggest demand. Wayne wanted to play in every single game so he understood it.

"In 2006 he was only 20 and went in with an injury – at that time the expectation was definitely unfair. England had a good squad with a lot of players at their peak and they had a responsibility to look after him in games so that he could be the best that he could. If opposition teams think Wayne Rooney's the danger man, they're going to consider it a job well done if they keep him quiet. At international level it's very rare that one player makes such a difference. There was too much focus on the idea of Wayne showing his magic but it was only reasonable to expect him to do that if the other players are doing well around him."

It was all academic now – Rooney was staying. He also appeared to reach agreement with Ferguson on another matter, that being his ankle injury. He would miss four weeks, one of which would be spent in Oregon for conditioning training.

There was no rush back; on November 20th, Rooney returned as a substitute in a 2-0 win over Wigan Athletic. There had not been enough time to heal raw scars – a section of the United support booed Rooney, at least as many as those who cheered. They perceived the transfer request as treachery. The abuse was a little more personal, considering Rooney's place of birth. He was a Scouser that United supporters had taken in as one of their own. Supporters forgave his personal transgressions and sung his name. Now they considered his act to almost be the ultimate betrayal.

Rooney was not the first top player at the club to threaten to leave. Denis Law had been publicly put on the transfer list after calling Sir Matt Busby's bluff in the 1960s. Bryan Robson had flirted with a move to Juventus, a club who were linked again when Roy Keane had a contract dispute in 1999. "In negotiations, you've always got to be prepared to walk," Keane wrote in his first autobiography. "It was up to me to make United understand that I would move unless I got the contract I felt the club could afford." Keane also went on record on more than one occasion to question the quality around him while he was still captain.

All three were still – and continue to be – revered, but there is no question that the events of October 2010 created a rift between the United support and Rooney that, for some, is still to heal. Perhaps it is because of where Rooney was born. Perhaps it's because in the eye of the storm, the fans had backed him when there was criticism over his national team performance and also for the rumours over his personal life, only to feel let down. Maybe it was the lack of apology – for many at the time, it certainly seemed this was the case.

After the Wigan game, Rooney had only heard the positive reception. "With the issues which have gone on for the last few months, I would be lying if I said I wasn't worried about the reaction from the fans," he said. "But overall, I thought the reception I got was brilliant. I can understand the fans' frustration with the contract negotiations; it happened in the public eye which made it a bit more difficult. But the main thing for myself and the club is that we managed to agree that deal."

United's travelling support usually provided the true voice of the terrace and there was no avoiding the division as Rooney started for the first time in a while against Rangers in the Champions League at Ibrox. Rooney scored a late penalty to win the game, but looked rusty. To his credit, he embraced both subjects in the post-match fallout.

"With everything else that has happened, it all goes a bit overboard," he said. "But I have been through patches before when I haven't played well and I've come through them. I feel like I have apologised to the fans but everyone keeps saying that I haven't. If that is the case, then I apologise for my side of things.

"I am just happy it is all over now. Could it have been the biggest mistake I ever made? Yes, of course. You see so many players leave this club and not do so well, so I am just delighted I have stayed. Everyone is saying that I was definitely going to Manchester City – but believe me, if I had gone, it wouldn't have been in England."

With the best of intentions, and an apology made – though many United supporters will still claim a true apology never happened – it was time for Rooney's football to do the talking.

Chapter Fourteen

THE REDEEMER

T he conclusion to the 2010/11 season bore more than just a passing resemblance to the 1995/96 campaign; a hero returning in the face of national criticism to have a definitive say in the title race.

Wayne Rooney was not Eric Cantona, but it did not mean the comparison wasn't valid. It even extended to the state of the Manchester United side – when Cantona received his suspension for his brand of vigilante justice against a Crystal Palace fan, he was used to playing alongside Paul Ince, Andrei Kanchelskis and Mark Hughes, none of whom were at the club when he returned. It took some time for Cantona to click with the Class of 92 graduates who took their place.

The Manchester United team Rooney was returning into had a different dynamic to the year before. It felt strange that things could have changed so much from when United were preparing to take on Bayern Munich in March; but changed they were.

The first major element was the broken leg suffered by Antonio Valencia. The winger's delivery from the right had proven to be a major asset; he would be out until March, but with the psychological impact of the injury taking longer to heal. United's attacking approach had almost entirely changed, too. Dimitar Berbatov had followed in Rooney's footsteps of the previous year to assume responsibility for leading the line – and he was doing a fine job. He scored four goals in his first five games of the campaign before a sensational hat-trick against Liverpool, which included an overhead kick which went in via the crossbar.

Three days after Rooney's goalscoring return against Rangers, Berbatov stated his own case for retaining his place, scoring five times in a 7-1 win over Blackburn. Rooney and Berbatov complemented each other well, taking it in turns to play as nine and 10. A more traditional partnership was available – Javier Hernandez had settled into life at Old Trafford with seven goals so far in his first season. Hernandez was most definitely a traditional number nine, a player who would run behind the last line of defence, with a knack of scoring scruffy goals.

Of the two, Berbatov's form made him the first choice to partner Rooney, although when it came to the game against Arsenal in mid-December, Ferguson went with that tried and trusted 4-3-3 shape with Nani and Park flanking Rooney. It worked – Park scoring the game's only goal. Rooney missed a penalty, but played well. United were playing much better football than the scorelines were suggesting – a Boxing Day victory over Sunderland deserved much more than just two goals.

Rooney himself had scored only one league goal all season – and that was a penalty against West Ham in August. It seemed as though it might be a case of 'new year, new me' when he scored just two minutes into the first game of 2011 at West Brom (a match made infamous for causing Gary Neville's impromptu retirement), but Rooney suffered another twisted ankle in training and missed a couple of weeks.

When he was back, he was asked to play wide at Blackpool – but the game was going horrendously for him and his team-mates, with the hosts taking a 2-0 lead. Rooney was brought off – United staged one of their memorable comebacks to win the game late on.

"We tried to use Wayne as a wide player and he was just not getting into the game in the first half," Sir Alex Ferguson complained. "It was no fault of his. The rhythm of our game wasn't right. We then tried to put him through the middle but, when we were still 2-0 down 20 minutes into the second half, we had to do something and had to gamble."

Rooney was given a rest from the FA Cup trip to Southampton and was recalled for the visit of Aston Villa on the first day of February. It was time for him to get his season going once and for all.

Within the first minute of the game, Rooney had his name on the scoresheet – from kick-off, Edwin van der Sar's long kick down the field was thumped into the net by the number 10. Just before half-time, Nani's arching cross from the right curled perfectly into the path of Rooney, who finished inside the six-yard box. Darren Bent pulled a goal back for the visitors before Rooney set up Nemanja Vidic to power in a third.

"Wayne was fantastic," Ferguson said. "Goals always help strikers. But Wayne still has the appetite to play, he never stops trying and he gets rewards eventually."

There are rewards, and there are rewards.

Sometimes in football there can be a case of the necessary elements combining to create the feeling of something special. Other times it just happens – with no word of warning and less than even a hint that it could.

Take Eric Cantona in 1996. When he scored his seminal winning goals in 1-0 wins over Newcastle in March and Liverpool in May, there was almost a sense of inevitability about it. That was probably because of what it was following; Manchester United 1-0, Cantona had become a staple of that season.

There was nothing that prepared anybody for what happened at Old Trafford on Saturday, February 12th, 2011. Manchester City had made the short journey across town and were competing in a tight 1-1 draw. The visitors had pulled level in the 65th minute when David Silva equalised Nani's first-half goal. Ferguson's response was to bring on Berbatov and switch from 4-3-3 to 4-4-2. Rooney was not playing well. With the Bulgarian on, United's players urged Rooney to stay closer to the box and try to get on the end of things. He took the advice.

With just under 12 minutes to play, Paul Scholes took control of a ball deep into City territory; he stabbed it out to Nani on the right-hand side of the box. The winger scooped in a cross from the inside-right channel, the ball deflecting up off Zabaleta's back. Rooney had been lurking, anticipating the tap-in. But the ball was now behind him, and much higher – high enough to evade the attention of Vincent Kompany, who turned his body to try and reposition. So did Rooney, albeit in more theatrical style.

The United striker pushed his right foot into the ground for momentum, propelling his left leg into the air for the swing. Up came his stationary leg, swinging with full force towards the ball. The timing was immaculate. The sound of the ball striking the very bottom of Rooney's shinpad was audible to the supporters

Wayne acrobatically adjusts to a deflected Nani cross to engineer one of the greatest goals ever seen in the Premier League, his derby winner in 2011

sitting in K Stand behind the goal. The sight of Rooney's body, limbs horizontally protruding from his torso at various angles, was indelible. The suspended motion of his frame, three feet in the air, was a physical phenomenon that caused 75,000 people packed into the arena to take a sharp intake of breath.

It was spectacular enough without the finish. But the connection was pure and full – and the ball flew past Joe Hart into the top corner of the net. The City players were stunned, still caught cold by Rooney in midair, almost like eleven Wile E Coyotes transfixed by the dust left by the Roadrunner in the shape of his body.

The actual Rooney was gone, sprinting over to the corner in front of the City supporters; he turned his back to them, and stretched his arms out like Christ the Redeemer, his head leaning back to soak in the adulation.

There were still more than 10 minutes to play, but the goal was a technical knockout; City were floored, and could not respond.

"I don't think Wayne played particularly well against City!" recalls Rene Meulensteen. "But then he went and scored this incredible goal. That summed up the sometimes erratic nature of his form. He was a little older now. He wasn't that unbelievable, unstoppable and almost naive guy who would just burst without thinking. Now he had all this experience and had more knowledge so he naturally changed a little."

But still with the instinct quite unlike any other player, coupled with the ability to pull off the outrageous.

"It was one of the best goals I've ever seen," says Rafael Da Silva. "It was a tight game. Then Wayne scored this goal. I was on the bench. It was something that happened so quickly, and yet remains strong in the memory. How did he get so high? It was a dream to watch, a dream to be there just to witness it. It's unforgettable."

Rooney had tried a couple of overhead kicks in his time at United and never came close to connecting, let alone this flush; he was more likely to be found trying to chip the goalkeeper almost every week, rarely with the same kind of success he'd enjoyed against Portsmouth and David James in 2007.

"I'm no different to anyone who saw that goal in how vivid it is," says Fabio Da Silva. "That's why I prefer him playing at number nine. When the ball comes in, his reaction is so fast. The ball is crossed but there's a deflection and he thinks so much faster than everyone else. It was incredible. It felt like we were talking about it for the rest of the season! I don't remember if he tried it in training that week, but I do remember that he tried the lobs – those were every single day! He was constantly trying it. In training he was pretty good at it. More successful than in games!"

The reaction on the day was just as strong – this was a moment which didn't need time to appreciate in value. "I think it's the best goal I've ever scored," Rooney said. "I saw it coming over and I thought, why not? The last time I scored a goal like that would have been as a young kid at school. Until then, I hadn't been pleased with my overall performance. Some of the lads told me to stay around the box and I would eventually get a chance. Nine times out of 10 of those go over the bar. It was all instinctive. It's got to be my best ever goal because it came in such an important game."

Sir Alex agreed with the quality and felt it was worthy of even greater praise. "I haven't seen anything like that, that's for sure," he said. "It was absolutely stunning, unbelievable. It reminded me of Denis Law in his prime. Whether Denis ever put away one with so much ferocity I am not so sure. It must be one of the greatest goals ever scored in this stadium."

Before United's next game – an FA Cup clash with Crawley

– Ferguson laid down a challenge to Rooney. "Until last season Wayne used to go on these scoring bursts," the manager said. "He used to score in five or six games and then go missing in terms of goals, before coming back. Last season he was far more consistent. I would be quite happy for him to go on a burst now because we have got some important games."

The City goal was just Rooney's sixth of the season, and Ferguson would have appreciated that the increased number of the prior campaign was mostly due to the different role the striker had played. Nonetheless, the manager was completely correct to note his previously 'streaky' form. Rooney responded in the best way – the City goal was the first of eight goals in 11 games. It felt, though, as if there was something decidedly more significant about these contributions.

You might attribute that to a new maturity, possibly as a con-sequence of living through a period where Rooney felt, if not quite adversity, then as close to it as a professional footballer in 2011 reasonably could. Rooney had more than done his bit in compensating for the goals lost by Ronaldo and Tevez. He had fully embraced the role as the leading striker and the injury he'd suffered created the biggest *what if* of the previous season. And yet it still felt as if the early spring of 2011 saw a different Rooney, a player who had embraced his role in a different way.

Perhaps it was a matter of discomfort; suddenly, Rooney's absence had been credited with United failing to achieve what was expected. He was being described as one of the greatest in the world, greater than even Ronaldo in the minds of some. To go from that to the national vilification through and following the World Cup, and then the trouble back in Manchester, well, it was bound to have an impact on his character – and it could be said that it shaped him in a new way.

"It had been almost two years since Ronaldo left… Wayne played brilliantly in the first year but I don't know if it was the best for him," says Rafael. "It took him some time to get used to being in the position of the main man. To grow into it. To say, 'okay, I'm the king here' and to embrace that responsibility in a different way.

"So I think what we saw in 2011 was the result of that – a player so used to being part of a team, to not having the spotlight on themselves. Now he was. He was almost growing back into it. So many players glow in that position – Ronaldo was one. Rooney had always been that guy since he came on to the scene. He was 16. Everyone in England talked about him. There was a brief moment where everyone spoke about Ronaldo, and now it was back to Rooney."

United's unbeaten start to the league season had crawled all the way, almost unnoticed, into February; before the City game, that record had been lost at Wolves, on March 1st, Rooney scored in a defeat at Chelsea which left United still within touching distance of the chasing pack. That was followed by a loss at Anfield – the game after that was an FA Cup quarter-final with Arsenal, won with goals from Rooney and Fabio. There was progress, too, in the Champions League – two Hernandez goals saw off Marseille to set up a quarter-final clash with Chelsea.

Before that, United played a crunch game at West Ham.

The feeling of persecution around Rooney had grown in the previous two weeks, in spite of his increasingly positive performances. There was a new report that Ferguson and Rooney had a rift and the contract had been a truce for public consumption; you could feel the frustration in Rooney's comments on the matter: "I didn't know anything about it until I was on the way home from training on Sunday. I stopped off to get petrol and a few people asked me if I was leaving in the summer. I said, 'Where did you hear that?' and a fella said it was in a newspaper. I've never heard such rubbish in my life.

"I get angry when people question my commitment to the club. I'll be here until I am in my thirties, that's for sure. My relationship with Sir Alex has no problems whatsoever. I'm enjoying my football here and if I was going to leave in the summer I wouldn't have signed a new contract. I intend to see it through to the end. Unless United ever say I'm not wanted, I'll be staying."

Back in East London, West Ham stormed into a two-goal lead through a pair of early penalties. Ferguson – who'd started with Park behind Rooney – brought on Hernandez at half-time. When that didn't work, he brought on Berbatov, with Rooney behind them. Within a minute, the switch paid dividends; United won a free-kick on the edge of the box, and Rooney struck it magnificently. The feverish travelling support behind the goal began to believe that more would follow; eight minutes later, it did. Valencia played a ball into the box. Rooney's balance and control was superb, as he finished with ease across the goalkeeper.

In the 73rd minute, Fabio won a penalty when his cross was handled – Rooney stepped up to take the kick, and sent the goalkeeper the wrong way. He ran to celebrate in front of the United support, and was duly joined by his team-mates and the television cameras. One cameraman got close and personal with the forward, who, for the second time in a year, gave a national address through the lens. "F****** what? What?! F****** hell." His 14-minute hat-trick (his fourth for the club) had turned around a result which was made secure by a late Hernandez goal.

"He was just being himself," says Fabio. "It was an emotional moment. He's scored these important goals. He's had criticism all season. I understand that players are role models and we have to set examples. But people have to realise we're still human beings, with human reactions, he's just like anybody reading this. Maybe I can understand a little, the fact that Wayne was a superstar. It makes it much bigger than it would be if it was another player. It was the same with England at the World Cup. He understood that responsibility, he understood that he needed to set an example. And as far as I am concerned he did. But, off the pitch he was just a normal guy and wanted to be seen as a normal guy with normal reactions."

Rooney was apologetic in the moment, perhaps understanding what was probably to follow. "Those goals gave me so much satisfaction, particularly the one that put us in front after being two behind," Rooney said after the game – and, when he was pushed on the outburst, he said: "I want to apologise for any offence that may have been caused, especially any parents or children watching. Emotions were running high and on reflection my heat-of-the-moment reaction was inappropriate. It was not aimed at anyone in particular."

Not for the first time, Rooney was given little slack despite showing almost immediate contrition. The chairman of the FA was David Bernstein, a Manchester City supporter and former chief executive of the club. Before that, he had worked for French Connection – the fashion retailer whose gimmick was the mischievous labelling of 'fcuk' in prominent lettering on their garments. This weekend, however, Bernstein was particularly sensitive to the word, and gave Rooney a two-match suspension. The second of those games? The FA Cup semi-final against Manchester City.

Perhaps Bernstein was just averse to unseemly acts when they were conducted in a red shirt: in March 2021, he described Roy Keane's infamous foul on Alf-Inge Haaland as 'the worst thing I've ever seen on the pitch… I have never forgiven Keane for that.'

There is certainly no defence for Keane – but perhaps Bernstein missed the time when Ronaldo trudged off the Eastlands pitch bearing Michael Ball's stud pattern on his abdomen. Or the time Ben Thatcher introduced himself to Pedro Mendes in a particularly violent manner.

"I'm gutted to miss two matches," Rooney said. "I'm not the first player to have sworn on TV and I won't be the last. Unlike others who have been caught swearing on camera, I apologised immediately. And yet I am the only person banned for swearing. That doesn't seem right."

Rooney would miss the next game against Fulham – in the press conference before it, Ferguson expressed how livid he was with the referee who had included the incident in his report, resulting in the suspension. "Lee Mason has now put himself in the spotlight," blasted the United manager. "If he doesn't send a player off for swearing the question will be, has he got double standards? He is in a very difficult position. I think he was put under pressure. Are we being victimised? I don't even need to say that. I believe there's an obvious trend at the moment.

"We've got motivation. Wayne is disappointed. He thinks he has been victimised. When I came home on Saturday night, my wife said, 'They'll do him'. I said, 'Don't be stupid. You can't do him for celebrating'.

"He wrote the letter to the FA. We discussed everything with John Alexander (United secretary) and David Gill. We put in a proper appeal and Wayne apologised. I don't know these people on the FA. Someone told me there were 14 full-time people in the disciplinary department but I don't know for definite. Fourteen full-time people? For what? Really, it's not worth bothering about. You've got to take your medicine and get on with it."

The medicine, for some, was hard to swallow. Dimitar Berbatov was again showing what he could do, scoring the opener against Fulham to add to the late winner he'd recently scored against Bolton. However, against Manchester City at Wembley, Berbatov struggled – there was a growing feeling that he was not a player for the big games. He was poor in the semi-final – even without Rooney available, Ferguson took off Berbatov for the goal-shy Anderson. City comfortably won 1-0.

Ferguson was starting to settle on the pace and power of Rooney and Hernandez. The pair showed how lethal they were on the big stage – Rooney scored in the first leg of the Champions League tie against Chelsea, and Hernandez scored in the second, as United qualified for the semi-final with a degree of comfort against the previous season's league champions. When Hernandez struck a late winner against Everton, Rooney tweeted that the Mexican was the 'buy of the century'.

"Rooney and Chicharito really liked each other," recalls Fabio. "They liked playing with each other. It gave Wayne the chance to play at number 10 and they were a really good match… You could put Rooney anywhere on the pitch and he would do a fantastic job. He became a number nine after Cristiano left and he was a natural at that. I saw it every day in training, just how fantastic he was at finishing. Playing at number nine he would have more opportunities to score.

"If I had the choice of where he would play it would probably be as that striker because I was confident if I crossed the ball, he'd be there to score. I'm not just saying that because I wanted the assists! It was not an easy choice. He was brilliant as a creator too, his ability to pass over long distances and his all-around game really did make him suited to different positions. He wasn't satisfied to just play up there and wait for the ball to come to him. He wanted to be involved, he wanted to tackle. I'm sure if you asked him he'd prefer playing at 10 because he could be involved more."

Rooney had praised the impact of Hernandez, but it was probably more true that his own impact was proving to be the most influential of the title run-in. His goal against City, the hat-trick against West Ham – it seemed that in the crucial moments, United's main man would deliver.

"When a player is in that kind of form, it gives a big boost to everyone," says Rafael. "You see one of the best players in the world playing so well and feeling good, it gives you extra motivation too. He feels like he's going to score important goals. You feel that every time you give him the ball he'll do something important. Even when you arrive for the game, you have an extra confidence. It's almost like a relief."

Rooney followed his goal against Chelsea with an important second goal in Germany against Schalke to give United a commanding advantage. "He really showed a great example in the Champions League and showed his leadership qualities alongside Scholes and Giggs," says Fabio. "Everyone counted on him to win games and lead the team. He took the responsibility very well. I think it showed his football intelligence. There is the fire that was present in the Premier League, he could speak to referees in a certain way. He knew that if he did that in the Champions League he'd be getting yellow and red cards. He was able to control himself more as he became more mature. That's why he was such a strong player in that moment."

The 2-0 win in the first leg put United in such a secure position that Ferguson could change almost his entire team for the return – a luxury that no-one would have ever expected for a Champions League semi-final. The 'reserves' did even better, winning the second game 4-1 – United were back in the final for the third time in four seasons, where they would face Barcelona at Wembley.

With three games left, United were in a commanding position in the league. They faced Chelsea at Old Trafford with a three-point lead – victory would mean they could not be surpassed in points, and they would need just one point from their last two games (at Blackburn and at home to Blackpool) to reach a milestone – the first English team to win 19 league titles, surpassing Liverpool to become the outright most successful club in English football.

Games against Chelsea had been traditionally difficult – but in the last few months, United had found joy in them, winning both legs of their Champions League tie. It was no different here – Ferguson's men scored in the first minute, and then again in the 23rd, to claim a comfortable 2-1 win and put them on the brink. Rooney was outstanding. "He could have scored six," his manager said afterwards.

It seemed as though being on the edge of history had put a spring in the step of the United players, but when it came to the potentially decisive day at Ewood Park, Ferguson's side were flat. Brett Emerton scored for the hosts early on. That much was no deviation from the script when it came to United's visits here – often they had had to settle for a point, usually thanks to the heroics from Brad Friedel in the home goal. Today they had Paul Robinson between the sticks, and he'd barely had to use his gloves. Rovers looked more likely to add to their lead.

With 18 minutes to go, Hernandez chased a through ball and was brought down in the box by Robinson. Both sets of players surrounded the referee Phil Dowd and the linesman – Dowd awarded a penalty. "I'm bricking it," Rooney confessed later. "I can't remember a time where I've been this nervous on a football pitch before."

He needn't have been – the spot-kick was good, and restored parity. For what it meant in terms of the current season and the historical achievement, it was as good as a winner. United kept the ball for the last few minutes, conserving energy and protecting their point.

Manchester United were champions of the Premier League again.

They were champions of England for a record 19th time.

Wayne Rooney, an Everton supporter, had scored the goal to take United past Liverpool – the most hated rivals of both his boyhood club and the one he played for.

"It wasn't something he spoke about all the time but we all knew he was an Everton fan," Rafael says. "So for him to score the goal that took us past Liverpool on league titles, it was an amazing feeling for everyone, and he had this feeling that was probably different to the rest of us. Maybe it was even more special for him."

It was. Unsure of how to mark the occasion, Rooney settled on something impulsive for a truly modern audience: that evening, he tweeted an image of his chest, which was shaved and trimmed to feature the number 19 in the midriff.

"Of course it was massive to him," says Fabio. "He grew up through Everton's academy and as an Everton fan. He understood that the rivalry between United and Liverpool was even more intense than the derby between Everton and Liverpool. For him to score the goal that took us past Liverpool. To make United the most successful club in England. Imagine that feeling. A dream come true. If he couldn't win the league with Everton then the next best thing has got to be winning it with the club that Liverpool hate more than anyone."

Even the United supporters who had vowed to never chant his name after the events of October were able to indulge in some good old schadenfreude at the expense of their most loathed rivals. In time, it would have been easier for those fans to acknowledge Rooney's crucial importance in the title run-in that season. His contribution had been significant, both in terms of goals and momentum. Those moments may not have been as prolonged as Cantona's influence in 1996, but they were no less definitive, and, especially when it came to the goal against City – which seemed to announce 'I am back' – no less spectacular.

It was also a significant moment for Rooney because it proved that with him, United could still achieve – that they didn't need Ronaldo or Tevez. They could rely on him. And, when he was at his best, so were United. They were going to need that to be the case as they prepared to face Barcelona in a rematch of Rome.

Chapter Fifteen

CAROUSEL

T he Champions League final of 2011 was an experience so harrowing for Manchester United that it remains painful for anyone connected with the club to speak about.

Three things are true – or as true as objective opinion can be. The final featured the best Barcelona team in history, which was at the time the greatest team in the world. It also featured a Manchester United team which was most definitely not the best team in history, even if it was, at the time, the best in England. The third truth is that Barcelona were thoroughly deserving winners.

Perhaps it's a tribute to how good Sir Alex Ferguson was as a manager that there have been so many autopsies afforded to a game where United had no real prospect of winning. With Xavi, Busquets and Iniesta in imperious form, the Spanish team dominated in possession. Ferguson used Carrick and Giggs, hoping for sensible economy of the ball; United were once again frustrated that they could not call upon Darren Fletcher. Fletcher had made the bench, but this was more through sentiment, with the Scot having missed a number of games with ulcerative colitis. He was, again, a significant miss. But even if he had been available and fit and well, he was still only one man, and Barcelona were simply better. In their key area, they were untouchable – and it was a strong foundation for Lionel Messi to showcase his own magic.

Ferguson had vowed that what happened in Rome would not happen again. But he had also watched Inter Milan achieve success against this Barcelona side through Jose Mourinho's defensive suffocation. Manchester United could not play like that. Ferguson was a winner at almost any cost, but not at the complete abandon of what United stood for. They could not be cowardly in a European Cup final. For Rooney, it was deja-vu before the team had even been named.

"We lost two Champions League finals going toe-to-toe with Guardiola's Barcelona, by trying to press high and get round them, which was suicidal," Rooney wrote in his *Sunday Times* column in 2020. "I remember Alex Ferguson saying, 'We're Man United and we're going to attack, it's in the culture of this football club' and thinking, 'I'm not too sure about this'. I think all the players knew, deep down, it was the wrong approach, that we were abandoning the way that had brought us success in that 2008 semi-final – and sure enough both times we got outplayed. There is being true to the club, but then there's sitting back afterwards and thinking 'we lost'. For me, it doesn't matter how you do it in these big Champions League games, as long as you win."

Pedro scored in the 27th minute. United rallied, almost like a punch-drunk heavyweight. Rooney played a ball in to Giggs in the box – he showed presence of mind to lay the ball back, and Rooney struck a fine first-time shot into the top corner.

"He gave us hope," Fabio Da Silva says. "When we were 1-0 down and hardly touching the ball, you start to lose hope. It made us believe again for a moment. It's a shame for him, a shame scoring a great goal like that didn't get a better reward."

United's optimism lasted until the break. They knew their best chance was to score again before Barcelona did – but Messi's strike in the 54th minute meant the Spanish side were able to restart the merry-go-round. When David Villa scored with 20 minutes left, the remainder of the biggest game in football played out like a painful testimonial. Death by a thousand cuts.

Before studying Rooney's more recent comments, it's worth journeying back to 2011 to consider his reaction at the time. "Barcelona are incredible and sometimes you've just got to hold your hands up," he told *TalkSPORT* three days after the final. "They were by far the better team. That's the level we want to be at and we need to up our level to be there. I'm sure the manager knows that and he'll be looking at what he is going to do to get us there. There's a bit of regret about things we didn't do that we talked about. We weren't there to make up the numbers. We wanted to win."

Similar remarks were made in Rooney's 2013 book – so is the more recent criticism of Ferguson's approach made merely with the benefit of hindsight?

"Those are Wayne's comments," says Rene Meulensteen. "It's a bit of an emotional reaction rather than a rational one after losing a final. Sir Alex Ferguson was spot on with his tactical approach and it comes down to fine margins in those games. Players will always be critical when results go against them."

Fabio Da Silva, who had to face Barcelona's front-line for the 70 minutes when they were in devastating form, appears to agree with Meulensteen: "In all fairness, Wayne hadn't been a coach by then. I'm not saying it's easy to criticise. I just think whenever you lose a game you can look back and say that if you had approached it differently, you would have had better luck. I'm sure even Sir Alex thought like that.

"The reality is that Barcelona were just too strong for us. It was their best ever team. What if we had done something differently? There is nothing to say we would not have been beaten by a heavier score. There was no guarantee that playing more defensively would have worked. Teams did that against Barcelona and still lost. We couldn't have played like Inter Milan. That's not Manchester United. We did have a great defence. They had the best midfield and best attack in their history. Maybe in the history of club football. I can understand Wayne's frustration, though, because I definitely share that feeling."

United were not as good as they were in 2009, or 2008. Ferguson responded to the disappointment with an injection of youth – Danny Welbeck was to remain at the club following a successful loan spell at Sunderland, and David De Gea and Phil Jones were signed, as was Ashley Young. There were outgoings. De Gea was replacing retiring goalkeeper Edwin van der Sar.

The Dutch legend was joined by Paul Scholes, who also hung up his boots. Scholes left with a parting message – considerable praise for Rooney. "He can still go up several notches," the now-former midfielder said. "There can still be an improvement in every aspect of his game and I think we'll see it. He is capable of being the same for us as Messi is for Barcelona. He can be United's Messi, that's how good he is. When his head is right and he is right physically he can do real damage to teams. He is still young and has not reached his peak yet."

United had spent, but whether they had strengthened was another matter. It did not need a debate to see that Manchester

City's first team would be much healthier – they had continued their Arsenal-pilfering by taking Gael Clichy and Samir Nasri, but it was the £38m acquisition of Sergio Aguero which was most noteworthy. That Aguero, Silva and Toure combined had cost City just £7m more than what United had received for Ronaldo two years earlier was not lost on United's support, who welcomed the summer investment but still felt concerned that it might not be enough.

The first test between the two teams came in the Community Shield. City led 2-0 at half-time but United came back with a spectacular response; Smalling pulled a goal back, then Rooney orchestrated the equaliser, combining with Tom Cleverley and Nani for the latter to score. In the last minute, Nani broke clear to score a winner – first blood for the season went to the champions.

Rooney was in fine form at the start of the league season, scoring in the first two games – wins against West Brom and Spurs. But it was the third game which really had people paying attention. United's football had been slick and rapid – almost as if they'd been provoked into playing well by the embarrassment of Barcelona at Wembley. The combination play of Young, Nani, Cleverley, Anderson, Rooney and Welbeck was extraordinary. Rooney's status in the dressing room arguably increased due to the transition. "He was even more of an idol to the guys who came in that summer, players who knew him as the star in the Premier League, the main player for England," says Fabio. "You could see it was an incredible experience for them."

Against Arsenal on the last weekend of August, United inflicted the worst defeat the Gunners had suffered since the 19th century. To say it was eventful was an understatement. Arsene Wenger was reeling not only from the loss of players to City, but Cesc Fabregas' transfer to Barcelona. The players he had left were torn to shreds by the merciless United stars, Rooney grabbing three of his side's eight. The first two were fantastic free-kicks. The first was his 150th goal for United.

"I was aware I was only one goal away from reaching 150," Rooney said. "And speaking to some of the players, I asked how many Bobby Charlton had scored for the club. Giggsy said, 'You need another 100 or so', so that's a target for me now."

The United manager seemed to have more sympathy than his players. "We could have scored more... but you don't want to score more when Arsenal have a weakened team like that," Ferguson said after the match.

Welbeck picked up a hamstring injury, so after the international break Hernandez was back in the team. It showed no disruption to United's rhythm as he scored twice against Bolton – but the main story was another hat-trick for Rooney, as United won 5-0. His third was a tremendous curling effort away from the goalkeeper from 20 yards, to make it eight goals from four league games. It was nine from five when United turned Chelsea over (it should have been ten, but Rooney missed a penalty).

The idea of Rooney becoming a goalscorer in streaks had almost self-perpetuated into existence – even by his high standards, there'd never quite been a run like this. "If you look at Pele, he was a very aggressive attacker who could also look after himself and so can Rooney," Ferguson said in September. "They have similarities that way, strength, speed, determination. Wayne has shown great maturity in his game. That's what happens when you reach your mid-20s, you get more authority, your timing becomes better, your understanding becomes better.

"There have been British players who have similar great qualities that make them great players. Whether it's a Paul Gascoigne, George Best, Sir Bobby Charlton, Denis Law, the similarities are that the boy has great courage, he wants to play all the time, he has incredible stamina. These are added extras to the talent he has."

Rooney could, in some respects, consider himself a victim of timing when it came to how he was perceived. In 2009 he had placed eighth in the Ballon d'Or rankings. 2010 promised much, but the injury and the disastrous World Cup meant he did not even feature in the top 23 for the award. He would come in fifth place for 2011 – behind Messi, Ronaldo, Xavi and Iniesta – a personal peak. Close to his 26th birthday, there was a universal acceptance that this was probably as high as could be hoped, considering the legendary company he was keeping.

There were plenty of landmarks available for Rooney to cement his own legacy. There was the creeping goal tally he was acutely aware of at club level. That was presently owned by Sir Bobby Charlton – as was the England record of 49 goals. That too was in reach, with Rooney notching 27 and 28 in Sofia on an evening where Bulgarian fans disgraced themselves with racist abuse to Ashley Young, Ashley Cole and Theo Walcott.

In addition, Wayne admitted that becoming captain of club and country 'full-time, would be an honour'. There was still some time before that could become a reality – at United, Nemanja Vidic was a lock, and for England, a red card against Montenegro suggested there was still a little growing to do. Rooney kicked out at Miodrag Dzudovic, putting a dark mood on a game which saw England qualify for the European Championship – he now faced the prospect of missing all three group games.

A dark October continued back at United, with a brief light in the Champions League when he scored twice against Otelul Galati to become the highest scoring Englishman in the competition's history. That was a pure rose in a whole bunch of thorns – United's

European campaign was disastrous, with Ferguson's side dumped out at the group stage. Either side of that record-breaking evening were two bleak days indeed. At Anfield, a 1-1 draw was blighted by Luis Suarez's racial abuse of Patrice Evra. Against Manchester City at Old Trafford, it was most definitely the football that was bad, with City striking a devastating blow by winning 6-1. United were already chasing the game when Jonny Evans was sent off just after half-time. When Darren Fletcher made it 3-1, United bombed forward, only to concede three more goals in the closing minutes. 'Suicide' was how Ferguson described it.

Self-inflicted wounds threatened to ruin Rooney's year, but he was given a slight reprieve when he was given just a two-match international ban. The miserable conclusion of 2011 came when Rooney, Evans and Gibson were fined for having a night out on Boxing Day, and subsequently dropped for the New Year's Eve home game against Blackburn. United lost 3-2 – Rooney, who'd scored four goals in four games (after almost two months without a goal) would surely have continued his latest streak.

The Blackburn omission was one of those which was only fully revealed some time later, with Ferguson telling ESPN at the time: "Wayne hasn't trained well this week, he's missed a few days... It's little strains here and there."

In his second autobiography, Ferguson explained that he did have some concerns about Rooney's lifestyle. "Wayne needed to be careful," he said. "He has great qualities about him but they could be swallowed up by a lack of fitness. Look at the way Cristiano Ronaldo or Ryan Giggs looked after themselves. Wayne needed to grasp the nettle. I would hammer him for any drop in condition. It was quite simple – he wouldn't play."

The Blackburn game had also highlighted United's weakness in the middle of the park. Michael Carrick was reliable, but

Anderson and Cleverley were not what one might describe as robust. Darron Gibson was a good squad player while Paul Pogba, a young reserve midfielder who had the talent, also had an agent who was agitating for a contract healthier than his player's status at the club. Ferguson turned to Paul Scholes, who came out of retirement at the start of 2012. It was a complete shock when he was named on the bench against Manchester City in the FA Cup – but Rooney stole the show, if not the headlines, scoring two in a 3-2 win.

The other scorer on the day was Danny Welbeck, who was the latest forward to find Rooney a compatible team-mate. "He was a good partner for Danny but I think this is the main point about Wayne," explains Fabio Da Silva. "He was at such a high level that he was a good partner for everyone in the team. When someone is as good as him he makes other players better.

"A player like Harry Kane or maybe Dimitar, they work better with other players who have specific qualities. Wayne didn't need that. He could play with anyone, and he was intelligent enough to understand the weaknesses of his strike partner and make them look good. Nobody gave him enough credit for that. Technically, people wouldn't appreciate Wayne. Perhaps his style wasn't always as beautiful to watch as Berbatov, for example. But people around the world never realised how important Wayne was in making his strike partners look good."

United were benefiting from Welbeck's confidence; his style was different again to Hernandez and Berbatov, giving Ferguson four good strikers to pick from. Rooney, though, remained the man for the big occasion, scoring twice in the poisonously tempered return match with Liverpool to earn three points, and then hitting a brace at Stamford Bridge to lead a fightback from 3-0 down to get a draw. Defeats in the FA Cup to Liverpool, and in the Europa

League to Athletic Bilbao (despite a stunning long range effort from Rooney), left United with only the Premier League left to battle for – it was a straight fight between them and City, with 10 games left.

It was starting to feel like two years earlier, with City scoring plenty of goals, and Rooney doing his best to single-handedly bridge the gap. Two goals against West Brom on March 11th took him to 26 for the season. After that game, Ferguson set Rooney a target of 40 goals, something he repeated after the striker scored the only goal of the game against Fulham. "He could get to 40," Ferguson insisted. "There are eight games left and he's capable of getting two goals in a game and has had two hat-tricks this season, so you never know."

His return was much more modest – perhaps Ferguson had hoped his words might rekindle the early season spark, but the matches were arduous slogs. 2-0 wins over Blackburn and QPR gave United what seemed like an unassailable lead of eight points with six games left – but what came easy went easy, as the same number of points were dropped in the next four games. It was excruciating. First came a defeat at Wigan. Rooney was brought off in the 65th minute with United desperate for a goal. "He just didn't look like scoring," said Ferguson.

He did score twice against Aston Villa in a 4-0 win, but was still brought off again. "He was careless," the manager blasted. "Wayne has to play on the edge of a game, when it is really close and competitive. When the game gets to that casual bit, he is worse than the rest of them. He gets really casual about it."

If that was a message for the rest of the team, it was not heeded – Rooney scored twice against Everton, but United threw away a two-goal lead with seven minutes remaining to draw 4-4. It was a personal landmark for Rooney, who surpassed George Best and

Dennis Viollet to move to fourth in United's all-time top scorers list.

Against Manchester City, Ferguson went pragmatic. With a three-point lead in the table, they just had to keep City at bay to have some comfort over their own destiny. But this wasn't 2010, and playing Park as a reducer didn't have quite the same impact. City took a lead on the stroke of half-time. United couldn't recover.

Level on points, the clubs were separated by a goal difference of six in City's favour – the October result once again coming back to haunt United. Supporters turned up to the penultimate home game with Swansea hoping to see a goal fest. They had to settle for two. Barring a landslide at Sunderland on the last day, United were left hoping QPR could get a result at City.

Ferguson's team did their own job – Rooney struck in the 20th minute with his 199th club goal, and 34th of the season. From then on United had one eye on the side of the pitch, looking for updates back in Manchester. News filtered to the players that QPR were leading; but when the final whistle blew, there was an ominous, anxious atmosphere coming from the United fans and the bench. Rooney confessed he had no idea what was going on until all of a sudden, Sunderland supporters started celebrating. City fans had adopted a goal celebration from the Polish team Lech Poznán, where they would all turn away from the pitch and jump up and down. Now Sunderland fans were doing it.

"My heart sinks," Rooney wrote in his second book. "I can see it's done, finished… I feel sick."

City had scored two goals in injury time. They were top on goal difference. Level on points stood for nothing – City were champions.

"Everyone was devastated," remembers Rafael. "The manager.

Ryan Giggs, who had won 12 league titles. Wayne, who'd won four. It was like a nightmare in the dressing room. It was a sad moment but we can also say it was a good experience for us."

That would indeed prove to be the case in hindsight, but the scars of the memory would remain. Rooney had described the previous season as 'a terrible year' considering all of the drama. But at least there was a title win to celebrate in May 2011, even if the events of the following twelve months were enough to make his head spin from start to finish.

Chapter Sixteen

HISTORY REPEATING

F ootball, like many sports, is cyclical. There are only so many times that scenarios can play out in a manner that feels completely fresh. While the 2012/13 season came dressed in new clothes, there were definitely moments where things felt very familiar indeed.

Much of the cast had changed for England, but the story remained the same when it came to their international tournament performance. The changes went right the way to the top – Roy Hodgson had become manager in the period between qualification and the commencement of Euro 2012. Fabio Capello had resigned as part of the controversy which surrounded allegations of John Terry racially abusing Anton Ferdinand. Terry was stripped of his captaincy and Capello cited what he deemed as 'interference' from the FA when he handed in his notice.

As part of the fallout, Rio Ferdinand was inexplicably omitted from the tournament (again), though Hodgson insisted it was because he didn't want to take the Manchester United defender as mere 'back-up' to his first choice selection of Terry and Joleon Lescott. It solved one dressing room headache, at least, for Hodgson. Lescott stated his own value by scoring England's first goal at the tournament, earning a 1-1 draw with France. Then Danny Welbeck scored the winner against Sweden in the second – providing a healthy scenario for Wayne Rooney to return into. If England avoided defeat from their final group game with Ukraine, they'd go through to the knockout stages.

Rooney hadn't scored in an international tournament since Euro 2004, but he scored a scruffy tap-in against Ukraine, the game's only goal. Hodgson said he would be happy for goals of that nature as long as they came in greater frequency. "If you take Pele for example, he was capable of producing his best football when it really mattered to help Brazil win World Cups," the England manager said after the game. "Let's hope Wayne Rooney can start to do that for us. If Wayne can produce his best he can help us keep going even further."

Rooney wasn't Pele, and the rest of the England squad did not resemble any of the Brazilian squads he played in. They were also not in Italy's class, which was inconvenient, considering they were the quarter-final opponents. England's maximum achievement as underdogs was to take this game as far as penalties; Italy had 20 efforts on target before getting deserved joy from the spot-kick lottery. Rooney at least scored his kick, but Hodgson was quizzed about the forward's fitness after the exit.

"When he missed the first two games, we were believing that what we need is to get to the third game and Wayne will win us the championship," explained Hodgson. "That, maybe, was too much to ask. He certainly tried very hard, but he didn't have his best game against Italy. I don't think that fitness itself was a particular factor. When you get to the big stage, you hope world-class stars show their world-class talents."

Maybe so – but perhaps the more relevant part of Hodgson's statement was the earlier part of it. Comparing Pele of 1970 with the England of 2012 was unrealistic and unfair on Rooney. Still, nothing of what happened to England or Wayne Rooney in Poland and Ukraine that summer was of surprise.

There was at least something new waiting back in Manchester for the new season. Not necessarily in starting the season wanting to retain the title – but in the identity of the new champions. It was the first time that a local rival had usurped them, and it was a matter of significant discomfort that the noisy neighbours had something to crow about.

Before the season got underway, Rooney discussed how he hoped the unfamiliarity might unsettle the new champions. "It'll be a different situation for them," he said. "Over the years everyone has tried to raise their game when they play Manchester United. City being champions, they'll have to face that now. Sometimes it can be more difficult. City have got some great players and Chelsea have spent a lot of money, so it'll be a close-run thing."

City's expenditure had been more modest – Jack Rodwell, Javi Garcia and Scott Sinclair the headline buys. Chelsea were also buying from a position of strength – they had won the Champions League in the previous season, but were showing their intent by signing Eden Hazard and Oscar for almost £60m.

When people were wondering how United would respond, most felt that Hazard, a tricky winger, would have been a natural buy. There was also annual speculation that Cristiano Ronaldo might one day return from Real Madrid. Sir Alex Ferguson signed Alex Buttner as back-up in defence, and playmaker Shinji Kagawa. The big signing, though, came in the form of Robin van Persie – a coup in several respects. First of all was prising him away from Arsenal, who were loathe to lose their star player to a hated foe. That hurdle was made easier with two key factors – the first, that the other interested club were Manchester City, who had already managed to get a few cut-price bargains from Arsenal. The second, that the player himself wanted to move to the red half of Manchester. United's pulling power was not something that could necessarily be trumped by money.

Rooney welcomed the prospective signing: "Of course he's a player that I admire. He's a fantastic player, he's been amazing for Arsenal over many years. If he does come here he would be a great addition to the squad."

Van Persie, after signing, repaid the compliment. "I'd love to play with Wayne," he said. "He's a world-class player, one of the best. He scores goals and makes assists, he can play for the team and works hard."

Van Persie would have to settle for a place on the bench for the first game of the season, which was at Everton. There was a poignancy to the occasion as it marked ten years since Rooney had made his senior debut at Goodison Park.

"It feels like a long time ago," he said. "It's great to have played in the Premier League for 10 years. It's an exciting league and I still get just as excited. I just hope I can play for another 10 years and have as much enjoyment as I did in my first 10."

Everton were still managed by David Moyes, and still played in the same uncompromising way. Marouane Fellaini had already been a headache for United in the recent past, and the Belgian scored the only goal of the match.

Next up were Fulham, with Rooney on the bench nursing a nasty cut on his thigh. But when Kagawa (from the number 10 role) and Van Persie both scored in a 3-2 win, it led to some mischievous speculation that Rooney was expendable and might even be sold before the end of the summer transfer window – something David Gill shot down quickly. "That's absolute garbage," he said. "Wayne is definitely not for sale and is integral to our team. He is a great player with a bad injury, but will come back without a shadow of a doubt."

The injury was severe enough to restrict game time for the following month; Rooney's re-introduction was gradual, in which time Van Persie was quickly getting to grips with his new surroundings. The Dutch forward scored a hat-trick at Southampton which included an injury-time winner, and followed that with a late winning goal at Anfield.

When Rooney was back in the starting line-up against Cluj in the Champions League, he described it as 'the start of my season'. He played in a withdrawn forward role, almost the head of a midfield diamond, behind Van Persie (who scored both goals in a 2-1 win) and Hernandez. Ferguson felt confident with the firepower at his disposal. "I don't think it matters that much who is getting the goals but Rooney will start scoring soon," he said. "I think he will explode. I think the two of them, Van Persie and Rooney, will go over 20 goals this season and if Danny Welbeck and Javier Hernandez get 20 goals between them, then we are in business."

Ferguson praised Rooney's attitude while recuperating. "He is fit, he has trained very well," Ferguson said. "Maintaining his fitness is going to be important because he is a stocky lad. He is going to have to train well all the time."

At Newcastle, Rooney was fantastic at the top of that diamond, with Welbeck in for Hernandez. United won 3-0 on a day where none of their strikers got on the scoresheet – a timely reminder about the importance of the team amid Van Persie's goalscoring heroics.

Having spent a couple of years moving around the front line, Rooney had spent the period of 2009 to 2012 exclusively as a striker, whether as a nine or a 10. He could clearly do both jobs proficiently – 34 goals in each of his seasons as a nine, and trophies galore as the heartbeat of the forward line. It was a strong enough sample size for people to have their 'favourite' version of Rooney, although some changed the parameters of the argument to say there was a version before 2010 and one after. That became associated with the more traditional conversation of peak and decline, and the idea that because Rooney's decade in the top flight had started much earlier than most players, because he was of stockier build, and because compared to Cristiano Ronaldo one could say his attitude to personal improvement was not as all-consuming, his natural decline would arrive earlier.

To most, though, Rooney was simply following the next stage of his natural career trajectory. He was now deemed old and senior enough – at 26 years old with 77 caps – to wear the captain's armband for his country as an official deputy for Steven Gerrard.

Rooney took the moment to pay tribute to his past influences. "Roy Keane was one of the best," he said. "He was vocal on the pitch and helped me off it. He was a great captain. Hopefully I can gain some of his qualities. He wasn't afraid to tell everybody how he wanted them to play. I fully respected him. I wasn't fearful. It was desire and passion."

He marked the occasion in style, scoring twice against San Marino – the second a special shot from the edge of the box. It was his 31st goal for England, moving him into the top five all-time goalscorers.

Roy Hodgson was very pleased, saying he saw 'the best of Wayne Rooney'.

Another goal followed in England's 1-1 draw with Poland –

Rooney gets ready to lead his country out for the first time as captain,
deputising for Steven Gerrard as England took on San Marino in 2012

back in Manchester, his club were hoping that those strikes would signal the start of another streak. Against Stoke, Rooney played up front alongside Van Persie, and scored two poacher's goals in a 4-2 win. But that was followed by only one goal – a penalty in Europe against Braga – until December.

Against West Ham in late November, Rooney had again played atop a diamond and it hadn't been as fluent as earlier trials. United won 1-0 with an early goal from Van Persie, but Rooney was brought off with 10 minutes to go. There was no doubting he had played his part in the team's steady performance, but Ferguson was keen to stress that he expected more. "He can contribute to the team's success fine but we would rather he scored more," the boss said. "He has missed the odd game and he is the type of player who can't miss games. The frame he has got, the type of person he is, he needs to play all the time."

Rooney netted twice in a crazy game at Reading that was 4-3 to United after 34 minutes – and remained that way at full-time. Ferguson was seemingly hoping that he'd play himself into form. He had the full 90 minutes against Cluj in the Champions League on December 6th, but was poor. The United boss was bullish about that. "Wayne Rooney has got another 90 minutes behind him. He is close to full fitness and hopefully he will be approaching top form come Sunday."

Sunday was the Manchester derby. For the big game, there was no experimentation. Rooney would start alongside Van Persie up front. While many focused on the goalscoring exploits of the Dutchman and Sergio Aguero, Rooney was keen to show that he had usually been the main man for this occasion. His eight goals in derbies made him the highest contemporary scorer in this fixture and he had a record-setting and record-breaking afternoon at the Etihad Stadium. After 15 minutes, he received Ashley

Young's pass from the left, moved infield and struck a low shot that seemed to roll slowly into the corner. The accuracy was exceptional. Fourteen minutes later it was two – Rafael's cut-back was steered across goal by United's number 10. In scoring, Rooney had surpassed Sir Bobby Charlton as United's record scorer in derbies.

City staged a second-half fightback, and looked as though they'd snatched a point with an equaliser four minutes from time. There was one last twist – Rafael was brought down on the edge of the box in injury time. Van Persie took the free-kick – it took a slight deflection and flew into the far corner to snatch victory.

"Obviously we took a bit of stick before and during the game from the City fans, so it was great to remind them who we are and what we are about – and it was great for our fans too," Rooney said after the match. "We've waited a long time for this to happen. They've had a great record at the Etihad Stadium and to spoil that is a great feeling."

Patrice Evra was keen to remind everyone of the role Rooney had played. "At the beginning of the season a lot of people were criticising Wayne but you can't forget Wayne – and he just proved it," he said. "He scored two goals in the last game against Reading and he's scored another two against City. In the big games you need big players – and Wayne is one of them."

Sunderland were the next opponents – and, because May was still fresh in the mind, this was no less an occasion than the derby. Rooney revealed before the game that it was something he was still dwelling upon. "When the final whistle went, we didn't really know what the score at City was. But then we heard the Sunderland fans cheering. It was sad to see that – they should be supporting their own team. They didn't have the best of seasons so for them to be cheering like that was sad. It was something the players won't forget."

Defeating Sunderland was not nearly as taxing a proposition as beating City – and United already had a two-goal lead before Rooney made it three, tapping in from his centre-forward's position. The eventual 3-1 win was enough to establish a six-point lead at the top of the table for Ferguson's men.

Rooney seemed to be in the middle of one of those goalscoring runs, but then had one of his worst games for the club in an early game at Swansea before Christmas. He subsequently missed United's festive calendar with a knee injury – it was a bad run of games to miss, even for a player of Rooney's stature, as United kept winning without him. The fixtures included a win over Liverpool. For the first time, it was beginning to seem as though United were capable of thriving without Rooney.

It brought to mind a moment in February 1997; Eric Cantona had largely cleaned up his act post-Selhurst, but was missing from a trip to Arsenal because of a suspension. The Gunners had one of the most miserly defences in the land. When Andy Cole and Ole Gunnar Solskjaer both scored fine goals in a 2-1 win at Highbury, Ferguson was given food for thought. It was not only possible to win without the Frenchman. United could also play attractive football without relying on him to orchestrate it.

Rooney himself had witnessed a similar moment when Ruud van Nistelrooy, still one of the world's premier strikers, was no longer deemed the most suitable fit for the style of play of Ferguson's side. The difference with Rooney is that he had proven himself compatible with all styles of player, and amenable to changes in position so long as it was for the good of the team.

By and large, he'd played well, adapting to the formation tweaks and even proving that he was the best partner for Van Persie in the traditional 4-4-2. When he was back from injury, Rooney set about showing his best form. He scored against West Ham, but was dropped to the bench against Spurs. Spurs manager Andre Villas-Boas would have been relieved, going by his opinion of Rooney, who he described as 'the heart' of United. "His role is always underrated but he makes United tick because of his movement and the way he always sacrifices himself for the team," he said. "He embraces all that United stand for. He has the team spirit, desire to win, and the focus. He has overcome some difficult moments in his career but he's a top quality footballer."

Rooney was back in from the start for the next run of games, scoring in an FA Cup win over Fulham, netting both goals against Southampton in the league (his first was his 100th goal at Old Trafford) and then a crucial late winner at Craven Cottage, scored in the same solo style of Ronaldo at the same venue six years earlier. After 25 games, United had a nine-point lead.

United were approaching the business end of the season, and had a Champions League tie with Real Madrid to look forward to. They earned a very good 1-1 draw in the away leg, and before the return, saw off Norwich with comfort at Old Trafford. Shinji Kagawa scored a hat-trick before Rooney hit a howitzer in injury time – a 25-yard stunner that flew into the roof of the goal. It took his tally to a commendable 14 for the season, considering the fractured nature of it due to injury and illness.

"It has been a bit of a stop-start season for me which has been disappointing," he said afterwards. "I haven't played as many games as I normally would have. But I feel fresh and ready for that battle until the end of the season. With the way the manager rotates there will be a lot of players feeling fresh. We should definitely be well prepared. I'm 27 now and that is the time when most players start to peak. Hopefully that will be the case and the team will benefit. It's great to have played so many games for this club and it would be nice to get to the 200-goal mark. Yes, of course, I can get the 25 goals the manager has asked for. But the most important thing is to keep playing well and winning games. Whether I reach that target won't really matter if we win trophies."

It's interesting to analyse the entirety of Rooney's statement because of how it paints the picture of how he felt things were at the club. He was singing from the same hymn sheet as he had all season; as he had for most of his United career. *We've got a great squad. I'm happy to play and do my part however I'm required. The most important thing is to win trophies.* These were the perfect responses that footballers are expected to dole out. Rooney was dutiful, of that there could be no contention. He was also back in form and looking sharp. His six goals in 10 games singled him out as the most in-form player when it came to goals – Kagawa's hat-trick put him in second place in that period with the three, while Van Persie, Hernandez and Giggs each had two goals. It made the next chapter of this story all the more perplexing.

Chapter Seventeen

ACRIMONY

S ir Alex Ferguson – that master of control – was the only one
prepared for the drama which would explode at 6.45pm on
the evening of March 5th, 2013. He made the bold decision
to drop Wayne Rooney from the starting line-up to face
Real Madrid in the last-16, second-leg clash at Old Trafford.

"I left Wayne out of that second leg because we needed someone
to get on top of Xabi Alonso," Ferguson wrote in his second autobiography. "The Ji-Sung Park of earlier years would have been
perfect for that job… there was no better player in our squad
to keep on top of Alonso than Danny Welbeck. Yes, we sacrificed Wayne's possible goalscoring, but we knew we had to choke
Alonso and exploit that gain."

It was not the first time Ferguson had dropped England's most
famous player in a big game against Spain's most famous team, as
a certain David Beckham would attest. If you were of Machiavel-

lian disposition, you might be inclined to suggest that this was in the manager's mind. He certainly would not have been ignorant of the significance.

The omission wasn't the only case of deja-vu. Now, as back in 2003 against the Spanish giants, United eventually needed to call upon the star man. Now, as then, it made no difference, and Real Madrid emerged victorious on aggregate to qualify for the next round. There were moments when United felt hard done by. The biggest came early in the second half, when Nani was controversially sent off. At that moment, United were controlling the tie, and were leading 2-1 on aggregate. The visitors scored twice in quick succession. Rooney was called upon – but it was too little, too late.

Rooney's place on the bench was scrutinised in the studio for ITV. "Maybe the writing is on the wall for him," said Roy Keane – a man well-versed in reading these particular signs.

Ferguson was said to be fuming with the referee's decision for the Nani red card. The reason the manager felt this setback more acutely than any others was yet to be revealed, but his assistant Mike Phelan was sent to face reporters after the match. "In that dressing room, everyone was fit," Phelan told reporters. "But big decisions have to be made."

In the dressing room, the decision wasn't necessarily received with the same shockwaves as it seemed to create for the rest of the footballing world. Ferguson had made bold selections before. This was one of those. "It's tough," explains Rafael Da Silva. "Every single player knew how good Sir Alex was, and how big his decisions sometimes were. So it is not always a big deal like it is seen by the media. Everyone respected the manager and whenever he made his team selection we respected it. For me, as a player, I love Rooney and I would always want him on the pitch. I know how much he helps the team. It is a natural thing – whenever you see that one of the best players isn't playing, you understand it's going to be a harder task to win the match.

"But I also understand that if the manager has decided not to play him, he has a reason. It wasn't the first time. Maybe Wayne would never understand that reason, because players want to play every game. You can say it didn't work out because we were eliminated. But we weren't eliminated because Wayne didn't start. We played well, we had some bad decisions against us…"

Rooney was back in the team for the visit of Chelsea in the FA Cup. In the pre-match press conference, Ferguson skilfully addressed the tone of the conversation. Some journalists had journeyed back to 2003, put two and two together and suggested there was a fallout between Fergie and his star boy.

"It's rubbish. It's because he's a stellar England player, that's the problem," he said. "He's the Paul Gascoigne, the Bobby Charlton. He's the best English player and any publicity about him will be used. Left out of the team on Tuesday night – that's the headline. You have to contend with that being news. To say I don't talk to him on the training ground is nonsense. It's an insult to me too but it sells newspapers. What can you do? I keep telling him he's too trusting. I told him, 'I don't know why you do things with the FA'. They've not helped him one bit. Every time he does anything, they punish him more than anyone in the game. He should be realising that. I wouldn't do a thing for the FA but they force him to do it… There's no issue with his contract. When it needs to be renegotiated it will be done. We don't want good players to leave."

It did seem, however, as though Ferguson had growing concerns about Rooney's physical condition, and they were expressed in the manner of someone who was open to the idea of letting a player go. "Wayne needed to be careful," Ferguson said in his 2013 book. "If he missed a couple of weeks for United, it could take him four or five games to get his sharpness back… He would receive no leniency from me. I would hammer him for any drop in condition. In my final year, I felt he was struggling to get by people and had lost some of his old thrust… as time wore on, I felt he struggled more to do it for 90 minutes, and he seemed to tire in games."

Rooney didn't appear to play with a chip on his shoulder. He scored against Chelsea with a free-kick that was surely a cross – it put United 2-0 up, but Chelsea levelled, and then won the replay to dump Ferguson's side out of the FA Cup and leave them with only the league to play for. They maintained such a strong position that even after losing to Manchester City at Old Trafford in the game after the Chelsea loss, United still had a 12-point lead with seven games remaining. They won at Stoke, and then drew at West Ham, where Rooney was brought off and looked decidedly unhappy about it.

Those results meant United welcomed Aston Villa to Old Trafford on Monday, April 22nd knowing a win would seal the title. Rooney was selected from the start, in a brand-new position alongside Michael Carrick in midfield. He was superb in his Paul Scholes imitation role. Less than two minutes were on the clock when his gorgeous cross-field pass found Valencia on the right. The game was opened up sufficiently for Rafael to then cross it to Giggs, who knocked it across goal for Van Persie to tap in.

It was Rooney's pass in the 13th minute which is most often remembered, however. It was something straight from the training ground. Rooney was inside his own half when he received a ball from Kagawa. From there, he struck a perfect 40-yard pass which arrowed down to Van Persie. The Dutchman was still outside the area when he connected first time on the volley – the ball flew cleanly into the net.

"Wayne was a creator as much as a finisher," says Rene Meulensteen. "He loved being a part of the game and involved in the build-up. He enjoyed playing passes and making assists. I can remember doing sessions where I would act as the centre-back positioned between two full-backs and we'd move the ball around to the midfielders; one would make a decoy run and the other would drop into the hole to receive the ball. The forwards would then make switch runs to spin across their defenders. Wayne loved playing as one of the midfielders in this, where he could ping the ball over the top for the attacker.

"In training before the Aston Villa game we were going through this exercise and we had talked about Ron Vlaar's positioning. Robin knew he would be making those runs across him. Wayne came deep to fill in one of those positions in midfield and then hit the pass perfectly for Robin. That was the difference between Wayne and the other forwards – none of them would be that bothered about playing the midfield role in the exercise. They wanted the goals, they wanted to be at the top. Wayne loved to play those balls. So even when he wasn't playing in midfield, he would drop to make those runs so that he could play those balls for the benefit of the team. That was a part of him, not something taught to him."

As someone who coached the many iterations of Rooney, which did Meulensteen prefer? "I think there's a case for them all," he says. "The versatile version contributed with goals and assists. But he was played where we needed him and there were seasons where we needed him to play as the number nine. I can remember Sir Alex explaining that when he was playing in that role he had to hold the line, we didn't want him dropping all over the place. He did brilliantly at what was asked and he did have to alter his game because his natural instinct is to be involved in the game. I'm sure if you asked him which side he would prefer, I'm certain he would say being more involved and scoring fewer goals. He loved scoring goals but he loved being part of the action."

Rooney had certainly revelled in the first half and his enjoyment had played a fundamental part in United's goals. They won 3-0, Van Persie getting a hat-trick to cement his place in the headlines. The former Arsenal man would quite understandably be perceived as the difference between failure and success for United. It's worth pointing out, though, that it was hardly as though Ferguson's side had struggled for goals the year before. They'd registered 89 in the league, one of their highest ever tallies.

Rooney may have been a player whose importance went under appreciated by the public at large, but, as always, never by his team-mates.

"I thought Wayne was still amazing in *that last year under Sir Alex*," says Rafael Da Silva. "We knew he had his ups and downs. A lot of people were talking about his relationship with the manager. I didn't see that on the training pitch. I thought he had some fantastic games. We're talking about the level of Wayne Rooney – many people would say Robin was the star of the season, but Wayne's importance was always clear. The most obvious example was against Aston Villa, with the incredible pass for Robin's goal. I was stood right behind it. It was the sort of thing Wayne would do every day."

That last year under Sir Alex. To stop that being a spoiler, let's cut straight to the chase. On May 8th, Ferguson shocked the world by announcing he would retire at the end of the season. It had been a decision he'd taken in the winter due to family reasons. He couldn't go on forever. Suddenly, his fury at having a last go at the Champions League taken from him due to a controversial decision was understandable. He would at least be bowing out a winner, with a 13th league title at United a fitting end to a glittering career. The day after the retirement was announced, Ferguson's successor was, too. It would be David Moyes of Everton.

It wasn't, however, the end of the story between manager and player.

Since the Madrid game, those rumours of Rooney's exit had inevitably come with suggested clubs. Paris Saint-Germain were one – there was even an announcement that a deal had been struck on French television, forcing representatives of the player to deny it. Rooney was on the bench for the visit of Chelsea and then omitted from the squad altogether for the final home game of the Ferguson era against Swansea City.

"I don't think Wayne was keen to play, simply because he's asked for a transfer," Ferguson told reporters after the match. "I think he wants to run it through in his mind."

This matter had apparently occurred after the Villa game. Ferguson had brought Rooney off because Villa "were a very fast young side, full of running, and their substitute was running past Wayne. He came into my office the day after we won the league and asked away. He wasn't happy after being left out for some games and subbed in others. His agent Paul Stretford phoned David Gill with the same message."

Ferguson said the request had been rejected and a club spokesman followed that by saying the player was not for sale. On the open-top bus parade the following day, Rooney was booed by some United supporters.

Rooney also missed the final game of the season at West Brom, with the club's official line being: "Wayne Rooney has been given permission not to travel with the squad as Coleen prepares for the arrival of their second child."

United drew 5-5, and just like that, the Ferguson era was over.

The fallout from his statement about Rooney's transfer request would be a more complicated matter to resolve.

In the days after the match, 'sources' close to the player insisted he had not requested to leave and did not wish to. It was clear the topic of his former player was going to be the biggest issue for Moyes to handle.

***

Reading between the lines, you would be forgiven for thinking that over the summer of 2013, Rooney had in fact come around to the idea of leaving Old Trafford. When David Moyes faced the press as Manchester United manager for the first time, he was pushed on the matter several times, never unequivocally stating that the striker wanted to stay. After dancing around the topic, one reporter asked him outright: "David, has Wayne Rooney categorically said that he wants to remain a Manchester United player?" To which Moyes replied, "I can tell you categorically that Wayne Rooney is training fantastically well. If I was Wayne, I would look at the legends who have played at this club. You can see their pictures at the training ground — George Best, Bobby Charlton, Roy Keane... Wayne is not too far away from that. It isn't too difficult to get the goals to reach the goalscoring record, and if he could do that he would be seen in the same light as those people. Wayne will not be sold by Manchester United."

Nobody was thoroughly convinced – and Rooney was said to be 'angry and confused' when Moyes told reporters on the club's pre-season tour of Bangkok: "My thought on Wayne is that if for any reason we had an injury to Robin van Persie we are going to need him. I want as many options as possible."

Talk of a transfer accelerated. United may well have been more amenable if an approach had come in from overseas. "I would have almost been interested to see how he would have done abroad," says Rene Meulensteen. "Cristiano never made a secret of his ambition and went on to prove his greatness in Spain and Italy. Wayne stayed for the best years of his career at United just like Ryan and Paul and all credit to him for doing so."

But Real Madrid were not interested. They wanted a British star alright, and were prepared to pay a world record fee for him, but it was Gareth Bale they'd set their sights on. Barcelona had already signed Brazilian starlet Neymar. Arsenal could not afford him. It left Chelsea, with Jose Mourinho recently returned as manager, as the club most keen to sign him. In fact, Mourinho had made it clear that Rooney was his only summer target.

They made an offer of £20m which was turned down. In early August they made a new offer of £25m but that too was rejected.

Rooney – who had missed the last week or so of pre-season with an alleged shoulder injury – was not in Moyes' first United team in the Community Shield, but was back on the bench against Swansea on the first day of the league season. He came on with his team winning 2-1 – and set up late goals for Van Persie and Welbeck. As the players celebrated the final goal, Rooney could be seen more than 20 yards away from them, trudging back to the halfway line alone.

United were due to face Chelsea in the following week's game. Mourinho, after spending the summer talking openly about the player he desired, now said he wanted his club to delay a third bid until after the game. "I don't want Chelsea to do it before we go there," he said. "I think this is a period where we're going to be quiet."

Michael Carrick insisted the speculation was not impacting the dressing room. "He is a big Manchester United player," Carrick said. "He's one of us and we all stick together. When we're on the pitch, we fight for each other and do what we can for Wayne. I thought he came on and looked good. He set up two goals and that's what he's all about. He got a bit of a whack when he made Danny's second but I'm sure he'll be alright. But he has given this club an awful lot so the fans support him and we support him."

Rooney played for England against Scotland in the midweek, and seemed to suggest that Moyes should have started him against Swansea. "You obviously need that sharpness," Rooney said. "I haven't had that many training sessions with the first team because they have been away. I might be lacking that bit of sharpness but hopefully that will come."

Before the Chelsea game, Frank Lampard was the latest representative from Stamford Bridge to have his say. "I think Chelsea have made their interest known and it's a decision for them and Wayne," the midfielder told *Sky Sports*. "If the manager wants to add another player, we all hope he gets his man. I didn't speak to Wayne about it when I was with England last week, he was training and he was focused, and I'm not privy to the transfer stuff."

The speculation was the most exciting thing about it all. United and Chelsea played out a dull 0-0, and the end of the transfer window came without another official offer being made by the Blues, in spite of the rumours that they'd make a £40m proposal.

Now he was bound to remain at Old Trafford in the short term, it was time to turn attention to his relationship with David Moyes. It had been far from perfect at Everton and following publication of Rooney's 2006 book, Moyes took legal action relating to the implication that he had relayed a private conversation to the *Liverpool Echo*. In court, Rooney's solicitor withdrew the accusation, apologised and paid damages.

Rooney might have had cause to reflect on many things in

the nine years since he moved to Old Trafford. He seemed to be uncertain, at the time of leaving Everton, about Moyes' capability and authority to manage a top club. He would have cause to question it again, if not directly. Moyes had brought his close aides from Everton to Old Trafford. It was an uncomfortable start which never improved. Jimmy Lumsden and Steve Round were capable coaches but did not have the experience to command respect from a dressing room of winners.

Rio Ferdinand is just one senior player to go on record as to the difficulty with this transition – the stories of the experienced defender being shown videos of Everton centre-half Phil Jagielka, and then being upset when the menu in the cafeteria at Carrington was changed, have gone down in United folklore now, but a crucial element which has gone under the radar is how unprepared the new manager and his staff were to familiarise themselves with the routine of the squad they were inheriting. Instead, Moyes imposed his own way of doing things. It gave the impression that he felt standards had slipped. Some senior players were bemused as he encouraged them to be better in training as 'this was Manchester United'. One can imagine how Rooney would have observed this.

Still, in spite of the numerous understandable reasons why there should have been difficulty in the relationship between Moyes and Rooney, the public perception was one of water having passed under the bridge. It's an interesting conundrum. On one hand, many supporters felt Rooney *had* showed signs of decline and that the summer was an opportune time to sell him for a sizeable fee. It could be argued that Ferguson had offered any incoming manager the opportunity to move on the player and start afresh. Perhaps selling Rooney might have given the impression that Moyes was ready to make tough calls from the off.

The appointment of David Moyes as successor to Sir Alex Ferguson in the summer of 2013 meant Wayne would be reunited with the manager he had a frosty relationship with while rising through the ranks at Everton

Instead, a different scenario played out. Moyes was not the only new man in power at United – David Gill had been succeeded by Ed Woodward. This new combination did not help with the summer recruitment plans. United were in need of a morale boost – a statement to inspire confidence in the new era. But in his first press conference, Moyes had seemed so uncertain, and from that moment on it looked as though the club were locked in a struggle to keep hold of their best player. In the end, the perception was that United's power in holding his contract was the only thing that kept Rooney at the club. Meanwhile Moyes was only able to sign Marouane Fellaini from his former club, at a fee that was several million pounds higher than his release clause had been at the start of the summer.

Now he was set to remain at Old Trafford, Rooney had a personal reason to show how good he was. Whether he wanted to stay or not, there was another question – was he good enough to? Ferguson's increasingly sparing use of him suggested he was dispensable.

On the last day of August, Rooney was involved in a training ground clash with Phil Jones, and suffered a deep cut on his forehead. It required 12 stitches but would rule him out of the international games of September. He would also need to wear a protective headband.

He played the full 90 minutes wearing the new black band in the first game after the break, scoring in the 80th minute against Crystal Palace. It was a clever free-kick to make it 2-0 and secure Moyes' first home win as manager.

"The headband didn't arrive until Friday but he felt all right with it and so we decided to give it a go," Moyes said afterwards. "I think it was what a sumo wrestler would wear! But he was fine. The hope is that we get a partnership where folk are saying, 'My goodness we are having to play against Van Persie and Rooney'. I can only see Wayne playing as a forward for us. To be successful you need to have people who can score you 20 goals. I am hoping that, with Robin and Wayne, you have two there who have that in them."

Two more goals followed in the Champions League win over Leverkusen – the second of which was his 200th goal for the club. Rooney was 'terrific' according to Moyes: "Not just for his goals, but his pass for Antonio Valencia's goal as well. He's got a very real chance of becoming one of the all-time goalscoring greats at this club. Being part of the history here was something we made him aware of.

"Any centre-forward who is scoring goals feels good about himself. I just wanted to get him back in really good condition and mentally right. All I know is that if you are going to win the Champions League, you need to have several world-class players and Wayne comes into that category."

Another record came at the weekend – but Rooney's 11th goal in Manchester derbies, making him the outright leading scorer in that rivalry, was very much a consolation (and possibly not even that) from an encounter in which United were already 4-0 down at City.

Rooney might have wanted to keep his head down, but October saw him propelled back into the headlines when Sir Alex Ferguson's second autobiography was published, featuring all of those statements about the player's supposed decline and alleged transfer requests. Ferguson was asked if he felt he'd done the right thing making it public. "When the club refused to sell him to Chelsea, he realised his only job was Manchester United, and it's brought back his focus, his work ethic and his purpose, and he's playing well again, so maybe that was a good turning point," Ferguson said, while admitting he hadn't spoken to Rooney since he retired.

"If in some way I've helped to bring his form back, I've done the right thing. Did it end badly? No, I don't think so. I think if Wayne walked in now, he would shake my hand."

Rooney was on international duty with England, and was asked to comment – he repeated the sentiment of his commitment, though did make some marked statements.

"I've been focused and I have wanted to prove to people that I'm a top player," he said. "I wanted to come back fit, sharp and scoring goals. I've scored a few goals and I'm playing every week so I'm enjoying it… I didn't feel I got a consistent run of games up front. I felt when I played in midfield I did okay but I didn't want to play there. I've had no problem in the past playing out of position, but I felt I deserved the right to play in my position and that wasn't happening."

He was asked if he had told Ferguson that he preferred to play up front. "Yeah, and…" he smiled, before expanding. "Everyone at the club knew that's where I wanted to play and I think that's why I was disappointed because I got asked – told – to play in midfield and I didn't want to. I'd always go and do it to try to help the team, but there had to come a point where, for my own career, I had to be a bit selfish really. David Moyes has come in and he's playing me up front and I'm enjoying it. I will have more discussions with the club and we'll see what happens from there."

When the opportunity next arose to put questions to Ferguson, the former United boss made some conciliatory noises. "Do you think I would drop Wayne Rooney the way he is playing now? Absolutely no way," he insisted. "This is what we want to see from Wayne Rooney, in this form all the time. The expectation on him is huge. He is the one hope for England, one of the great players for Manchester United, and when we see him in this form we see a different player…

"Wayne asked away. He felt he was unfairly played out of position and I can understand that. But at the time Wayne wasn't playing well enough. That was my judgment. He asked away because he said he wasn't getting played in his proper position. This is the nub of it. If you write a letter and ask away you lose all of your signing-on fees. He has never admitted that and never put in a written transfer request."

The 'spat' was apparently concluded by that crucial last sentence. What Ferguson was keen to point out as a misunderstanding, Rooney saw as a clarification. "He's got his own opinion and I've said nothing about it," he said. "But thankfully he came back and corrected the story that I put a transfer request in and proved I haven't. I'm thankful to him, he's corrected that. No, it hasn't reignited a feud. I haven't seen him since he retired. I'm happy under the new manager. I'm looking to the future now. A new coach has come in and it's given me a new lease of life. We're trying to be successful as a team. He's got a lot of players hungry and you could see tonight they are fighting for places."

United had picked up after that damaging setback to City (which was followed by another embarrassment, the first loss at home to West Brom since the late 1970s). Inspired by the rookie Adnan Januzaj's double at Sunderland, Moyes' team went on a 12-game unbeaten run. Rooney's form was okay if unspectacular, although his contribution in the home game against Stoke turned the match in his team's favour, inspiring Ed Woodward to describe the England forward as 'irreplaceable and phenomenal to watch' on the day fresh rumours linked Chelsea and Arsenal with January moves. If United were keen on renewing Rooney's contract – and those talks would have to be fairly imminent – then Woodward had done much of the arguing on behalf of the player.

Moyes, too, could not have been more complimentary. "Wayne and Robin, on their day, will be a match for any player in the world," he said in November. "When those two are firing, they are the best." He followed this later in the month describing him as 'a big leader' in the team, that he was 'in top form' and 'first class'. When Rooney could have been sent off for a swipe at Cardiff's Jordon Mutch, his manager defended it as 'hunger, desire and commitment'.

The indulgence seemed to be having an impact. In the return against Leverkusen, Rooney was superb, setting up the first four of his team's five goals. "Wayne doesn't need a rest," Moyes said after the match. "He needs to keep playing. He gets better the more games he plays. I just want to make sure he keeps playing as well as he is doing – and if he does that then I don't need to worry about resting him."

Rooney's importance to the team was underlined by a few moments in early December. First, he scored twice in a 2-2 draw at Spurs. He played when United fell to a shock defeat at home to Everton, but was suspended when they lost by the same 1-0 scoreline to Newcastle at Old Trafford three days later. That made it five league defeats for the season – after just 15 games, United were in ninth place in the table, 12 points behind leaders Arsenal, and seven points behind Manchester City in fourth. Describing the form as a slump would have been generous.

It was never more important for United to appear powerful, which was not the image projected when it was reported that Rooney's camp had rejected the initial offer of a new contract. If they couldn't convince their own player to stay, then what hope would they have of persuading top talent to come? The indulgence of the player had cultivated a school of thought that Rooney was almost bigger than Moyes in terms of stature at Old Trafford.

Moyes was banking on the title of manager of Manchester United being enough of a status, but with Rooney playing so well while United underperformed, the need to secure him to a new deal seemed paramount. Losing the player at this stage was not a battle in which Moyes could avoid defeat.

Over Christmas, he gained some breathing space with four consecutive league wins but any hope the new year would bring a fresh page was extinguished by the end of the first day. United lost at home to Spurs, and Rooney picked up a groin injury. He was sent for a warm weather break to Egypt to recover.

Moyes was questioned on reports that Rooney had asked for assurances over the players that the club were targeting, and had also expressed his desire to wait until the end of the season to see where United finished before making a commitment. "We would have to wait and see what happened in that situation," Moyes said – but it appeared he understood there was a more pressing need. Before the end of January, Moyes broke United's transfer record to sign playmaker Juan Mata from Chelsea. Mata was undoubtedly one of the best players in the league but it seemed a confusing one for a club that traditionally played pacy wingers – Mata seemed more of a signing to take the place of Rooney rather than complement him.

There was an air of desperation around United's new acquisition – Moyes had suffered a disastrous month, losing to Swansea in the FA Cup, being beaten heavily by Chelsea in the league and losing an embarrassingly poor League Cup semi-final penalty shootout to Sunderland.

So, Mata had been brought in very much with the future in mind. It was of sufficient intrigue to attract Rooney back to the negotiating table. The Spaniard made his debut in a 2-0 win over Cardiff, but February started in calamitous fashion, with a defeat to Stoke and a home draw with Fulham that felt like a defeat. The Cottagers were managed by Rene Meulensteen, the coach Moyes had allowed to leave when Ferguson retired. Meulensteen predicted that Moyes' team would cross the ball and then repeatedly cross it when they got frustrated. In the end, United threw 81 crosses in, a record for a Premier League game. Most of them were dealt with easily. They were now nine points away from fourth place.

Moyes, keen to generate some positivity, made it clear that although he wanted to strengthen the team, the biggest investment and reward would come for Rooney himself. A contract was presented that would make him the highest paid player in the country. It was an offer he could not refuse. A curious episode – in which all parties might have said it was an opportune time to part ways – concluded in mid-February, with the announcement that Wayne Rooney had signed a new long-term contract.

"Wayne has been the best player in England since I put him into the Everton first team in 2003," Moyes said in an official statement. "He is a vital part of my plans for the future and I'm absolutely thrilled he has accepted the challenge. I said last July that Wayne has an outstanding chance to be a true legend of this club. He came up to my house. I said to him, 'If you ask me what's missing, I think you've gone a bit soft'. I said, 'I've watched you, I just think you had better get back to the old aggressive Wayne Rooney'.

"But he had to get to a level of fitness where he was able to produce again. And that's what he has done. He hadn't been the hard-working, aggressive player he was. It's his work-rate, not just for himself but for the team. He's become an all-round team player who is also a technically gifted footballer. I felt as though he nearly had to reinvent himself again. Go back to being the old

Wayne Rooney, aggressive, fighting for everything that's there, but with the level of technical ability of a top player. I think he's done that."

Rooney said he was 'made up' to sign the new deal. "In August I will have been at the club for 10 years and I have played with some fantastic players and won everything that I hoped I would," he said. "I now have the chance to help the younger players coming through and to be a part of another great United team. I am convinced this is the start of another successful chapter in Manchester United's history. The future is bright for United."

Chapter Eighteen

NOOSE

wo months to the day after Wayne Rooney's new contract at Manchester United was confirmed, David Moyes was sacked as manager. Although their history might have suggested otherwise, there was never any hint in this admittedly brief period that Rooney had ever undermined or questioned the boss; there was never any moment where he had expressed any public doubt or made things difficult for Moyes when it came to his relationship with the existing squad at United.

"There was speculation that he was going to leave but I don't think that was anything to do with David coming in," says Fabio Da Silva (who did leave the club in January 2014). "He was the most important player in the team, and David gave him this big contract, so I am sure that the relationship between them wasn't difficult."

Fabio's sibling, Rafael, concedes there was naturally a feeling that Rooney commanded a respect through his achievements that Moyes was unable to match. "I didn't know what to expect from Wayne and David Moyes' previous relationship and I still don't know if they were close," he says. "When David arrived Wayne was the main player at Manchester United, almost the main man. Giggsy was still there but towards the end of his career. Wayne was *the* guy. When so many things had changed, Wayne had been there for nine years, had won everything and scored all the goals. He had so much experience at the top level."

When the pressure was at its most intense for Moyes, Rooney was the player doing more than anyone else, almost as if to prove any dissenting voices wrong. There was even one of his most memorable moments in Moyes' darkest weeks. Early in the game at West Ham, Ashley Young hooked a ball upfield, and Rooney tracked the bounce and outfoxed his marker, James Tomkins. Rooney turned and saw that goalkeeper Adrián was just out of position. The forward was five yards or so into West Ham's half, but sensed the opportunity, and struck the ball on the half-volley. It wasn't the height that beat the goalkeeper, but the swerve which pulled it back ever-so-slightly. In fact, the ball still bounced before it went in, but go in it did, for a remarkable memory made sweeter by the fact Rooney added a second later on to secure victory.

"I was just behind him when he struck it," remembers Rafael. "My immediate thought – *ooh, I'm not sure.* I looked at the goalkeeper. He was in a decent position. Then you see him lose his feet. It was amazing. His imagination was so incredible. He scored goals other players wouldn't even think of trying. I would say he tried it at least three times every season. It was more impressive that he did it in the early stages of a tight game, when most players are just getting into the match."

It truly was a rose among thorns; United suffered one humiliation after another, with even the faintest of hopes being trampled upon ruthlessly. 3-0 home defeats to Liverpool ('One of the worst days I've ever had in football' – Rooney) and Manchester City were chastening. A 2-0 loss at Olympiakos was followed by an unlikely second-leg turnaround. Hopes were raised for a similarly unrealistic push at the Champions League as a whole, especially when Patrice Evra scored a thunder-blaster against Bayern Munich in Germany, in the second leg of a tie that was 1-1 from the first leg. It was the best minute of the season – Bayern responded with three quick goals to knock Moyes' side out of the tournament.

Goodison Park was a fitting venue for the final act of Moyes' reign. On April 20th, 2014 – less than a calendar year after he'd been confirmed as manager – United lost 2-0 at Everton to confirm firstly that they would not mathematically be able to qualify for the following year's Champions League, and secondly that Moyes would be out of a job.

One report in the *People* the following week said Rooney was unexpectedly emotional at the decision. "Although several senior United players were clearly anti-Moyes and agitated for the manager to be replaced," Steve Bates wrote, "Rooney gave the doomed boss his full support and was said to be 'raging' at some United players who are rejoicing in his departure."

With four games left of the season, Ryan Giggs took temporary charge – Rooney got this mini-era off to the strongest possible start, scoring twice against Norwich to take his tally for the season to 19 in all competitions. He was comfortably the team's top scorer, and perhaps the only player who'd performed to a standard expected of them. With a brand new contract, there was no possibility he would be agitating for a move in the summer. He, like everyone else, was anxious to see who would be named the new permanent manager.

He didn't have to wait long.

***

The biggest charge levelled against David Moyes was that the stage seemed too big for him. The job needed a man with experience, a man who exuded control – few men fitted the profile better than Louis van Gaal. The Dutchman was renowned for his discipline which had seen him upset players and staff at his previous clubs; but it was thought that this was exactly what United needed.

The decision was made to hire him in mid-May. United's clear-out had already begun. Club legends welcomed in the first wave of transition were now seeking pastures new. Nemanja Vidic had already announced that he would be joining Inter Milan, thereby vacating the club captaincy. The other senior figures who would maybe have assumed that responsibility were Rio Ferdinand – but he moved to QPR; Patrice Evra – but he moved to Juventus; and Ryan Giggs, but he retired from playing in order to be Van Gaal's assistant, with a purported succession plan in place after Van Gaal retired.

It was wide open for Rooney to get the armband. "Of course I would be interested," he said from his position with the England team ahead of the World Cup, but in the short term, he was concentrating on England's chances that summer. The World Cup was being held in Brazil, so perhaps a relevant moment to recall all of those previous comparisons to Pele at international tournaments, made after Euro 2004 and before almost every one Rooney had played at since. Expectations had changed. The remnants of the 'golden generation' were Steven Gerrard at 34 and Frank Lampard at almost two years older. England's group included Italy – who had humbled them at the Euros – and Uruguay, blessed with world class strikers in Luis Suarez and Edinson Cavani. Their chances of qualification were slim. It was accepted that Roy Hodgson and company would be coming home earlier than they would like.

There was the reality, and the usual hope that England could overachieve. And if they were going to, why would they not be inspired by Rooney, who was coming off a strong individual season and also going into the tournament with no injury concerns? Well, Paul Scholes was quick to tell us: "There's a chance Wayne is worn out. His peak may have been a lot younger than what we'd expect of footballers traditionally."

On the same day, Rooney had expressed his satisfaction with his own condition. "In the previous tournaments I've had little injuries which have stopped me from training in the first week," he said. "I feel fresh, I feel fit, I feel ready. So really, this tournament, there will be no excuses from me. I want to prove myself at this level."

Rooney's comments had been coincidentally timed with Scholes', so weren't in response – but Roy Hodgson, a week later, addressed the statement. "Of course I don't think Wayne is past his best. I have selected him in a 23-man squad that I'm very proud of. I believe in Wayne Rooney. He is still only a young man."

It was hardly a ringing endorsement, and as ever, if you were to give the merest of molehills to the press pack following an England team at a World Cup, they could construct their very own Sugarloaf. In early June, Hodgson was asked if he thought Rooney was an 'exceptional' player, and gave a garrulous response: "With respect, you make him an exceptional player when you want to make him an exceptional player and when you want to make him a player that you don't think should be in the team, you make him that as well. I have to allow you to decide whether he is exceptional. You're saying he is an exceptional player. I'm not saying if he's exceptional or not. I have picked him because he is a very good player and I think it's wrong of you quite frankly to use words about him that you either want me to refute or agree with.

"I am only prepared to talk about Wayne Rooney as one member of my squad and a player who I hope will help us have a good World Cup. You decide the epithets, you make him exceptional or, after the last game, I understand quite a few people made him less than exceptional. That's your decision. I make my decisions on his performance. Is that okay?"

Crystal clear, Roy – or clear as mud, given he went on to describe Raheem Sterling just moments later as… 'exceptional'.

The conversation found its way to Rooney. Now it seemed his lack of a Ballon d'Or, the absence of any major European individual awards, was being used to suggest he hadn't achieved what many had projected for him. "Listen, I am not a player who needs that like Cristiano does," he said after a blistering training session in Rio. "He has to have that and you admire him for having that. But I'm more about winning things as a team. He wants his moments. It's more important for me to win trophies as a team. I have won PFA Player of the Year but it's nowhere near as good as winning things with Manchester United. I know if I have a good tournament here the team will play well."

England's opening match was against Italy at Arena da Amazônia. Their performance was much better than it had been at the Euros, but they still fell behind after 35 minutes. Rooney was playing on the left wing, and from that position, played a fantastic cross for Daniel Sturridge to tap in two minutes later. But Italy scored early in the second half – Rooney found himself increasingly central as his team pushed for an equaliser, and he had the best chance, firing just wide. He was one of the few positives from a disappointing result, but it was put to him in the tunnel after the game that he should not consider his place in the team was 'guaranteed'. "I've never felt that," he responded angrily. "I work hard to try and get into this team. I have never said my place is guaranteed. I don't expect to play, but I work hard. I want to play. I enjoyed the game. Obviously we lost, but I was involved. I could have scored, created the goal and felt I had an influence."

Rooney proved himself again, against Uruguay. He went close with a free-kick and then hit the bar, before the South Americans went up a gear and went in front. England were facing elimination already. Their response was hardly spirited – but they got a reprieve in the 75th minute when Glen Johnson crossed and Rooney was in the six-yard box to score his first ever World Cup goal. With five minutes to go, poor defending let in Luis Suarez to score his second, and knock England out.

Posting on his Facebook page after the game, Rooney issued an apology. "Absolutely devastated to be out of the World Cup," he said. "Going into each game we had great belief in ourselves but unfortunately it hasn't worked out. Sorry to all the fans that travelled and at home that we haven't done better ... gutted!"

Germany legend Michael Ballack told *The Times* that far from trying to fit Rooney into the team, Hodgson should have built it around the United man. "For me the only player who looked like making a difference for England was Rooney. He is the only one who can hurt teams, and the only one who is really world class," he said. "Some people are saying he should be dropped, which is crazy. Despite all these problems England look better than they did two years ago and Roy Hodgson should build his team around Rooney and tell them to do everything they can to play for him."

Rooney played 15 minutes of the dead rubber match against

Costa Rica. It finished 0-0 – a drab way to conclude England's World Cup campaign. His experience with the biggest international tournament had never been favourable. The previous two, he'd gone into with or recovering from injury. Somehow, despite there being little expectation this time around, England had found a way to disappoint, and when it came to forecasting the future, Rooney – just 28 – was cast as one of the players who formed the past. His status as the young pup of the Golden Generation placed him with the old guard now Gerrard and Lampard were having to accept the consequences of time. Rooney, with 95 caps and 40 goals, was not quite ready to do that.

Chapter Nineteen

GOING DUTCH

I t was a new era at Manchester United, one where Rooney was
going to be front and centre. England's dismal World Cup
showing meant their players were available to take part in the
entirety of their club's pre-season. It was safe to say that the
preparation fixtures under Louis van Gaal bore no resemblance
to what was to follow. After inheriting a squad that had lost so
much experience and gained only Ander Herrera and Luke Shaw,
nobody could have expected the new manager would have a team
that would win games against Real Madrid and Liverpool, much
less play them off the park. United were electric. Rooney netted
five in six pre-season matches. He'd also worn the captain's armband, and after the final warm-up game, Van Gaal confirmed this
would be the case for the foreseeable future.

"Wayne has shown a great attitude towards everything he does,"
he said. "I have been very impressed by his professionalism and

his attitude to training and to my philosophy. He is a great inspiration and I believe he will put his heart and soul into his captaincy role." Rooney spoke of his own delight, describing it as a 'true honour'. Philosophy was a word that was entering the Old Trafford dictionary. Nobody was quite sure what to expect, but on the opening day against Swansea it wasn't only the faces which were unfamiliar. United had always traditionally played 4-4-2, with flirtations with a 4-3-3 in the Ronaldo years. This was drastic in comparison, with a 3-4-1-2 shape. De Gea was in goal, with Jones, Smalling and Tyler Blackett in defence. Ashley Young and Jesse Lingard were wing-backs, with Fletcher and Herrera behind Mata in midfield. Rooney and Hernandez led the line. The game was broadcast live on BT Sport, with former Liverpool winger Steve McManaman describing it as 'the worst I have seen as a Manchester United eleven' and Paul Scholes saying only Rooney and Fletcher would get into 'his' United team.

The shape was changed twice in the game – United looked thoroughly uncomfortable, and, at times, like strangers. Swansea had a half-time lead, and although Rooney levelled with a smart overhead hook from close range, Gylfi Sigurdsson scored a late winner to embarrass the hosts on Van Gaal's big day.

"It is always a bigger story when United struggle," Rooney said afterwards. "You are going to get ex-players going over the top and having their say. We have to accept it. This is a really bad result for us… we need to do better."

Van Gaal discussed the value of his system and why it would take a while to bear fruit. "I think it is a departure from what they are used to," he said. "What is important is the quality of the players. That is why we are playing the system we have at the moment. If I played 4-3-3 instead, I would have to choose between Wayne Rooney and Robin van Persie. The only surprise last week was ourselves. Swansea played as we expected."

It was do as I say, not as I do – but a different sort of autocracy to the one experienced by the players under Ferguson. Van Gaal wanted patience but was not going to exercise that virtue himself. His spending spree in the last 11 days of the window was remarkable. The defender Marcos Rojo arrived for £16m, followed by the club record signing of Angel Di Maria for £59.7m. Daley Blind, at £14m, came in from Ajax. On deadline day, Monaco striker Radamel Falcao signed on loan. It was not a transfer strategy that seemed particularly well-planned, but it was the club's biggest spend (adding the £60m spent on Shaw and Herrera) by a considerable distance.

It would be mid-September before all of these players could play together for the first time. Rooney knew, at least, that as captain he would be part of the team when they did, so could feel as much optimism as anyone. That good mood would have been boosted by a true show of faith in him by Roy Hodgson, who announced that not only would Rooney continue to be a part of his post-World Cup rebuild, he would be captain.

His time as skipper got off to a strong start – he scored a penalty against Norway at Wembley, although only 40,000 fans were there to see it; a visual indication of the lack of interest in the England team at that time. That was followed by a win in Switzerland, earned by goals scored by Danny Welbeck (who had recently moved to Arsenal to make way for Falcao). The European Championship qualifying campaign was off to a flyer.

At United, Van Gaal's latest new-look team included three of the players he'd just signed (with a another coming off the bench) and strolled to a 4-0 win over QPR. Rooney, playing as a striker alongside Van Persie, scored the third just before half-time.

The following game was arguably one of the most definitive of the entire post-Ferguson era at United. Leicester were the opponents, and Rooney started behind Falcao and Van Persie. Mata was the player who lost out. In the build-up to the game, Van Gaal had effectively said Rooney was undroppable. "I don't think any player is fixed," he stated. "Only the captain has more privileges."

For an hour of the match at the King Power, United's attack was thrilling. They were leading 3-1 and looked so dangerous that they might score with every attack. The problem was that for the next half hour, Leicester *did* score with just about every attack *they* had. United were paying the price for losing so much defensive experience in the summer. Worse still, Van Gaal appeared to not be a fan of Jonny Evans or Rafael, who, to most observers, were probably the best defenders still at the club.

After losing 5-3, Van Gaal explained that although Rooney would stay in the team, it didn't necessarily mean he would remain as a centre-forward. "I was not so satisfied with Rooney as a striker," he said. "Rooney can play in more positions, he's a multi-functional player and I have tried him in a striker's position. He's played well but not spectacular and Falcao is a striker and I think he can do it better."

Rooney showed that instinct for knowing where the goal is after just five minutes against West Ham soon after. Later, with a 2-1 lead on the hour mark, the Hammers broke, and Rooney cynically disrupted the play, bringing down Stewart Downing – he was dismissed by Lee Mason. "It was probably the right decision," Rooney admitted. "I saw the West Ham player making a counter-attack and I tried to break up the play, but I just misjudged it. I expect people to say it's a sign of the old temper flaring up again but I was trying to break up the play. I don't think it will benefit anyone to appeal."

He could not have admitted his guilt any more than he did. On Monday, however, he was not criticised by his manager. That privilege was reserved for Rafael Da Silva. His crime? Setting up Rooney's goal. The Brazilian had crossed first time, from an area that was not under Van Gaal's strict instruction. His philosophy contained two key elements Rafael had betrayed – to control the ball in order to make more considered decisions with your second touch, and to stay very close to the positions laid out in the system. No roaming was permitted. These were not merely instructions – it was the law.

But if these things were against Rafael's natural impulses, it stands to reason that they must have been against Rooney's, too. Rooney liked to go where the ball was in order to be more involved in the game. His most legendary moments were of impulsive brilliance. Van Gaal's demands were less autonomy and more in line with totalitarianism. One would have thought it would be anathema to a player of Rooney's spirit. And yet – possibly because such faith had been entrusted in the player by the manager – there was an immediately strong bond between United's highest profile player and their new boss.

"Wayne loved Van Gaal and it seemed like the feeling was mutual," Rafael says. "Van Gaal was a coach who liked players to play in different positions. The other thing is that it would have been impossible for Van Gaal to clash with Rooney. He needed him as an ally. Wayne had just signed his new contract, he was the main man. I didn't see eye to eye with him, but Van Gaal was no fool. He couldn't take him out of the team. He did it with Rivaldo at Barcelona and he was fired."

However, what might have felt good was not necessarily the best thing for United or for Rooney. In 2015, Rene Meulensteen observed for TalkSPORT that Rooney did not 'look the same'.

Does he credit that to Van Gaal's philosophy? "One hundred per cent," he said. "You start to tell him what he needs to do, he over-thinks. The play of the team becomes laboured, too slow, and against Wayne's instinct and quality." Could it be said, then, that whatever perceived decline there was that followed, it was emphasised due to the nature of the coaching? "Probably. It's a fair observation," Meulensteen adds. "When you drag a player so far away from their natural instinct and nature they're bound to underperform. It was not only Wayne."

That said, it would have been premature to think Rooney was in any sort of decline in the winter of 2014. He was in rude health for club and country, scoring goals 42 and 43 for England against San Marino and Estonia respectively. The latter came in his 99th appearance. Roy Hodgson appeared more appreciative of the quality of his skipper than he had seemed in Brazil. "When I came into this job I didn't know quite what to expect of Wayne," he said. "My knowledge of him was shaped by TV, radio and newspapers. He is a very different person than I thought – a very driven, very professional person. Since he's had the captaincy, he has taken on even more responsibility and to get 100 caps for your country will be some achievement."

Rooney's drive was evident to see as he was comfortably United's best player in a defeat in the derby; but that fire was crucial to instigating a sequence of six successive victories. He went on one of his goalscoring runs here, netting five goals in seven matches as United ended 2014 on a high.

"Since he has been made captain, he has taken a step even further," Van Gaal said in November. "He is someone who has attracted the headlines over the years. It comes from starting a career so early and being branded a wonderkid at 19. He has had his fair share of ups and downs but I think that has hardened him."

His 100th cap arrived in November, against Slovenia at Wembley, and came with goal 44 in a 3-1 win. "It's a great honour and I'm extremely proud to be able to achieve it," he said. "It's a special moment for me, but I don't just want to be remembered as one of the players who gets 100 caps or more. You want to be successful. That's the main aim."

International level for Rooney had proved a puzzle. He'd been the best player in the best team he'd played in, and, like Paul Scholes before him, had strangely found himself moved around just when it seemed they needed him most. Because winning things for your country is such a limited experience, international matches have a life of their own, and come with their own reputation. Rooney scored twice in a memorable win against Scotland a few days after his special day against Slovenia (he had become the youngest player to reach 100 caps), to mark one of his best weeks playing for his country. Now on 46 goals, the record of Sir Bobby Charlton was tantalisingly close.

Rooney had netted the first goal in a big 3-0 win over Liverpool in December, before concluding: "We are getting better and better. The results are coming and the gap to the top is only eight points. Some of the games haven't gone the way we would like, but we are winning them and that is a great quality to have. Everyone can see Van Gaal has an aura about him. He has experience. When things weren't going great for us earlier on in the season, he knew what he was doing. He knew the form would come back and that we would win games. There was no panic because he has been through it all before."

The result against Liverpool, however, was more of an indication of how badly things were going for the Merseyside club. Their title challenge of the previous season was as much a distant memory as the sight of Luis Suarez in Liverpool colours, with the

Uruguayan having moved to Barcelona. They had lost six of their 15 games before facing United.

Maybe Rooney was right – maybe Van Gaal did have an aura about him. It would go some way to explaining some of the unlikely results, such as the 2-1 win at Arsenal in which Rooney scored a late winner (overtaking Jack Rowley in the histori-cal goalscoring standing for his club) with a team that included Paddy McNair and Tyler Blackett in defence. But the spirit in those games was replaced by an anxiety in others. A dreadful 0-0 draw with Spurs on December 28th was followed shortly after by a home defeat to Southampton where United failed to register a single shot on target.

Supporters were increasingly unconvinced by the laborious style of football, exacerbated by the manager's apparent lack of confidence in players he'd only just brought to the club. Concerns over Falcao were understandable considering he had been recovering from a serious injury, but Di Maria had arrived as a record signing and had been the best player on the park in the previous season's Champions League final. By January, he was already in and out of the team.

United's ambitions had been refined by the turmoil of the previous season. The loss of experience and the scale of the turnover meant that qualification for the Champions League had become a priority, which would have been a very difficult concept for the serial winners still at Old Trafford such as Rooney, who main-tained ambitions of being the best in the country. Ed Woodward had made a number of big-money signings but the lack of genuine strategy seemed obvious. United had become tougher to defeat as a result of Van Gaal's post-Leicester pragmatism, but they had also become tougher to watch.

In early February, Rooney played in a strange right-sided

midfield role at West Ham; the shape of the team seemed to be experimental and narrow, and it took a rudimentary route-one approach to snatch a late point. Van Gaal explained why his captain was moved into an area which, at times, seemed to be an abyss. "It's about communication and me giving my arguments why he has to do that – and, yes, sometimes convincing him he has to do something for the team," Van Gaal said. "Not many players can play in as many positions as Rooney but that is not always a benefit for him. A player doesn't always like it so I have to take care of that. But I don't think he ever complains about where he has to play."

On the last day of the month United welcomed Sunderland to Old Trafford. Rooney was back in his comfortable position just behind Falcao, and scored the goals in a 2-0 win. Afterwards, he said: "I was obviously pleased that the manager played me up front. It's down to the manager whether I stay there. It's his decision where he sees me playing and I will respect wherever he wants to play me."

United were knocked out of the FA Cup by Arsenal – so, after a humiliating 4-0 defeat at MK Dons in the League Cup, were left without anything to play for other than Champions League qualification. It wasn't the only blow that week. Rooney was allegedly knocked out by his friend and former team-mate Phil Bardsley in a play fight at home. A video surfaced of Bardsley punching Rooney; Bardsley's wife Tanya posted on Twitter that Rooney had 'jumped straight up'.

In the 2020 book *LVG – The Manager and the Total Person*, Van Gaal was quoted as saying the incident suggested he had not succeeded when it came to his reasoning for naming Rooney captain.

"I could not fault Rooney's professional attitude on the field for one second," he said. "But the way he lived his life off it was a totally different story. So I made Wayne captain to try and get more control of him away from football. Unfortunately, we did not quite succeed."

Rooney recalled that Van Gaal didn't seem to take it so seriously. "If we have a few days off, I like to go to a mate's house and we drink and we put boxing gloves on," he said. "Though when that clip went viral I thought, 'Jesus, I'd better tell the manager'. But when I walked into the manager's office, he burst out laughing. It was totally not a problem for him. The media made it much bigger, but Louis just laughed."

There was a dire need at the club for some positivity. United had a horrid run of fixtures which threatened to rule them out of the fight for the top four. First they faced Tottenham at Old Trafford (Spurs having won their previous two visits), then they went to Anfield, had back-to-back home games against Aston Villa and Manchester City, then trips to Chelsea and Everton.

At the Lowry Hotel before the game against Spurs – as those Bardsley stories dominated the newspapers – Rooney gave a rallying cry to his team-mates.

"He was a good captain," says Rafael Da Silva. "Different to Vida. He was more demonstrative. Maybe it was a language thing. Wayne took it very seriously. I can remember him talking to Adnan Januzaj, trying to explain things to help him settle into life as a senior player. He did it with the other young lads who came into the team as well."

There was a new system against Spurs. The three-man defence was a thing of the past. Now it was a 4-2-3-1, with only one of the manager's signings (Daley Blind – if we're discounting Ander Herrera as one he technically inherited) in the team. Herrera and Carrick were in midfield, with Mata, Fellaini and Young as the three behind Rooney; although at times it was difficult to know which of Fellaini and Rooney was meant to lead the line.

That confusion spread to the Spurs defence – after nine minutes, Carrick played a through ball, and it was Fellaini running on to it to finish clinically across goal. Fellaini then won the ball for Carrick to score a clever header 10 minutes later. Old Trafford was bouncing – for the first time in over a year, United were playing with chemistry and cohesion. The mood was euphoric when Rooney rolled back the years to steal the ball off a defender, shrug off a challenge and then finish with confidence to make it three. He celebrated by running to the corner, throwing a flurry of punches into the air, and then falling dramatically back in the same fashion as the video which had gone viral. After the 3-0 win, Fellaini told reporters of Rooney's 'very important speech'.

The ball was rolling. United won at Anfield thanks to magnificence from Mata, and then another Rooney stunner settled the result against Aston Villa. Rooney was not on the scoresheet, but was in great form again, as United hit four past City to record their fourth consecutive win. The run of form meant Van Gaal's team were nine points clear of fourth place with six games remaining; their qualification for the Champions League effectively assured with such comfort that they could afford the end-of-season slump that followed.

It was unfortunate for the dynamic of the team that Carrick had come off with an injury towards the end of the City game, necessitating a switch for Rooney into deep midfield again, with the ineffectual Falcao brought in to do the job that the captain had been doing. The groove was well and truly gone. United lost three in a row without scoring, despite bossing the ball in each of the games.

Despite this, they did indeed qualify for the Champions League, thereby meeting the minimum expectation for Van Gaal's first season, and permitting him a second on which to build. Reflecting on what had gone right in his first year in England, the manager paid tribute to Rooney. "Wayne is a very good captain," he said. "I am very proud. He is very good in the dressing room, he is always an example on the training pitch and in matches, he always fights to the end. Wayne has also played in a lot of positions for me without ever complaining. I think I made a very good decision with Wayne."

For the second year in a row, Rooney finished as top scorer, though the diminishing returns (14 in all competitions, 12 in the league) were reflective of the new attitude of the team that seemed much more cautious. He was now on 230 goals for United. Against Slovenia in June, Rooney scored a late winner to register his 48th for England. With Sir Bobby Charlton's goal records standing at 249 and 49 for club and country respectively, there was every expectation that Wayne Rooney's 2015/16 season would be record-breaking.

Chapter Twenty

SWINGING THE AXE

At the time, it felt as though Manchester United's approach to incoming transfers was much more sensible than it had been the previous year. First of all, the club seemed quick to admit to its mistakes, which felt like a good sign. Angel Di Maria got the move to Paris he'd hoped for, and the loan for Falcao was not renewed. Despite the high hopes that came with the pair, there was no great sadness when they moved on. The same could not be said for the more brutal swinging of Van Gaal's axe, which led to some very uncomfortable departures. Nani, Van Persie, Rafael, Hernandez and Evans were all permitted to leave – each of them out of favour with the manager.

Collectively, the money received for the group did not even cover the fee to sign Morgan Schneiderlin of Southampton, the midfielder who would hopefully bring the screening and water-carrying midfield qualities that Van Gaal's team seemed to lack. Darren Fletcher had been permitted to leave earlier that year, so

Bastian Schweinsteiger seemed like an exciting replacement from Bayern Munich. Matteo Darmian was signed as right-back to be much more obedient than Rafael. And, with United now heavily reliant on Rooney to score goals, some of that creative weight was lifted by the acquisition of exciting winger Memphis Depay.

The main transfer saga of the summer was centred around David De Gea, who was coveted by Real Madrid, but not to the extent that they would offer a reasonable fee. De Gea eventually stayed at United, and signed a new long-term contract. The episode was an interesting contrast to how Rooney's similar incident, five years earlier, had been received.

Argentinian goalkeeper Sergio Romero was brought in as cover for De Gea, while United also swooped for teenage forward Anthony Martial on transfer deadline day. The tone was set on a difficult opening day where United won 1-0 against Spurs thanks to an own goal. Van Gaal confirmed afterwards that he intended to play Rooney as the main striker for the coming season. At Aston Villa in the second game, the captain had a poor match, with little fluency between him, Mata, Depay and Januzaj.

Rooney was marginally better in the Champions League qualifier first leg in Bruges. He was brought off with five minutes to go – his replacement, Fellaini, scored in injury time to secure a 3-1 win. "I'm an honest guy, I know when I haven't played well and against Aston Villa I was below my standards," he said. "I've had one bad game this season and everyone's all over it. I had a much better game against Brugge and could have got a goal or two, but that's football. It's still early in the season, so it's down to me to keep going. It would be nice to get off the mark but I've experienced this before and the goals will come. I'm confident I'm still capable of getting 20-plus goals this season."

He played the full 90 minutes against Newcastle, but that

merely meant his goal drought for his club stood at 858 minutes. His team, too, failed to score, with one of those controlled but laborious performances that frustrated fans so often in the previous campaign.

The dry run ended in spectacular fashion at Club Brugge in the return; Rooney netting a hat-trick before the hour to ensure qualification for the Champions League group stages. "I am delighted to get the goals," he said. "If I did not have a strong character, then maybe the drought would have affected me but I know my quality."

There was no such drought for England. Rooney netted with a penalty against San Marino – the sixth successive game in competitive matches where he had scored at international level, which was an England record. It was also the 39th different game he'd scored in – also a record. It was his 49th goal for his country – not quite a record. England won 6-0, and Rooney was brought off for a rest before the hour mark, with the opportunity to surpass Sir Bobby Charlton's goalscoring landmark against Switzerland at Wembley a few days later.

Before that match, Rooney admitted he would be 'disappointed' to just reach 50 goals. "I feel I've still got quite a lot of games left to play for England," he said. "If I was sitting here saying 'I just want to get 50 goals' then I'd be lying. I want to kick on and try to score as many as I can."

Against Switzerland, England were not particularly convincing. It took until the 67th minute to get the breakthrough, with Harry Kane grabbing his third goal in just four caps. Before long, his name would be mentioned in sentences including the words 'England' 'goalscoring' and 'record'. With the game drawing to a conclusion, there was a slight feeling of anti-climax. Hodgson had taken Rooney off against San Marino with getting the record at Wembley in mind, and the evening had almost seemed set up for that, especially considering qualification had already been achieved. David Beckham's son Romeo had been one of the mascots that came out with the team. The contriving of an occasion seemed as if it would pass unrewarded.

In the 83rd minute, Raheem Sterling found himself in the box, crowded by Swiss players. Granit Xhaka made a rash tackle. Italian referee Gianluca Rocchi blew for the penalty. Seventy-five thousand fans in Wembley cheered the moment as if it were a goal.

Gary Lineker. Alan Shearer. Michael Owen. There were many other great strikers England produced in the same period, but these were the three who had been expected to surpass Charlton's record and get to 50. Lineker came closest with 49. Owen reached 41. Shearer bowed out on 30, having reached the esteemed company of Tom Finney and Nat Lofthouse. Those at Wembley knew they could be witnesses to history.

Rooney stepped up – nobody else was going to take it.

His kick was strong and on target – to the keeper's right, and high. Yann Sommer got a finger to it, but the ball was already moving past him at a ferocious speed. England were 2-0 up – but for once, an individual moment was more important than what it meant to the team.

"Wayne is the story of the night," Hodgson said afterwards. "We are so delighted for him. We made a small presentation in the dressing room to Wayne, a football shirt with 50 on the back. He gave a very good speech in accepting that. I don't think Sir Bobby Charlton will be too disappointed."

The speech was filmed and shared on social media.

"Thanks to every one of you, coaches, players, the staff who I've worked with for such a long time," Rooney said. "This is such a

Wayne races off in celebration after converting the penalty that took him past Sir Bobby Charlton as England's all-time leading goalscorer

huge moment for myself, and my family, in my career. Hopefully for the team and for myself there's a lot more to come. We can be successful and hopefully there's a lot of young lads, Harry, Ross (Barkley) and Raheem coming through who can come close and even pass me in the future, so I'm grateful, it means the world to me, and thank you very much."

To the press, Rooney confessed his nerves, and shared that Sir Bobby had sent him a message of congratulations.

Before he was back in action for his club, there were rumours of another dressing room address – this time, it was reported that after United's opening day game against Spurs, Rooney and Michael Carrick had approached Louis van Gaal to discuss concerns about training and the mood at the club. Under Ferguson, such leaks were notable by their absence. But since he had retired, there was a much greater transparency about the club, and so it surprised few when van Gaal openly discussed what had gone on behind closed doors.

"Rooney and Carrick warned me that the dressing room is flat," he said. "It is alarming when your captains come to see you and that's why I went to the dressing room. It's a positive thing that the players are coming to me... but it was Carrick and Rooney and that was alarming for me because they are the captains. They are coming to my office. I am not a dictator, I am a communicator."

In 2017, Carrick explained more about the meeting. "We just spoke to him as the senior players, to have a conversation to say that everyone wanted to be better," he said. "It was a fair conversation, nobody went in there fighting. It probably sounded like a big deal, but it happens all the time at clubs all over the country. Sometimes a manager will pull you aside in training or in his office, but it just so happened that me and Wayne went to chat to him."

Victory over Liverpool was achieved without Rooney, who had a hamstring strain, but with Martial, who scored on his debut with a great solo goal. England's leading scorer was back in the goals for his club in 3-0 wins over Ipswich in the League Cup and then Sunderland in the league.

With five goals for the season, Rooney was United's top scorer in mid-October, although only one of those goals had come in the league, so Van Gaal was asked if he felt the forward was in 'subdued' mood before the game at Everton.

"I don't know why he has looked subdued," he said. "It is not so important who is scoring. We have scored a lot of goals. He's our No10, our second striker. That's my preference but sometimes I need another type in midfield. At the start of the season you were criticising us for not scoring enough goals. Now we have scored a lot you are picking on an individual player and I don't like that. He's our captain so that's very important because his influence is bigger than every other player in our group. He's a very important player for me, his colleagues, everybody. It's true the captaincy can burden some players but I don't believe it with Rooney because of his personality."

In any event, Rooney answered the critics – getting a rare goal at Goodison in a rare recent win at his old ground, and celebrating in muted fashion considering it was the first game after the passing of legendary Everton boss Howard Kendall.

Van Gaal beamed with pride about 'the example' Rooney had set for "everybody – not only his team-mates, but also for players from other clubs. And also for the manager."

Rooney clearly had a kinship with the boss, but that feeling was not shared by all at the club. The minor alleviations from the 'intervention' of Carrick and Rooney quickly dissipated and the status quo was resumed; the manager intense, critical and demanding in training. It translated into performances. Three consecutive 0-0 draws summed up the mood. United were heading for a fourth before a Rooney goal ten minutes from time eked a home win against CSKA Moscow in the Champions League. It was another landmark day for Rooney, who now was on 237 for United, tied with Denis Law as joint-second top scorer.

It was brief respite. Further goalless draws at Old Trafford against PSV and West Ham were followed by defeat in Wolfsburg which caused ejection from the Champions League. Dismal defeats at Bournemouth, at home to Norwich and then at Stoke made it seven games without a win and seemed to put van Gaal on the brink of the sack. Matters were made worse by Jose Mourinho's availability following his recent dismissal from Chelsea. The Blues – reigning champions – had a catastrophic title defence and came to Old Trafford to contest a 0-0 draw to signal a miserable end to 2015.

At least 2016 seemed to promise more in its early knockings. Rooney established himself ahead of Law, netting the winner at Swansea on January 2nd. Against Sheffield United in the FA Cup, Van Gaal's team put on another poor showing. With 71 per cent possession, his side had only two shots on target against the League One Blades to a backdrop of boos and chants of 'attack, attack, attack'. At least the second of those – a penalty from Wayne Rooney in the 92nd minute – went into the net.

"It is not only frustrating for the fans," Rooney admitted afterwards. "Players and staff are frustrated as well."

The strike was compared to Mark Robins' goal against Nottingham Forest – a goal in the FA Cup which is largely credited with saving Sir Alex Ferguson's job. If this could kick-start a successful cup run for United, then Van Gaal might still have a future in Manchester. If there was talk about the players downing tools for the Dutchman, that charge could not be levelled at the captain, who put in some of his strongest performances for a while in January 2016. Two goals in a 3-3 draw at Newcastle were followed by a dramatic winning strike at Anfield. For the first time ever, Rooney could celebrate goals at both grounds in his home city in the same season.

It was a strange period in Manchester United history. They went on to lose 1-0 at home to Southampton again – a replica of the fixture from the previous season – before a raucous away crowd followed them to Derby in the FA Cup. Rooney's stunning curled effort from the angle of the box got the ball rolling in a 3-1 win.

United then drew at Chelsea – the Blues getting an injury-time equaliser – before losing 2-1 at Sunderland, to leave them in fifth place, six points behind Manchester City in fourth, and having played a game more. Qualification for next year's Champions League was looking more likely through the Europa League. They'd have to do it without Rooney, though, who suffered a knee injury at the Stadium of Light and struggled through to the end. "It's difficult to say how long Wayne will be out," Van Gaal said. "The fact he played on is typical Wayne. He's a guy who wants to go until the end."

The injury kept him out for exactly two months. In the meantime, a young hot-shot by the name of Marcus Rashford had been rushed into first-team action due to an injury crisis at the club. He had made himself practically undroppable with some electric form. He scored twice on his debut against FC Midtjyl-land, then twice on his league bow against Arsenal. A few weeks later, he scored the only goal in the Manchester derby, and, before he was replaced by a returning Wayne Rooney for the final seconds at Upton Park, had scored a dazzling solo goal to help knock the Hammers out of the FA Cup. Van Gaal – an advocate for youth players – knew he had to control the lightning, and that meant installing Rashford as his number nine.

The cup run had galvanised the support; the injury situation had inspired their voice. Some of the fanbase fell a little back in love with Van Gaal, if not his brand of football; there were a number of reasons for this. Rashford was just one of a number of young players who were given a chance. Andreas Pereira, Donald Love, James Weir, Joe Riley and Cameron Borthwick-Jackson were all among the rookies who were forced to play, and the support – as ever – got behind them. Additionally, Van Gaal's relationship with the press had always been volatile, and United supporters appreciated a man who would stand up for his players. So when he was reported to be on the brink of dismissal, and reacted by responding spikily to reporters, and – perhaps best of all – falling to the ground on the side of the pitch to imitate what he perceived as simulation in the Arsenal game, some United fans couldn't help but feel a little fonder of him.

There was a little ring rust for Rooney after his return. He played as a number 10 against Aston Villa as Rashford scored again. Roy Hodgson insisted it would take more than 'people doubting his form' to convince him not to take Rooney to the upcoming European Championship. "He has got one great advantage over everybody and that is his record of 109 caps and 51 goals," he said (Rooney had scored in the friendly win against France in November). "He also has worked very hard at the other side of being an England captain: needing to stand up, to lead from the front; needing to be the first one into a press conference if things haven't gone well. He merits a place amongst the 23."

Where he would play was another matter, especially as his position at club level was undecided. In the FA Cup semi-final, he played in central midfield against his former club, after a successful trial against Crystal Palace.

"I've known for a few years I can play in that position," said Rooney. "I always knew that one day that is where I would play so I've tried to watch and learn what Paul Scholes did. It is early days, but hopefully if I keep playing there I can get better. We've got pacy, exciting players in the attacking positions so dropping deeper allows me to get on the ball to try and have a big influence on the game."

It was as a defender Rooney made his most crucial contribution at Wembley; with the game goalless, Romelu Lukaku rounded De Gea, and shot towards goal – only to be denied by the United skipper who had got back to clear away from the line. Rooney wasn't the only player in red featuring against his old club – Marouane Fellaini, playing further forward than his skipper, opened the scoring. Everton equalised through a Smalling own goal – in the last minute, Rooney was the first of three players to exchange one-twos with Martial, as the French forward danced his way through the defence to score a fantastic winner. For the first time in nine years, United were going back to the FA Cup final, where Rooney was hoping to claim the one domestic trophy which had eluded him.

When United lost at West Ham in the league to end their chances of getting into the Champions League (Liverpool had come out on top in an all-English Europa League clash), Van Gaal was almost certain to lose his job. If that wasn't enough to disrupt preparation for the final, a bomb scare caused the last league game of the season to be postponed and moved four days before the final. The eight-week layoff had derailed all reasonable momentum of Rooney claiming Charlton's goal record for United too, but he still claimed another record when he scored against Bournemouth for his 100th league goal at Old Trafford, and 245th overall for the club.

In the FA Cup final, Rooney started alongside Carrick in the middle of the park, giving an assured performance. His experience was necessary when Jason Puncheon gave Palace a 78th-minute lead. Where other players would have lost their cool, Rooney had a moment of class – a cross-field dribble where he evaded the attention of no fewer than six Palace players, and still had the presence of mind to place his cross with accuracy rather than thrashing at it. Fellaini chested it down for Mata to smash in a quick equaliser. The game went into extra-time and Chris Smalling was sent off. United, though, had one more go at it – and what a go. Valencia's cross was hacked clear, but only to Jesse Lingard, who struck the ball as sweetly as he ever could into the far corner. Rooney, meanwhile, had already done enough to claim his second man-of-the-match award in an FA Cup final. Unlike 2005, this time he was heading home with a winner's medal.

"Yes, it was a long time," Rooney admitted after the game. "I grew up watching FA Cup finals and it is a competition I have always loved. I lost two finals and at one point here I thought it was going to be a third, so I am just delighted."

Controversy had interrupted the celebrations. Van Gaal had not even collected the trophy when a statement was leaked to the press, allegedly from sources close to Jorge Mendes, the agent of Jose Mourinho, claiming he was to be the new manager of Manchester United. The speculation made it to Wembley quickly enough for players to be questioned about it in the post-match moments.

"It is unfair after we have just won the cup for me to speak about his future," Rooney said when questioned. "It is an important moment for the club, it is the first trophy since Sir Alex. We've got a lot of young lads who haven't won anything. I remember winning my first trophy and it spurs you on, it gives you that desire, determination and belief that you can go on and win more. There has to be an improvement. Certainly in the Premier League it wasn't good enough. You have to set yourself standards and we fell below them. You have to make sure we start challenging for the main trophies."

It was clear that there was an acceptance about what the league performance could mean. A fifth-placed finish was accompanied with a Premier League-low for United of just 49 goals. Only once – under Moyes – had they achieved less than 66 points. If the club had progressed or even stabilised from those days, it was not enough to save Louis van Gaal his position as Manchester United manager. Old Trafford – a byword for continuity – was set to welcome its third new manager in just four years.

Chapter Twenty-One

CAVEATS

I n spite of all that was expected from his former coaches and former team-mates, the relationship between Wayne Rooney and Louis van Gaal had been very strong. Perhaps it shouldn't have been too much of a surprise when considering the qualities of the individuals Van Gaal named as the top five he'd ever coached: Rooney alongside Ronald de Boer, Luis Figo, Philipp Lahm and Bastian Schweinsteiger.

As far as Rooney was concerned, Van Gaal was in his top one.

"Van Gaal is by far the best coach I have worked with – 100 per cent," he told *De Telegraaf.* "His tactical skills, his way of preparing and his attention to the finest of details, I found amazing. Van Gaal knows that the way he works is tough for players. I made him aware of that. I regret how it all ended, yet I know I have learnt a lot from him and I am definitely going to use those lessons when I am a manager."

In 2020, Rooney elaborated on his 'devastation' that Van Gaal had been dismissed.

"For me, it was an absolute joy to work with him," he said. "We should have kept him for a third season. We would have been so much stronger. I felt things were improving and players started to understand his vision. In those two years I learned more than under any other manager. This is why I will be forever grateful to him. Not just for making me captain, but also for all the trust and belief he had in me. At the time I'd decided that I wanted to become a manager. And working with Louis was priceless, because I could learn so much from him. I could not have wished for a better example."

Some might wonder if those comments are completely straight-forward. One could easily feel it was a subtle dig at Sir Alex Ferguson, considering the difficult way that relationship had ended; that was not necessarily the case. After all, it's fair to say Rooney had more direct experience with knowing exactly what Van Gaal wanted as a coach, whereas Ferguson was more of a manager, working with the likes of Queiroz and Meulensteen to delegate and discuss matters of tactics and so on. It wouldn't be disingenuous for Rooney to categorise Van Gaal as a coach and Ferguson as a manager, if only for matters of diplomacy.

No matter how he perceived it, the powers that be at Manchester United decreed that Louis van Gaal was no longer suitable to be the manager of the club. His abrasive personality and dour football was thought to be an ill fit. Jose Mourinho's style of manage-ment is characterised to be the same, which would make someone wonder why he was chosen as Van Gaal's successor. Mourinho, though, was an imposing personality in British football, with only his most recent last five months at Chelsea a period that could be categorised as an unmitigated disaster. Mourinho guar-anteed trophies. It was a risk Manchester United felt they had to take. One could even look at the nuances, the subtle differences between Mourinho and Van Gaal, and deduce that the outgoing manager was more adventurous.

Rooney may not have been happy with Van Gaal leaving, but he seemed content with his replacement, commenting: "It's exciting times for Manchester United. Jose Mourinho is one of the best managers in the world. I'm looking forward to working with him."

The forward was speaking from England's training camp in France ahead of the European Championship. As captain, he gave a pre-tournament speech to the squad.

"He was just giving us past experiences and what to look out for because there's a lot of us who haven't been to a major tournament," Harry Kane said. "It was great of him to stand up and give us an insight into what he's been through."

His place in the squad was guaranteed but his position in the team, as usual, was not. England were blessed with in-form forwards. Harry Kane, Jamie Vardy and Marcus Rashford had momentum and confidence. Raheem Sterling, Dele Alli, Ross Barkley and Adam Lallana were also competition for attacking midfield or wide positions. Rooney's comments earlier in the season, about Scholes and Giggs, had been misinterpreted as an admission that he was considering a change of role – and he was keen to put the record straight on the eve of the tournament.

"Everyone who watches football is entitled to his opinion," he said. "But I know the qualities I have. Firstly I never said I've changed my position. I've changed my game slightly. I've played with players who have changed what they did and become better players. That's natural. I've played in midfield for the past few months at United and it's a natural way of football. I feel, with my football intelligence, I can play there and further my career there as well. My favourite position is being on the pitch, to be honest.

And my ambition for this tournament? That is to do as well as we can and try to win it."

England were in Group B, with Russia, Wales and Slovakia. It was an expanded tournament to include a second round, which meant four of the best third-placed teams from the six groups would qualify for the knockout stages. It didn't lessen the frustration of the first game, when England conceded a late equaliser to Russia. Rooney had started in midfield and had played brilliantly before he was strangely substituted in the 78th minute. Afterwards, the Three Lions lost their composure and were left gutted when their opponents grabbed a goal in injury time. Afterwards, Roy Hodgson claimed he'd made the decision because Rooney was tired. Quizzed on this, the captain simply said 'no'. "That's the manager's decision, I respect it," he added. "He's doing what he feels is right at that moment and that is why he's paid to be manager, to make those decisions."

There was no arguing with the figures – Rooney made 38 of his 55 passes in the opposition half. But it was clear that being Wayne Rooney came with special criteria. The BBC's Phil McNulty gave a curious assessment, admitting it was a 'midfield masterclass' before qualifying that with the following: "Rooney's display must be placed in context. It came against a very poor Russia side who allowed him time and space."

It was the sort of backhanded compliment Rooney had become used to receiving. A strange juxtaposition of events had created a scenario where Rooney's status and accomplishments were now almost public property, subjected to continuing arguments about whether he had met, surpassed or failed to reach his potential. On the one hand you had the trophies and the personal accolades. Five league titles, a European Cup, a Club World Cup – the full house of domestic trophies. The goalscoring record for England. The inevitability that Wayne could have his poorest goalscoring season and still break the United goalscoring record in the coming months.

On the other, you had the last three years – a moment in time when the greatest manager of all felt he was dispensable, a moment in time that almost caused the groundswell of opinion about an alleged decline. That this moment took place when Rooney was just 27 meant that the following three years – in which he was, to most observers, the best outfield player in his team's inarguable decline – were pitted against a backdrop of Ronaldo and Messi continuing their personal wrestle over the Ballon d'Or.

Balanced against that was the idea of what everyone felt Rooney should have been. For a good few years the sight of Rooney in England white or United red was aposematic; recently, however, he had been seen as representative of his team's fall from grace, in spite of his efforts usually making things look better than they actually were. Football nostalgia is rarely sympathetic. Rooney's accomplished style of finishing, his fine range of passing, his ability to score goals that didn't even enter the consciousness of his contemporaries – these qualities still existed, but the appreciation for them diminished in the light of what people expected him to achieve.

It could be said that Rooney himself fed into that narrative. A few beers every few months over a few years didn't seem like the biggest crime but he may as well have been propping up the bar at the Rovers Return in comparison to the clean living Lionel Messi, who himself might have blushed at the dedication to physical development shown by Ronaldo. But there is not being one of the greatest two players on the planet, and there's the perception that was often projected onto Rooney – that he was unintelligent and yobbish, a representation of the worst parts of British working class culture. This was, of course, grossly unfair, as anyone who shared a training pitch with him attests.

The point remained – sometimes it didn't seem to matter how well Wayne Rooney did. Every piece of praise had to come with a caveat.

Back at the Euros, Hodgson could not afford to take off Rooney against Wales, who went into half-time ahead. The captain was inspirational in a second-half fightback that saw Sturridge net a late winner. "The one who really deserves a pat on the back is Wayne," said Hodgson. "We thought that if we could get him being Wayne Rooney doing his job here, we'll get a lot out of it. We'll get a goalscorer from distance, we'll get a passer and we'll get the benefit of his experience and captaincy. He showed work-rate, desire and composure. When you have a lot of the ball, it is very easy to lose composure but we didn't. Wayne was prepared to stay on the ball that little bit longer and make the extra pass, and not be tempted by the killer pass or killer shot.

"When he is having bad moments we ask questions, but we never get swept along in that tide of 'Rooney The King' or 'Rooney shouldn't be in the 23'. If you are England captain you are never far from headlines but we don't pay attention to those things."

Again, it seemed strange for Hodgson to state '*bad moments*'. The bad moments were England's collectively – Rooney himself did not have a catalogue of performances that were so notably poor that they were worthy of reference. At his worst, Rooney was still tireless in his effort to improve, never a passenger and never a handicap.

After a dour draw with Slovakia (in which many players, including the captain, were rested, though he did come on for the last 34 minutes) secured qualification to present a second round clash with Iceland, Rooney was in upbeat mood. "We want to win it and that's the aim," he said. "I'm not going to say we are a group of young players so we'll be happy to get to the quarter-finals, the future's bright over the next two to four years and all that. You don't play for the achievement of getting to a quarter-final. What would myself and the other players get out of that?"

England did make a quick start against Iceland. Raheem Sterling was brought down in the third minute. Rooney's penalty was low, strong and good. But Iceland's response was equally impressive – they levelled within a minute, and then capitalised on poor goal-keeping to score in the 18th. England's own retort was poor. With five minutes left, Hodgson took off Rooney for Marcus Rashford, who was unable to make a difference. England were out – and, for serial underachievers, this was the greatest humiliation since the 1950 World Cup defeat by the USA.

Roy Hodgson resigned almost immediately after the game. Rooney was not quite ready to throw in the towel. "It's a sad day for us," he admitted. "Sometimes not always the best team wins. Once they got in the lead we knew it would be difficult to get the goal back because they are well organised. There are always upsets in football – it's not tactics, it's just unfortunate. I'm still available to play. It'll be interesting to see who comes in."

That incoming manager was to be Sam Allardyce, whose greatest achievement in football was arguably getting a modest Bolton Wanderers to overachieve for several years. He had most recently engineered a 'great escape' at Sunderland with just a few months in charge.

With all the change at Old Trafford, Rooney was looking to the future there too, despite the award of a testimonial which normally serves as a cause to reflect. The opponents, inevitably, were Everton, just a few days before the season – which gave home fans the first opportunity to see a brand new strike partnership.

Jose Mourinho had made four summer signings. There was the world record return of Juventus midfielder Paul Pogba, the defensive arrival of Eric Bailly, the creative trickery of Henrikh

Mkhitaryan and the free transfer of Swedish legend Zlatan Ibrahimovic. At 34, Ibrahimovic was four years senior to his new
captain, but had the confidence to boast that this was not going
to be a Dad's Army frontline.

"I said many years ago the perfect partner for a striker is Wayne
Rooney," said Ibrahimovic. "He works not only for himself but
for the striker and the whole team. I'm absolutely happy to be one
of the guys beside him. Every big player can work with other big
players. That's not a problem. It's up to the coach what he wants
but, with him, I see no problems. Only success. He has had a
fantastic career. It's not easy to be in top clubs for so many years.
He has performed at the top every year. He is a perfect example
for young players."

After the testimonial – a poor 0-0 game – Rooney's agent Paul
Stretford commented: "Should United make it clear they want
Wayne to stay beyond 2019, we will be sitting down very quickly
and ensuring that will happen."

The Rooney-Zlatan show got off to a flyer, with both scoring in a
3-1 win at Bournemouth. It was the first time for a while that there
was a traditional look to their link-up. Mourinho still played his
favoured 4-2-3-1 formation, with Rooney as a number 10, but he
and Zlatan would get involved in the play, even if the new arrival
was definitely more inclined to be the natural number nine.

Ibrahimovic scored in the first half of the first home game
against Southampton, and when a penalty was awarded early in
the second, Rooney showed some of the deference displayed in his
earlier career by allowing Zlatan to take it. He did, and scored. So
there was not necessarily a problem with age – but Mourinho was
accused of sacrificing youth for experience, and with Rashford
and Martial now contesting one position on the left, it meant one
star's potential was likely to be curtailed.

That was the same in many of the forward positions. Many felt Pogba would be a better number 10 than Rooney. Juan Mata was still at the club and would inevitably enter the conversation. Then there was Mkhitaryan, Lingard, Young, and that was before considering the options of Carrick, Herrera and Fellaini in the middle. One of the most frequent observations of Rooney at this time was that his willingness to do anything for his team was effectively taken advantage of; as before under Van Gaal, he was the player who found himself moving around to accommodate players when either others were not playing well or the system did not appear to work. Mourinho's strong start of four successive wins was followed by three consecutive defeats, including one against Manchester City – now managed by Pep Guardiola – in which the tactics appeared to be all wrong.

During this period Rooney was moved back into midfield and then to the substitute's bench, from which he came on in four successive matches as United turned their form around.

There was a similar positional debate as Sam Allardyce made his England bow against Slovakia. Rooney made his 116th international appearance alongside Kane in a traditional 4-4-2. England had to wait until injury time for their winner through Adam Lallana. Before the match, Allardyce could not have spoken more glowingly of the man he said would remain captain: "I've seen Wayne play for United up front, in the hole, down the right, central midfield. All the managers that he has had will play him anywhere to get him on the field."

After it, however, the manager said Rooney had played 'wherever he had wanted to be'. The accusation of indiscipline – or that Rooney saw himself as the player who picked the team – seemed to dog the player for the next month as he was phased out of the United side. Before Allardyce had a chance to publicly explain, he was sensationally sacked from the England job after being set up by a newspaper sting. His replacement was Gareth Southgate, who made a remark about players needing to show 'positional discipline', apparently in direct reference to Allardyce's comments.

"Wayne can play any number of different positions," Southgate said. "The only thing I would say is that I go back to one of the things we work on with the team, which is tactical discipline, positional discipline, in and out of possession."

However, Rooney was quick to reveal that the outgoing manager had actually said sorry to him. "It was a bit of a misunderstanding after the last game, when Sam came out and said I play where I want," he said. "I played exactly to instructions. That was a big misunderstanding that I seemed to get slaughtered for. Sam knew he made a mistake. He said that to me on the plane home. I got battered for my performance, which I felt was actually a decent performance."

If Rooney was hoping for support from his club manager, he would presumably have been bemused to hear Mourinho's take: "Honestly, there was a Wayne before the Slovakia-England match and a Wayne after it."

Asked if he would play Rooney against Zorya Luhansk in the Europa League, the boss said he was going to 'protect' him. "I am not sure if I will play him from the start because of the situation the media created for him," Mourinho insisted. "He can't afford to have a performance that is not really good. Because I am here to protect him, I have to analyse whether the best thing for him is to start the game."

Ask anyone who had spent a concerted amount of time with Rooney and they will speak of his incredible awareness of the game. Many also spoke of their surprise that the player they got to know was much different to the personality who had been portrayed in the press. It seems that Allardyce, Southgate and Mourinho were all guilty of allowing their preconception to become a misconception.

At club level, at least, it didn't appear to be personal. "When you leave a player out for a game, sometimes for a player it gives them freedom of the mind when the manager says, 'I'm leaving you out for this reason or that reason.' The players didn't get that," Rooney told BT Sport, recounting this period in 2018. "That's the most difficult thing for a player to work out, why you're not playing. There was nothing like, 'You're not doing this, you're not doing that.' It gives you something to work on.

"I knew Zlatan was one of his big signings, he came in and was scoring goals and I maybe wasn't playing to the level which I knew I could do. I think it's only right for a player to know why they're not playing. I knew myself that if I wasn't performing well enough, I wasn't going to be in the team. That's what happened. The big thing with Jose was the communication with the players. I know the players, they weren't happy with that."

Rooney had been questioned before but never had his place in the team – for club or country – been in significant doubt, other than the late days under Ferguson. But he was booed by some of the crowd towards the end of England's game with Malta at Wembley, and was then dropped to the bench for the trip to Slovenia. He insisted he wouldn't retire from international duty – and was cheered when he came on with the score at 0-0 (which is how the game finished).

The omissions invited speculation on Rooney's future – especially when he was back to his role as a bit-part player for United after the international break. Mourinho insisted that he was not prepared to allow a transfer. "It's not true at all – he is going nowhere," the manager said. "He's 31 now but I know he can play at the top level. What's going to happen at 32, 33, 34, 35 – I can't make this mental exercise. What I can say is that he's a very good player and a very important player for us. I know he's the type of player I need. He's my captain, he is the team captain and he behaves like that."

He was given two starts in the Europa League games with Fenerbahce – the first won at home, the latter lost away, though he did score in that defeat – 'finally' according to Mourinho, who added, "Maybe it's also a key point in terms of his self-confidence."

Rooney was recalled to the starting line-up for England against Scotland. "He is a big-game player with big-match experience," said Southgate. "A night like this will be perfect for him… Class is permanent." It was an understated performance in his 119th cap – extending his record with the most for an outfield player – as England won 3-0.

The following week, Rooney was pictured on the front of a tabloid newspaper looking bleary-eyed and wearing England training clothes. The player's representatives issued an instant apology. "Wayne is sorry that pictures taken with fans have been published today," the statement read. "Although it was a day off for the whole squad and staff, he fully recognises the images are inappropriate for someone in his position. Wayne spoke privately to both Gareth Southgate and Dan Ashworth to unreservedly apologise. He would like to further extend that apology to any young fans who have seen these pictures."

Rooney was omitted from the England squad that had played against Spain the evening before the pictures were published, though it was unclear whether this was in anticipation of the controversy or just part of Southgate's continuing process of moving on without the player who was still officially the national team captain.

United faced Arsenal the following weekend. Mourinho launched a passionate, if contradictory, defence of his player. "I learned since I was a kid that if someone lends me a pencil or something I have to take even better care of it than if it was mine," he said. "I think you have to build something to protect what is not yours. When my players go to the national team they belong to the national team. What happens there, for good or for bad, I don't interfere."

He was asked if he felt Rooney should have been drinking on his night off, and replied: "I would have a great answer for you but I don't want to speak about it. But if you go one by one, to see where these 23 players were, some of them were in worse places than the hotel bar. Even if you build a wall around you to try to feel protected from what people write and say about you, that wall always has points of fragility. It always has some little holes and we are not [made of] steel. We are flesh and blood so it has an effect."

Rooney did not start against the Gunners – Mourinho explaining afterwards, bluntly: "I believed Anthony Martial, Marcus Rashford and Juan Mata were faster than Wayne, better attacking opponents one on one" – though he did come on for Martial with 27 minutes remaining of a game that ended 1-1. The result left United in sixth place, eight points behind Liverpool and Manchester City.

Rooney broke his personal silence the following week. "What has been going on is disgraceful," he said. "I feel as if the media are trying to write my obituary. I love playing for my country and I'm proud of my achievements to date, but I haven't finished yet."

More achievements followed. Rooney started against Feyenoord and was in great form, scoring the opening goal. To call his interchange with Zlatan in the build-up a one-two would be reductive to both parties. First of all, Rooney did marvellously to spin clear of a challenge on the wing before playing the ball to Ibrahimovic. The return pass was delayed and timed perfectly. Rooney, free of a challenge, clipped the ball over the keeper with a touch of class. The goal took him past his first strike partner at Old Trafford, Ruud van Nistelrooy, as the club's record goalscorer in European competition with 39, and one behind Sir Bobby Charlton's overall record of 249.

"I'm proud and pleased," he said after his team scored three more times to win 4-0. "It is always a great feeling to score goals – and to score them for this club. I am sure there is plenty more to come. I am happy with the win first of all, but also the goal."

It had taken a while, but now Charlton's club record was finally within touching distance. Mourinho was not about to be swayed by sentiment, so Rooney was back to his role as a substitute against West Ham in the league – against the same opponents from the start in the League Cup, he was fantastic. But in his eagerness to impress so that he could earn a starting role at Goodison Park and hopefully make history there, he was booked – so would miss out through suspension.

Rooney was recalled afterwards but was not greatly influential in wins at Palace and West Brom, so he didn't even make appearances from the bench in the next three games as United extended their winning run in all competitions to seven.

His next game came against Reading in the FA Cup in the first game of 2017. His moment of history came just seven minutes in – Martial dribbled on the left and played the ball to Mata. The Spaniard clipped a ball across to Rooney, who stuck out his right leg. The connection off his knee was strong enough to take it into the net for goal number 249 for Manchester United. Like his most famous goal, that came in the same corner of the same goal in the same stadium, it was not struck with the intended body part – but, just like that goal against City, would be no less memorable for it.

He had continued to talk of the future, but Rooney would have been acutely aware that events of the present meant his days at United could very much be of the past. Marcus Rashford scored his 13th and 14th goals for the club in another 4-0 win to show that at the biggest clubs in the world, time just keeps on moving, and today's records are merely tomorrow's goals for the next group of starlets coming through.

"The ones who are closest to the record have left the club so, especially in modern football, it will be really difficult to beat it," Jose Mourinho said. "But Marcus is only 19. If he plays for United until the end of his career, maybe he can do it, but Rooney and Sir Bobby scored a lot of goals. Whether Wayne plays or not, he's always positive with the group, a good captain, a good pro, a team player and a humble guy."

It had been almost a month between goals 248 and 249. Rooney started against Hull in the League Cup, but was brought off. He was brought on as a half-time sub in a 1-1 draw with Liverpool, and he was again called on from the bench to rescue the game at Stoke after United had fallen behind to a Mata own goal.

In injury time, United were awarded a free-kick on the left hand side of the box. It was not quite on the angle – much better positioned for Rooney, who was standing over it, to whip in a cross to the back post, where Ibrahimovic was. Rooney, though, went for goal. His strike could not have been more perfect. The technique to whip the ball high over the defence and get it back down quickly enough to kiss the crossbar on the way in was simply masterful. The euphoria in the away end behind the goal was both at avoiding defeat and at seeing a moment of history. Rooney – true to character – celebrated just a moment, but immediately turned back to the halfway line, gesturing for his team-mates to recover the ball in the hunt to turn one point into three. It was not to be, but it did not sour a historic day for club and player.

Wayne steps up deep in injury time to whip home a fierce free-kick against Stoke City – his 250th goal for Manchester United and one that took him past Sir Bobby Charlton as the club's all-time leading goalscorer

"I want to win my place back," Rooney said afterwards. "I just have to keep going. I need to keep trying to perform and score to make sure I stay in the team."

Others were quick to play up the significance of his achievement, even if the man himself had seemed quite reluctant to. "It's a big thing – many great players have been here at this club and his name is right up on top," said Ibrahimovic. "I'm very proud to have been on the same field when he did it and hopefully he can continue to do what he's doing. He's a complete player. Everybody knows what Wayne is. But this country has to appreciate him. I don't see any other strikers like him today."

From contemporary legends to those of years gone by. Darren Fletcher now played for Stoke, but had recovered from the disappointment of the dropped points to pay a tribute to his close friend: "Getting the United goalscoring record will get Wayne more recognition now. But when he has retired people will look back at what he achieved and look at all his records and will be talking about one of England's all-time greatest players – and one of Manchester United's all-time greatest players."

And Sir Bobby Charlton – who had been one of the first to congratulate Rooney for passing his record with England – was quick to pass on his good wishes again. "All records are lovely but especially his," he said. "I had a word with him and congratulated him. What a goal it was too. Right in the top corner. Anyone would have been pleased with that one."

Rooney did feature in the next few games but then picked up a problematic ankle injury which effectively ruled him out for two months, although there were various moments where he was called back into the squad. He won a League Cup medal as a non-playing substitute when United defeated Southampton, but remained determined to show his worth to the club.

Mourinho seemed open to the idea of using him if needed; against Anderlecht in the second leg of the Europa League quarter-final, he was named on the bench. "His experience can be useful and if he comes through the training session in a positive way, I'll select him," Mourinho said in the pre-match press conference. "If we need a goal, he can help us, and if we need to keep a result, he can help us too. When you get to a certain age, and I'm not saying he's old, it's a bit more difficult to recover. We need everyone we can. Hopefully he can be a help."

United did need that experience – they needed extra-time – but still did not use Rooney as they squeaked through 2-1. He was recalled as one of eight changes for the next league match at Burnley, but now it seemed as though Mourinho was rotating his squad with the emphasis on keeping his preferred players fresh for Europe. There was, however, the chance of a reprieve. Ibrahimovic had suffered a serious injury against Anderlecht and would be out for several months. There was a place up for grabs in the first team. Martial and Rooney both scored at Burnley – Rooney's goal a scuffed opportunist's take that just crossed the line after a defensive error – to state their case.

If there was a place up for grabs, it could well have been Rooney's. He had a mini hot-streak, scoring a penalty in a 1-1 draw against Swansea and then the consolation goal in a defeat at Spurs, which turned out to be the last ever goal at the soon-to-be reconstructed White Hart Lane. It was a goal from point-blank range which indicated all the instincts of a predatory striker were still intact.

Earlier that week, Rooney had made his feelings clear. "Would I like to stay? I've been at this club 13 years, but I want to play football," he said. "Here? Of course. I think football changes. You have different challenges in your career. This season I haven't played as much as I would have liked to. I've tried to help the team on the pitch and off the pitch. I haven't thrown my toys out of the pram but I'm a football player and I want to play football. The more I play, the better, and the more I feel I can help the team."

United finished sixth in the league, with the last few games effectively sacrificed for a calculated push at the Champions League through winning the Europa League. In the final league game of the campaign (against a Crystal Palace side now managed by Sam Allardyce), Rooney started, and was brought off with two minutes to go. The supporters at Old Trafford had a fair idea they would not be seeing Rooney play for their team on that pitch again – and so, when he left the arena, he received a warm reception from a fanbase that had a mixed relationship with him over the past seven years.

Jose Mourinho tactfully avoided questions about the player's future by nipping in and out of the press conference room while most of the journalists were still watching the players do their post-season 'lap of honour' around the pitch.

United headed to Sweden for the Europa League final amidst the backdrop of a city in mourning; the Manchester Arena was targeted by a terrorist, and 23 people, including the culprit, were killed. Stockholm – the host city for the final – was still in shock of their own attack a few weeks earlier, when five people were killed.

The decision was taken for the game to go ahead, but there was an understandably sombre mood as the football world came together at the aptly named Friends Arena; United triumphed in a low-key game they controlled from the moment Paul Pogba struck an early goal. Mkhitaryan added a second in the 48th minute – Mourinho's side were able to see the game out in professional fashion. In injury time, Rooney was brought on for Mata, and was handed the captain's armband by Antonio Valencia, despite the Ecuadorian staying on for the remainder of the game.

It was such a public statement that neither Rooney nor Mourinho could avoid it in their post-match interviews, even though they were both non-committal.

Mourinho: "Wayne Rooney was ready to play, he was a big option. But I didn't need to attack at 2-0... He is a very important player for us. If he stays next season I'd be very happy."

Rooney: "I don't know... I've got decisions to make over the next few weeks, I'll have a word with my family, and then I'll decide. As soon as I know what's going on then, I'm sure you'll know."

Pushed if he had made that decision already, he admitted, "More or less, yeah... First of all I've always been a team player. This year, I've never once sulked, I've understood what was best for the team, I've tried to help when the manager's played me. I think a younger me would have been a lot more frustrated. I understand what's right and what's needed for the club and I respect that. I've been happy to help the club win trophies and that's the way it's been over the last 18 months. And that's a decision I have to make now – whether I want to continue doing that or go on and play more regular football."

The conclusion to this saga seemed obvious. The only thing that wasn't certain was Rooney's destination, considering he still had time on his contract. Ibrahimovic's injury had necessitated a push for a top centre-forward, and Mourinho's first choice seemed to be Romelu Lukaku of Everton. It would be convenient all round if those strikers exchanged dressing rooms. Ultimately – although the deals were conducted separately – that is what happened. With much less fanfare than the noise that surrounded his departure, 13 years after leaving Goodison Park, 'the boy wonder' was going home.

Chapter Twenty-Two

ALWAYS A BLUE

A t Manchester United, Wayne Rooney had experienced success to place him in the company of football's elite. You always need luck with these moments – the first two and last four years could not be construed as the glory days. But the seven in between, from 2006 to 2013, were some of the greatest days in United history. The condensed two-year spell from 2007 to 2009 was probably the most successful ever, when Rooney won five of the 12 major trophies he would claim while at the club. At the time of his departure, his 253 goals were the most anyone had scored for United. His 559 appearances placed him at number six in that chart – behind Gary Neville, Bill Foulkes, Paul Scholes, Sir Bobby Charlton and Ryan Giggs. He won twice as many trophies as Bryan Robson and scored more than three times as many goals as Eric Cantona.

Rooney contributed to that period of success as much as anyone.

His highlights reel was just as spectacular as Cristiano Ronaldo's. Throughout his entire spell at the club, he was moved around to benefit the team. At first, that was partly to accommodate the bulging talent in the side. As time wore on, it was clear that Rooney was so good that where there was an emergency, he was the player most capable of standing guard and fulfilling his team's needs. When the greatest days had passed, Rooney was the figurehead and talisman, inspiring his club to historic landmarks, and passing them himself. In the process, he achieved one of the most coveted records in international football, despite being written off on more than one occasion, and despite playing in a relatively poor team for most of the last half of his England career.

Opinion on whether or not he had fulfilled his potential would still be divided and likely will be for years after this record of his career is published. Perhaps if it were not for Ronaldo and Messi, Rooney's accomplishments would have been seen in a different light, for when you really take time to look at it, they were simply remarkable.

In the time between Wayne Rooney leaving Manchester United and him eventually retiring from playing, United did not win another trophy. You could call that coincidence. You could also say it was possibly a fair assessment that without Rooney's personal drive to do better as a team, without his relentless quest for more, United were far worse off. Talent is easy to acquire – character is not.

In the summer of 2017, as he moved back to Goodison Park, he revealed that even though he had a trophy cabinet the envy of any player in English football, the one medal he would treasure more than any other would be the one he could win with his boyhood club.

"Winning trophies with Everton would be the pinnacle," he

admitted. "I want to be part of it. It's a great feeling to be back. I'm ecstatic."

Rooney revealed he hadn't told his son, Kai, about the move. "I've known for the last couple of weeks but had to keep it from him. I kept it quiet from Mum and Dad too because I knew they wouldn't be able to hold it in. I didn't tell Kai because I didn't want him speaking to his mates at school but when I told him he was made up. He jumped on me. It will be great for him to come back and watch his dad play – he'll be buzzing."

He said that he had realised before Christmas that he would have to move on from United. "I understand managers have to make decisions but I knew I also have to make decisions for my career," he said. "I spoke to Jose in January and he always said he wanted me to stay and help the team until the end of the season. I have done that but I knew I had to leave to move forward for my career. Coming back here is the right place for me but I have to go and prove myself. It will be a big challenge – I've not come to a retirement home – and a lot of pressure but I've had that my whole career."

Everton were now coached by Ronald Koeman. The Dutchman had been rewarded for a seventh-placed finish with a huge transfer kitty, partly funded by the sale of Lukaku to Manchester United for £75m. Rooney on a free transfer was a relative bargain, and Koeman showed the club's ambition with the £25m signing of goalkeeper Jordan Pickford, the same fee for Burnley's defender Michael Keane, and roughly the same again for Ajax schemer Davy Klaassen. Rooney looked to be the headline capture until Gylfi Sigurdsson was brought in for £40m in mid-August. With the scale of the investment, Koeman needed to achieve.

Rooney's injury issues had presented an opportunity for Gareth Southgate to quietly usher the player out of the international picture, but his new manager was keen to talk up the striker's chances.

"First of all, if he plays really good football for his club it is possible that he will come back to the national team," Koeman said after watching Rooney net in two pre-season friendlies. "But it always starts with his performances for the club."

Everton's preparations for the campaign included Europa League qualifiers, which they navigated with comfort to qualify for the group stages. In the league, they faced Stoke at home on the opening day – a homecoming for Wayne Rooney. In the 45th minute, he scored the game's only goal, a classic header thumped with the power of a volley.

"There is a lot of expectation," Rooney admitted after the game. "There are still some fans who maybe thought I wasn't good enough to come back here. But it's up to me to prove myself. I could have gone to another Premier League team and taken my foot off the gas. But coming back here? I've got to be the best I can be. It's the club I grew up supporting, the club I want to play for."

There was an almost audible tinge of sentiment attached to the cheer which greeted Rooney's goal; an affectionate resonance you would not associate with someone who was returning to a place he was hated.

"I don't think today you'd find any Evertonian with many bad things to say about Wayne," says Nick Chadwick, the former striker who played alongside Wayne in his early weeks in the first team. "I'm sure if he could he'd be sat with his kids in the Gwladys Street End cheering his team on. That was always genuine. He was often left out of trips back at Everton by Sir Alex and I always felt that was a mark of respect. He would have understood the pressure Wayne was under and the conflict within him. But it was great for Wayne that he was able to go back and I'm sure that any anger towards him softened over time."

Scoring a winner against Stoke was all well and good. But

Rooney steps out at Goodison for his first game back in the blue of Everton,
a Europa League qualifier against Slovakian side MFK Ruzomberok

Everton had brought Rooney back with the hope that he would elevate them to achieve positive results in games where they had traditionally struggled – that he would provide the touch of class required to take them into the top four. From the second game to the ninth, he was going to have a chance to showcase that influence, with games against all of the major contenders (bar Liverpool) for those positions.

The first was a trip to the Etihad Stadium – and the visitors survived a flurry of attacks from Manchester City before gaining a major reward on the break. Dominic Calvert-Lewin's cross found Rooney lurking in a pocket of space – he made no mistake with the finish, to notch the 200th league goal of his career. City's domination finally earned them an equaliser, but that Everton were strong enough to come away with a point was seen as a positive result.

Rooney's own start to the season was seen as impressive enough for Gareth Southgate to reconsider his stance; Rooney, though, shocked many by announcing that he was no longer going to play for his country. "It was great that Gareth Southgate called me to tell me he wanted me back in the England squad," Rooney said. "However, having already thought long and hard, I told Gareth that I had now decided to retire for good from international football. It is a really tough decision and one I have discussed with my family, my manager at Everton and those closest to me. Playing for England has always been special to me. Every time I was selected as a player or captain was a real privilege and I thank everyone who helped me. But I believe now is the time to bow out."

Koeman welcomed the news. "It's a good decision for him and for Everton," he said. "Wayne spoke to me about this, he had a talk with the national coach and he made his decision. He thinks it's the best for Everton. I didn't give him advice. I'm not the right person in his decision. There's always the decision by the player and I respect that."

Just when things seem to be heading in a strong direction, they fell apart. Everton travelled to Croatia after the City game, and got the draw needed to get through to the Europa League groups – but three days later, they went to London to face Chelsea, and looked leggy in a 2-0 defeat. Rooney cut a frustrated figure and was eventually booked for dissent.

That was merely the beginning of his disciplinary issues. During the international break, Rooney was arrested and charged with drink-driving. He admitted he'd made a 'terrible mistake and let down his family'. Everton fined him two weeks' wages.

September was a desperately poor month – losses at home to Spurs (0-3), and then in Atalanta by the same score, projected a lot of pressure on Koeman, who admitted he was 'worried' about going to Old Trafford in the next league game.

Jose Mourinho was pleased to see his former striker, admitting earlier in the summer that he missed him. "I'm not the kind of guy that normally gets emotional in my job but I did when he left," he said. "I miss him a lot because he's a fantastic guy. Wayne deserves what he got – and what he got was our desire for him to stay and our respect by making it completely clear that we would have liked him to stay."

After the pantomime booing that comes for every returning player, Rooney was given a generous reception when he was taken off close to the end of the game. It helped that United were already ahead in a game they went on to win 4-0. The painful result plunged the Toffees into the relegation zone.

Insult was added to injury in the next league game. In the first half against Bournemouth, Rooney was caught by Simon Francis' elbow, causing a cut which bled profusely above his eye. He played on, though when The Cherries took the lead in the 49th minute, Koeman made the shock decision to bring off Rooney and replace him with Oumar Niasse. The decision was vindicated – Niasse scored two late goals to give the manager a crucial win.

It meant a place for Niasse in the starting 11, and a place for Rooney on the bench, in the following game at home to Burnley. The visitors took an early lead – Rooney was brought on with 25 minutes to go. He could do nothing to alter the result.

"The reason was to change and bring a second striker in, I had to make a decision about the midfield," Koeman explained afterwards. "I opted for Gylfi Sigurdsson and I thought Nikola Vlasic did well on the ball last Thursday and that was the reason not to start with Wayne. I explained the situation, that we were changing the style of play and like every professional player he accepted it."

Rooney was back in the team for the trip to Brighton – and scored a last-minute penalty to snatch a point. Koeman described his player as 'world class' after the match: "Taking penalties is not the most difficult job but at this moment yes, because it's totally different, it's 1-0 down in a difficult situation and the team needs points. If you keep your calmness in these types of situations that is experience and world class. Let's hope today gives the boys confidence and calmness to play and be more comfortable."

It didn't. Everton were beaten at home by Lyon, with Rooney not in the team. He was back in from the start against Arsenal, and scored the opening goal from midfield. It was almost exactly 15 years to the day since his goal against the Gunners which made the entire world take notice. His strike here was special, too – taking a touch to get it out from his feet before curling the ball into the top corner from outside the box. Unfortunately, though, it did not result in a win for his team this time around – Arsenal responded with a number of late goals to inflict an embarrassing 5-2 defeat on the hosts.

Everton fans were furious and Koeman was dismissed later that day. It seemed a reluctant choice, as apparently proven by the time it took the club to appoint a successor. That man was Sam Allardyce, who of course had that brief moment with Rooney a year earlier. He was appointed five weeks after Koeman was sacked, and was watching from the stands as David Unsworth took charge of his last match as interim manager against West Ham – who were, in one of those strange twists of fate, now under the leadership of David Moyes.

Everton enjoyed the new manager bounce before he was even installed – after 18 minutes, they were awarded a penalty, which Rooney missed, but then converted the rebound. Shortly afterwards he got his second, a more straightforward finish from 10 yards. The hosts were in control from that moment, though there was nothing to suggest what was going to follow in the second half. In the 66th minute, Hammers goalkeeper Joe Hart rushed out of his goal. A similar impulse had cost his team the earlier penalty – this time he came out of his box, but the risk seemed to pay off when he cleared the ball over the halfway line and so away from danger. Or so he thought.

The ball dropped almost perfectly for Rooney, six yards inside his own half. What followed was a showcase of vision, talent and technique; all elements perfectly combined and demonstrated, as Rooney struck the ball first time towards goal. Hart was still out of his box. All the shot needed to have was the right blend of power and accuracy – and it did. For the second time in his career, Rooney had scored from the halfway line in the Premier League.

It was his first goal at the Gwladys Street End since he had returned to the club. His first hat-trick for Everton – and completed with one of the greatest goals ever seen at this famous old stadium. It was, however, familiar territory for West Ham – who had conceded a similar goal to him when he was playing under Moyes at United. It was also familiar for Joe Hart, who had been the goalkeeper when Rooney scored what was described as the best goal in Old Trafford history, the overhead kick against City.

More firsts followed. At Anfield in December, Rooney scored his first Merseyside derby goal to earn his team a point. Liverpool boss Jurgen Klopp had said before the game: "I'm not sure if it's allowed, but I like Wayne Rooney as a person. I've always liked him as a player. I would be silly not to worry about him. But if you only worry about him that would be another big mistake." He presumably wasn't quite so fond of the striker after he cost him two points.

The rich run of form continued. At St James' Park – such a happy hunting ground in his United days – Rooney scored the only goal, a poacher's finish after the goalkeeper spilled his header. He made it six goals in five league games when scoring from the spot against Swansea – a 3-1 win helped move Everton into the top half for the first time since the second week of the season.

Sam Allardyce seemed very impressed with Rooney's form, but stressed that he might have to get used to being brought off in games to keep him fresh now he was 32. "What can I say, (Jay-Jay) Okocha and (Youri) Djorkaeff were the two easiest players I've ever had to handle in my career," said Allardyce. "Wayne is very similar. But I think it's all about the 30 games we've already had and managing that situation. So if I can afford to substitute him, then it gets him rested a little bit more for the next one. I wouldn't say he was that happy with me. He's never happy, Wayne! But he's a great professional."

Allardyce expressed that he felt the return to Goodison had come at an ideal moment in Wayne's career: "The move looks like it was perfect for Everton and perfect for him – and he's proving that now. We need him at that level for the rest of the season."

More tributes were paid to Rooney over the coming weeks. Dominic Calvert-Lewin was just five when Rooney made his professional debut, and admitted it was 'surreal' to line up alongside him. "He's taught me a lot," he admitted.

In January, Theo Walcott was signed, and though he had played alongside Rooney for England, he admitted the former United man was an 'inspiration'. "Without a doubt – just having him putting his arm around me at times with England, looking after me and learning from him in training," he said. "He hasn't come here to put his feet up at all."

With the form stabilised, Everton were content to see an uneventful conclusion to the campaign – picking up some decent wins, but still lacking something against the better opponents, and occasionally dropping silly points.

Rooney was visibly frustrated to be taken off in games, especially against Manchester City and Liverpool, where he was substituted with less than an hour played. "We needed more legs and as talented as Wayne is, we needed to get him about more," Allardyce said. "Nobody is too big to be hooked off… I can agree with you, to a certain degree, that Wayne struggles against the very best opposition. He didn't play very well in the first half against Manchester City but, before that, he had been outstanding and we had been a little bit short in midfield in recent weeks anyway."

He was now playing in that midfield area, with Allardyce later praising him as 'one of our best passers'; and despite Rooney's obvious dissatisfaction, he repaid the compliment to the work Allardyce had done after a banner had been displayed by fans showing their own discontent with the manager in their 2-0 win at Huddersfield in late April. "He's thick-skinned," Rooney said. "I think he has the full support from the team. Since he has come in, we'd be sixth if that was the start of the season. We're moving in the right direction, but that takes time and we're improving every game."

Rooney had been brought off with 63 minutes played of that game. It invited speculation that he might already be looking to leave as he was not quite ready to accept a role as a bit-part player. There was interest from the MLS, with D.C. United rumoured to have put in an offer.

Ahead of what was anticipated to be his last game – for good this time – at West Ham, David Moyes paid a glowing tribute. "I always thought Wayne could play in goal, as a right-back or a cen-tre-half," he said. "It was because he was a footballer, a genuine, old-fashioned street footballer. When Wayne was playing for the first team he would go back and kick the ball with his pals in the street. Those stories are ones we all hope still exist but I don't know that they do now. For me, he was the last of that type.

"When he was only a boy he would kick all the balls away on the training ground and I would get annoyed. But one day we had a small eight-a-side game and he scored by chipping the goalie right from the byline. It was one of those moments where the staff were looking round at each other and saying 'did he really just do that?' It was a moment when time nearly stood still for us. I don't want him to do to us what he did the last time so I would rather him not playing if I'm honest. He will always be a legend at Manchester United and respected for what he has done but he will always be an Evertonian."

Rooney didn't play – so the Huddersfield game ended up as a low-key way to bow out, although Allardyce insisted it was not a foregone conclusion that the player would be leaving. "There appears to be an interest from D.C. United," he admitted. "But Wayne has not asked to leave, and neither has he had a confrontation with me or been in any difficult situation since I've been here."

A few days after the season concluded with a 3-1 defeat at Upton Park and an eighth-placed finish, one departure from Goodison at least was confirmed when Allardyce was relieved of his duties. He insisted that there was no difficult relationship with Rooney that might have contributed to his exit.

"If anyone suggests there was any rift between me and Wayne Rooney I would one-thousand per cent refute that," he said. "I had several conversations with Wayne and said very recently that we conducted ourselves amicably. Whatever happens with Wayne now I wish him all the best, whether it is at Everton or somewhere in the United States."

Rooney had already made his mind up to listen to the offers that were going to come his way. His departure from Everton was certain. His return home had been relatively brief, but he'd ended as the top scorer (despite not hitting the net since before Christmas) and had at least one moment that would be remembered forever.

According to former youth team-mate Scott Brown, his second spell at Goodison was unforgettable. "Once he came back and had that Everton shirt on, all of that earlier frustration was gone," Brown says. "It was forgotten. As an Evertonian I was made up that he came back. He scored that hat-trick against West Ham. I'm not sure anyone will ever score a goal like he did that night."

Chapter Twenty-Three

WASHINGTON

'The Beckham effect' is a term coined to describe the impact David Beckham's move to LA Galaxy and the MLS had on the North American game. Beckham spent five years in Los Angeles and there could be no denying the many aspects which seemed to be changed by the end of that spell – the profile of the sport, the extra credibility, its competitive nature. That does not mean it was a runaway success. Beckham faced so many struggles during his time in America, including conflict with his own team-mates and supporters, that are sometimes forgotten when measuring how beneficial that period was. By the end, though, it was almost universally agreed that the 'experiment' had paid dividends.

By contrast, Wayne Rooney spent just two seasons in the MLS and despite arriving with an incredibly high profile, was not expected to have the sort of commercial influence Beckham, the global marketing icon that he was and remains, had. The story of Rooney's short spell in America almost warrants a book on its own due to how he embraced life in the MLS – we'll try and do it justice in the space we have.

Talk of the move to D.C. United picked up pace as soon as the English season concluded. Rooney had a family holiday in Barbados in May and flew from there to Washington for talks. On June 28th, he was greeted by a crowd of hundreds at Dulles International Airport amid speculation he was going to be presented later that day.

United published a statement: "It's official: Wayne Rooney will be suiting up in Black-and-Red. D.C. United announced on Thursday they have signed the English star on a permanent transfer, inking him to a three-and-a-half year deal after weeks of speculation."

Rooney told the club's website that he was looking forward to joining at a time when they were opening a new stadium, adding: "Moving to America and MLS fulfils another career ambition for me. When I visited earlier this summer I was really impressed with everyone I met, and of course the new Audi Field. Now I can't wait to get on the pitch and bring success to this club."

General Partner and CEO Jason Levien described it as a 'seminal moment', adding: "Wayne is a global soccer icon and his presence at D.C. United will elevate our product on the pitch and soccer as a whole in our city and in this country. We're thrilled to have his leadership as we enter this new era at Audi Field."

Rooney was unveiled at a press conference on July 2nd. Mayor Muriel Bowser proclaimed it 'Wayne Rooney day', much to the man's embarrassment, according to Levien. "He's humble," Levien told *City Paper*, revealing that he had rejected offers from the club to try and arrange for him to wear his normal number

10 shirt, which was currently worn by Argentine forward Lucho Acosta. "He said, 'No. I want to fit in. What's the right number for me? You guys let me know.' It's all been that way. People have wondered if he's going to fly differently from the rest of the club for away matches – he's like, 'No, I want to be with the team.'"

Rooney admitted that moving to the capital had greater appeal for him than the hustle and bustle of LA or New York. "It's too hectic," he said. "It's like London. I've never fancied going to live in London. I need my own space and to get away from things when I need to, and D.C. seems to give me that opportunity."

On July 12th, as he was preparing to make his debut, he explained his reasons for leaving England to *ESPN*. "Obviously at Manchester United I wasn't playing as much as I would have liked and I could have stayed there with two years left on my contract and picked up the wages," he said. "But I wanted to play, went back to Everton and had a year there, then Everton made it clear they'd be happy for me to leave. I felt I was doing okay, I was top goalscorer playing most of the season from midfield. But that's football. So, this option became available and I just felt this was the right one."

It would be fair to say that it was more about the league and the location than the form of the team and the calibre of players D.C. had which convinced Rooney to make the move. It was a squad of modest talent – most of their American players were uncapped, and the bulk of the international experience came in Jamaican strikers Darren Mattocks and Dane Kelly. The star of the team was arguably Lucho Acosta, who had come through the ranks at Boca Juniors and had a loan spell at Estudiantes before moving north. Prior to Rooney's signing, D.C. had won just two of their first 13 games. It didn't appear as though Rooney was going into a team that could win the MLS Cup, so there was a feeling that

that was an opportunistic move by the team in order to guarantee fans in attendance at the new stadium.

"There was definitely a feeling it went hand-in-hand, you had the opening of a new stadium and the opportunity to sign a player like Wayne," says Ian Harkes, midfielder at D.C. at the time and son of Sheffield Wednesday legend John Harkes. "The history of D.C. United is that it was such a strong club in the early days of the MLS and they were wanting to get back to that. This was a huge push to get back. They were obviously hoping Rooney would elevate that."

Harkes admits that he wasn't sure what to expect at first, but Rooney quickly won them over: "The buzz around the club was huge. The players were so excited, so were the coaching staff, it was amazing for the whole city to have a star like that join the team. No-one really knew what to expect but just seeing him in training every day, you learn so much from observing the way he carried himself. He was a top pro and gave everything... you know, all that talk about it being a retirement league… that wasn't how he saw it. Maybe he didn't want to go that route, to LA or New York, because others had gone there before. I'm sure Wayne was looking for a team that he could help. We were struggling when he came in."

It certainly felt a world away from what Rooney was used to. He couldn't have been more out of his comfort zone. That feeling would have been exacerbated on the morning of his debut, as he watched England lose their third place play-off in the World Cup on television in his hotel room. If he had accepted Gareth Southgate's invitation earlier in the season, there was every reason to believe he could have been part of a Three Lions side that got to the semi-finals and actually took the lead, before eventually losing in extra-time. Harry Kane, his successor as the talisman up front, scored six goals, taking him to 19 international strikes in just 27 caps. Rooney had been right in his prediction that brighter days were ahead with the young England squad. Now he hoped his judgment on moving to the MLS was equally sound.

In training for the few days before his debut, Rooney had made an instant impression. When David Beckham made his move to the MLS, there was an immediate rift in the dressing room, as Landon Donovan – the poster boy of the American game – was put out at being upstaged. There were no Donovans at D.C. United, and there was no negativity from the squad, just an appreciation for who was now with them.

"There was no resentment as far as I'm aware," says Harkes. "He'd experienced things we could barely dream of being close to. There were no real clashes or egos. He was a leader in his own way because of those experiences and the way he carried himself. He wasn't vocal, he was a quiet guy, definitely in comparison to what we had expected.

"He was so humble, especially considering what he'd achieved. He was a top class person. He was a legend of the game already but he didn't carry himself in that way. He wanted to be one of the group. In one of his first training sessions we had a finishing drill. He didn't miss once. Every touch he had was special. It was one of the best sessions I'd ever seen."

With the game against Vancouver Whitecaps being the first game at Audi Field, the existing D.C. team were 'rewarded' with starting the historic fixture, with Rooney on the bench. The hosts had a 1-0 lead at the break. In the 58th minute, Rooney – sporting the number nine shirt – jogged on to the pitch in front of 20,504 fans who had been chanting 'we want Rooney'. Within a minute, his team were awarded a free-kick 35 yards from goal. Rooney stepped up to take it, but it hit the wall and bounced to safety.

Wayne takes to the field as a second-half substitute on his MLS debut for DC United in a 3–1 win over Vancouver Whitecaps in July 2018

He was involved in the build-up for his side's second goal, and set up the third, laying it off for Paul Arriola to strike sweetly from the edge of the box. "To be honest I've never played with players the calibre of Wayne," Arriola said after the 3-1 win.

"I've said since I came here two weeks ago I want to win," Rooney said. "I'm vocal on and off the pitch. Vocal with the coach. Vocal with my team-mates. We speak about which is the best way to win a football match. My team-mates might look at me as someone who has had a career with Manchester United, Everton and England and they haven't got to that level yet. But I am a D.C. United player now. And I want to win."

The team coach, Ben Olsen, described his new striker as a 'high-quality, elite soccer player' and admitted he would probably ask him for advice. "I would be silly not to," he said. "My approach has always been to have an open-door policy. I am looking to improve as well and while I am still the coach I am sure there will be plenty of dialogue."

Once upon a time, one might have considered that a concern – it would have been easy to imagine Rooney being frustrated with an inexperienced coach, especially taking into account his first time around with David Moyes. This was an older Rooney, but there was a definite curiosity as to how it would all go down.

"We were all wondering how the dynamic would work between Wayne and Ben," says Harkes. "I think there was an understanding that players might be more inclined to appreciate what Wayne had to say more than the coaches. But from Wayne's standing, he was always appreciative of what the coaches and what Ben wanted. He'd give his opinion on things that could be done better but he'd always voice it in a very respectful way."

The reality of how difficult things were at present came as D.C. lost their next two games. It wasn't until his fourth game that

Rooney got on the scoresheet, with a goal that seemed to be from the training ground – he latched on to a through ball and finished through the keeper's legs. The goalkeeper was Tim Howard – his former team-mate from his first few days at Old Trafford. The goal was taken with the sort of familiarity one would expect considering the hours they would have faced off every morning at Carrington.

That match against Howard's Colorado Rapids went to the wire – D.C. winning in the last minute, and Rooney showing such commitment to the cause that he was throwing himself into every challenge. In one such moment, he collided with an opponent and suffered a deep cut on his head, as well as a broken nose. "It shows you what this means to him," a concerned, but proud Olsen said afterwards. "He's in the box, putting his face on the line, understanding that's a big moment...we needed that play. He's selfless."

Big moments and sacrifice – if Rooney's contribution was worthy of praise on that occasion, then what of the next time D.C. played at home, against Orlando City on August 12th? The talk pre-match was of a new tactic Olsen had deployed – taking advantage of their new player's attitude, Olsen wanted his team to play with an aggressive high line.

Rooney was finding himself with a regular problem when he was playing as a striker, as he did here. Several times he would receive the ball and try to go at the Orlando defence. Within seconds he was crowded out. In the 21st minute he was given the ball with just one man on him; within moments there were five bodies suffocating him – he did well to get a pass away to a team-mate. This extra space was going to have to be a side-effect that the D.C. players could take advantage of. Just before half-time, Rooney had the ball in the net, but it was ruled out for offside. There was still time in the first half for Rooney to lay on a goal for

Acosta. Orlando levelled, and the teams exchanged another goal each to go into injury time at the end of the game at 2-2.

There were six minutes of added time; in the sixth, D.C. had a corner, and their goalkeeper David Ousted came up to try and snatch a winner. Orlando were able to clear to their wide left. Will Johnson, their midfielder, chased the ball and was in control of it, although he was still wide and still in his own half. Earlier in the broadcast of the game, the Fox Sports commentators had remarked upon the first-half Rooney crowding incident and discussed that this was the product of degeneration. He no longer possessed that physical burst. He simply did not have the power, the speed to get away from opponents the way he once did; or so they thought. Rooney had not been aware of these comments. What happened next was not borne from desire to prove anyone wrong. It was simply the will to win; the competitive spirit within him that had never gone away.

The pair were midway in the Orlando half; Johnson a good 15 yards closer to the ball than Rooney. The Orlando midfielder tried to take a touch, slowing down on the halfway line. By now, Johnson was in control of the ball, and Rooney was still more than ten yards away. Johnson took the touch. As he tried to take a second, Rooney launched into a desperate slide tackle; it was strong, and successful, with Johnson losing his balance and giving the D.C. player full control of the ball just inside his own half. Rooney took three touches, advancing into the Orlando half, and launched a tremendous cross-field pass with power that seemed impossible to generate considering the lung-busting sprint he had just performed. That whole passage – from the clearance that started the dash to Rooney playing the pass – took 10 seconds. It would have been remarkable in itself. But the pass sailed perfectly into the path of Acosta, the shortest man on the field, who –

perhaps sensing that in moments like this, the footballing gods will smile upon you for taking a chance – got an opportunistic header to it, and the ball was almost carried by the frenzy of the crowd into the far corner.

Acosta's hat-trick won the game – but Rooney's almost superhuman feat was almost instantly recognised as seminal. This would be the moment everyone talked about. This would be the passage of play that would go viral and then be replayed when people wanted to reminisce over one of the most sensational examples of ball recovery and desire ever seen on a football pitch.

"I told him he looked like he was 18 again," defender Kofi Opare told the *Washington Post*. "He said, 'Man, that's the fastest I've ever run.'"

It was more than a passage of play to win a game. It was a moment where the penny – or cent – dropped for Rooney's teammates. This was the best player in the team, doing something that was above and beyond what was expected of him. Because of that effort – because of that *sacrifice* for the team – the reward was significant. "It was huge for everyone involved to see that kind of commitment," admits Harkes. "Seeing his work-rate and his desire to win was the most valuable thing. To track back and win the ball, and still have the quality to get the pass right and contribute at the other end. It showcased what he was all about as a team player. It was a joy to watch.

"It was the kind of moment that makes you think you've all got to put that extra five per cent in. It had a big impact on our mentality. It was a huge driving force for us, a turning point in the season. We witnessed the sacrifice he'd made to get us a result. It was also a message to some of the better players in our team – if Wayne was working that hard, then everyone had to. Nobody had an excuse. It had a big influence on our form."

It had also been a defining game for the growing partnership with Acosta and Rooney. Harkes: "When Wayne first came into the team he played as a lone striker. I think that was difficult because of the quality of passes that were coming in to him, so he seemed to find more joy when he dropped into deeper positions. He was so tactically and technically aware that he was able to control the pace and rhythm of the game more. He seemed to really enjoy that part of it.

"The hardest part seemed to be that difference in quality around him so I know there were conversations with the coaches about where he should play in order to have the best impact. There was a little bit of a feeling-out period between Rooney and Acosta. Lucho was obviously a very talented player. Once Wayne came in and they developed that understanding, that they would help each other out. Their skill together was going to help us tremendously. Once it did, it really clicked."

And once it clicked, so D.C.'s season finally got off the ground. Three days later, Rooney netted two in a 4-1 win over Portland Timbers. The first was taken with all the experience of a top striker; the second a superbly struck free-kick.

The goals continued – a penalty in a win over Atlanta United, and a stunning volley with his left foot in a 3-3 draw with New York Red Bulls. A brace in a 5-0 win over Montreal Impact included a very clever lobbed finish from 35 yards. Two more goals gave his team a 2-1 win over Chicago Fire. Perhaps the very best of the lot came against Toronto in mid-October – in the 18th minute, D.C. were awarded a free-kick 35 yards out. It was to the right side of the goal – if it was there to be struck by anyone, one would have thought it would be better for a left-footer. But Rooney stepped up and curled it with power and precision, over the wall and into the near top corner.

"His class and technique were on show there," recalls Harkes. "It was an illustration of how it was the next step above the players around him. It was world class regardless of the goalkeeper or league. It was a joy to watch."

Rooney's inspiring contribution had lifted D.C. up the table in the Eastern Conference. The poor start to the campaign suggested they would finish outside the play-offs, but seven wins and three draws from the last 10 games had not only got them into the play-offs, it was a run of form that suggested a rosy 2019 was around the corner. In the penultimate game of the season, D.C. won 3-1 over New York City – Rooney scoring twice and Acosta getting the other. The combination was working to thrilling effect, especially for Rooney's opener after eight minutes – Acosta danced around a number of challenges close to the touchline and pulled it back for his strike partner to convert. Acosta had flourished, gaining interest from European clubs, with his confidence through the roof.

The pair faced the media after the game. "We just enjoy playing with each other," Rooney said. "We both play to each other's strengths. It's great to play with players like that because they're always going to create your chances and create chances themselves."

Acosta, through a translator, agreed. "I don't have to say anything about it," he said. "It shows itself on the field how well we connect. He's a great player, very easy player to play with. He makes everything easier, makes us better as a team."

D.C. were knocked out of the MLS Cup in the preliminary round, with Rooney missing one of the penalties in the shoot-out victory for Columbus Crew. There could be nothing held against him – it was obvious that without his contribution, they wouldn't be there in the first place. One D.C. United player told the press: 'Before Rooney, nobody was talking about us, now everybody is'.

"It did feel like that," says Harkes. "Wayne's influence changed that completely, not just because of who he was, but in the form that he brought, the way he lifted everyone around him. We didn't win the play-offs, but just to get us there, just to see the way the team was playing, it was a huge difference."

It was still a strange scenario for Rooney to be in. He was not David Beckham and he was not playing in Los Angeles, or for a team who would seriously challenge for the MLS Cup. So there was a contrast – where Wayne himself was able to still enjoy some of the relative anonymity, but his team-mates were able to feel a much more intense spotlight.

"The difference in media attention stepped up after he signed," Harkes explains. "The whole team felt it. There was a demand on all of us to step up our game. But I'm sure he enjoyed the lifestyle in Washington. Being able to walk around with his family. To go out and do normal things that he'd never been able to do before. I remember one time he went bowling and he came into training talking about how great it was. To the rest of us, we were confused, it was difficult to appreciate just what he'd been through. It used to be strange for us, too, if we'd be travelling. Because soccer players don't have the same sort of fame, sometimes people would just pass by. It would be so strange to be sitting with one of the greatest players to ever play the game and people just walking past as though he was just an ordinary person, not realising who he was."

The off-season came with a peculiar reward. England faced USA in a November friendly at Wembley, and it was announced that Rooney would be called into the squad for the first time in two years. This was no ordinary comeback – this would be a farewell

Rooney is presented with a lifetime achievement award after bringing the curtain down on his international career in the 3-0 friendly win over the USA

performance in Rooney's 120th cap. With England 2-0 up in the 58th minute, Rooney came on for his former team-mate Jesse Lingard, and was given the captain's armband.

Once a divisive figure for the Wembley fans, every touch was cheered, most with the ironic encouragement to 'shoot!' He didn't – and admitted afterwards that he was almost fearful to score, considering the backlash from England legend Peter Shilton, who had heavily criticised Rooney's recall.

England won 3-0 – and Rooney was thrilled to have had the opportunity to have that last game. "Being back at Wembley, in front of the home fans... they gave me a great reception," said Rooney. "It is a moment to savour."

Though some had disregarded it as a farce, to others, it was an opportunity that might not come around again, such as for Jadon Sancho, the 18-year-old Borussia Dortmund winger. "Playing with Wayne Rooney was really great – a dream come true for me," he said. "He's a role model. I told Wayne that I was nervous in the dressing room. He came over and told me to be confident, that I had nothing to lose. I have to say thank you to him."

Rooney – who had predicted big things for England when he had opted out of selection 18 months earlier – again suggested success was on the cards for Gareth Southgate's squad. "England are in very safe hands from what I've seen this week," he said. "The way they are being coached is brilliant. It's a great group of young players who have a bright future. They will go close to being the next team to bring a trophy back for England."

There was no suggestion that Rooney would 'do a Beckham' and go back to a European club on loan for the winter. He was back, fit and ready to help D.C. United from the start of the 2019 campaign. There were new faces there for him to play alongside too. Kelly and Mattocks had departed, with experienced forward

Quincy Amarikwa coming in. The big story was the mooted transfer of Acosta to Paris Saint Germain. The oil-rich club apparently agreed a fee of under $10m to bring in Acosta as an understudy to the injured Neymar, and Acosta travelled to France – but the move did not go through before the end of the January transfer window, and Acosta would line up alongside Rooney once more.

Rooney had struck up a good bond with the new boy Amarikwa. "I'll always speak very highly of him because he's a very genuine guy, he's very open," says Amarikwa. "I found him to be like me in a way that he was naive because he believed in the best intentions of other people. That doesn't always pan out in the positive light you would like... but I liked it a lot about him because it's rare to find people who are genuine and want to do the right thing, especially in professional sports."

Much of the talk in 2019 would centre around how settled Rooney was in America, but his new colleague found the legendary striker to be much more interested in the health of the US game than most would credit.

"The MLS is a league that's been fighting to get its own market share, its own attention and respect. It's a struggle and identity crisis," explains Amarikwa. "A lot of foreign internationals who come here encounter great difficulties navigating the system. It's not as established as they're used to. There isn't as much money. Things that you don't even have to think about in other leagues are things that are massive hindrances to players.

"I started calling it the MSL, the Mental Strength League, because in order to survive you need mental strength. If you come from a place with higher standards it's not until you go to a place where it isn't like that, you're met with the same sort of issues you faced when you were first coming into the professional world. It's a rewiring.

"Take the Premier League – there are consequences. If you lose too many games you'll get relegated, you could lose your job. If you have a bad performance there are a million analysts ready to tell you how bad you are. There is a level of pressure and expectation. When you come to the States it's the polar opposite. You could have the worst game in the world and nobody really cares. Nobody's dragging you for your performance. That creates an issue with your own accountability. You have to hold yourself to standards."

This is where Wayne Rooney's relentless desire for excellence came to the fore once again, as Amarikwa explains. "A lot of players struggle with the fact there are no expectations for them," he says. "Because you showing up was all that was necessary. But in professional sports just showing up is not enough. So a player comes in with the ambition of getting to the play-offs, but that's not necessarily the ambition of the squad they're walking into. Play-offs matter because you want to win an MLS Cup. But if you don't make play-offs you get an extra month's vacation. It's an $800 bonus to get to the play-offs, and sure if you win maybe a $10,000 bonus and after taxes, $5000, but you've taken two months of your time. If you don't make the play-offs you get all this time off and nobody is really going to talk about how you didn't get there.

"And so I appreciate what Wayne did even more, because he did want to win and he was trying to make a positive change. He was trying to positively influence the league, the players, to make everything better. I hadn't seen nor heard of a player of that profile coming into the league and show such a willingness to engage with players, to learn about the players' association and attend some of the meetings, asking questions. Nobody of that profile had even cared to ask those questions.

"I cared, so it was liberating to see a player with Wayne's profile making the same stand. We'd have the conversations and Wayne would vent his frustration. My response would always be, 'Bro, I know, MSL.'. He was a catalyst for conversations like this. The league needed someone like David Beckham for that first big boost. It put MLS on the map.

"What it needed next was a player like Wayne who was coming in with the right intentions. He would speak up on things that were wrong about the system so the league could realise its ambition of being one of the better leagues in the world. Beckham's impact can be seen based on where we got to as a result of his time here, and I feel that Wayne's will be viewed similarly and I believe it should be perceived as more powerful and more valuable."

Amarikwa admits that he was not a big watcher of soccer growing up. "I hadn't ever seen Wayne play until I played against him and then trained with him," he laughs. "I had as unbiased a view on him as possible because I didn't know what came before, other than everyone saying he was one of the greatest of all time, I just assessed the person and player who was in front of me. I could see that his vision was greater than 99.9 per cent of any players I'd ever seen. I watched the passes he made, his movement, the way he approaches the ball to also create space on the opposite side of him to get players to commit because they believe he's going in one direction… the only time I'd seen a player with such a high level was with Thierry Henry at New York Red Bulls.

"He talked to me about how he'd been playing since he was 16. I was asking how many games he played every year. I imagined what his athletic ability must have been like when he had only half the miles on his body, compared to now, when he was still more athletic than most guys on the field. Even where he was at in 2019 it was such a high level. He had developed an efficiency in his game. People would talk about his pace diminishing. But he was timing his runs and passes so well. He was working for the team to help us."

The season started well. A 2-0 win over Atlanta kicked it off, and two weeks later, Real Salt Lake came to the Audi Field, where the pressing game inspired by Rooney paid rich dividends, most notably in the move for his second goal in a 5-0 win, when his team-mates pushed the play up high, winning the ball for their celebrated striker to finish cheekily over the keeper. Rooney followed that with a tap-in in the second half to complete his first MLS hat-trick.

The following week in Orlando, Rooney scored what turned out to be the winning goal with an outrageous free-kick almost from the corner flag; it looked to be a deliberate shot, struck with accuracy into the far top corner.

When D.C. travelled to Ohio to face Columbus Crew in late April, he found the visiting team ready to shower him with compliments. "His track record speaks for itself," said Crew captain Will Trapp. "But what I think he does so well is bring other players into the game. And then that can be a focal point and can make other players shine."

Columbus head coach Caleb Porter paid him a compliment at the same time as seemingly hugely underestimating him. "I think that's the biggest thing with him, he's just a fox in the box and he's just going to get to his spot and he's not going to miss much," Porter said. "He's deadly. When you look at him, he's strong but he's not all that quick and he's not a dribbler. He's just a box striker and he's just lethal and he can just crush a ball with both feet, placement, power."

He was deadly alright – Rooney scored the only goal of the match, another free-kick from the edge of the box. And if there was anyone left who doubted his ability as a top-level player, they were left to eat their words in late June, as Orlando City once again found themselves victims of a remarkable act of brilliance from the legendary England forward. There would be no tracking back to regain a seemingly lost ball and create a last-minute winner. No free-kick from an impossible angle. Somehow, he found a way to top both of those moments.

Just 10 minutes had been played. Orlando were on the attack. D.C. cleared their lines – the ball bounced off an opponent and towards Rooney, 15 yards inside his own half. It was rolling with a generous momentum, but everybody in the stadium expected Rooney to try and push the play upfield. In between the time the ball had bounced off the opponent, and the time it took to fall under Rooney's control – we're talking less than a second in real time – he had already decided to try something different.

Goalkeeper Brian Rowe was on the edge of his box.

Rooney swung back his right arm, as if his foot was connected to it by a trigger. Audi Field roared with anticipation. Rowe knew immediately he was in no-man's land.

There was a time when scoring from the halfway line was considered so unthinkable that for a generation, Pele's mere *attempt* at it in the 1970 World Cup was heralded as one of the pinnacles in footballing imagination. When David Beckham scored from that area of the pitch in 1996, it was seen as a once-in-a-lifetime achievement. Other players had done it since. Beckham himself had done it again – and on these shores. Balls were lighter now. It was easier to do. Easier, but still not easy. And Beckham's MLS version came in an unguarded net. Rowe was still in attendance – he was not in an irresponsible position. Rooney's ingenuity needed to be matched by excellent execution.

A superlative simply does not exist to do justice to how incredibly perfect his shot was. Rowe was beaten from the moment the ball was struck. All that was left was for it to be struck true enough to be on target; and, of course, it was. A once-in-a-lifetime goal which Wayne Rooney had now scored for each club he'd played for.

"It was a ridiculous goal," says Ian Harkes (who, by this time, had left D.C.). "But in a strange way you almost expected it from him. He'd mess around in training and try things like that. His technique was just a joke. It was a goal for the ages."

Because Rooney was the ultimate team player, a great goalscorer and a scorer of great goals; because he had been a world-class number nine or 10, he was many things to many people, and it's not quite as clear cut as saying one moment in his career was definitively better than another. Take the opinion of Amarikwa, who still has a fondness for the assist against Orlando, and he wasn't even at D.C. at that moment.

"It's a matter of taste because I really appreciated what Wayne did where he raced back to the halfway line and tackled," he says. "But, the goal against Orlando was impressive in its own way and what I really appreciated is the moment where Wayne identifies there's a chance to score. He looks to see where the goalkeeper is. The accuracy was incredible. The sight of the goalkeeper trying to get there when you know he's already beat… it makes the camera angle even better on the replay. But even with that goal there's a sequence of events, almost a chess move, that have to pan out for it to work. It's his awareness and control of the situation to make it happen. To create that set-up. I'm impressed with that almost more than the execution."

What is possibly the most impressive element of all is that it came from intuition and not strategy. It was more refined than the wildebeest that was wrecking professional defences as a 16-year-old, or scoring Champions League hat-tricks as an 18-year-old. But it was still a part of the core Wayne Rooney, the inimitable quality he possessed that nobody else on the planet did. Not Ronaldo. Not Messi. This was something he was capable of that even they were not. To have the imagination and awareness to go from receiving a ball deep in his own half and, within a second, decide to go for goal from over 75 yards – what more could one do but simply be grateful to watch it play out?

It was that instinct which had elevated everyone around him. It didn't always translate into results. But it did help his team-mates enormously. The timing of his runs made passes look better. The timing of his passes made his team-mates' positioning look better. In a mid-July game against New England Revolution, Rooney's team were losing 2-1 with four minutes remaining. It had been a bad-tempered game, with Rooney growing frustrated with what he perceived to be poor officiating standards. The ex-England man stood over a free-kick; it looked as though he would swing it deep to the far post, where all the tallest players were congregating.

As he prepared to strike the ball, he noted Amarikwa had pulled off to the near post. The kick was so far out that the Revs had not even bothered to assemble a wall, instead packing out the danger zone. Rooney's decision-making here was as ingenious as his goal against Orlando; he played the ball to Amarikwa, who pulled away from the defender closest to him, and found just about the only space there was to find in a packed penalty box, hooking the ball on the volley into the goal.

It looked as if it had been crafted through hours of practice, but according to the goalscorer: "It wasn't from the training pitch. I had positioned myself left of the box. It takes a highly-skilled player to be able to both see the pass and execute it. It wasn't a matter of going through it in training, it was more a result of general awareness. Wayne's ability to process that information and in the heat of the game, take the chance to try something different."

From the way things were going on the pitch, anyone would have thought Rooney was on his way to surpassing the feat of any Premier League player who had made that transatlantic move. However, the day after Rooney's worst result in America – a 5-1 home defeat to Philadelphia Union in early August – D.C. issued a statement that shocked fans. Rooney would be returning to England at the conclusion of the 2019 MLS season, to become player-coach at Derby County. At least, the timing of the announcement was a shock – it had been rumoured for weeks that Rooney's family were growing homesick.

"My time in Major League Soccer is something I will always be proud of," Rooney said. "The supporters in the Screaming Eagles, Barra Brava and District Ultras have made my time in America so enjoyable. While the decision to move home was a tough one, family is everything to us. I would like to thank everyone at D.C. United for the incredible support."

Rooney missed the next game against Los Angeles Galaxy with a reported sickness; he certainly appeared to have a greater liberation with expressing how sick he suddenly felt with aspects of the game in the MLS. He was back for the following game against Vancouver, but was brought off when it seemed he might be sent off for continual arguments with the officials. As he stormed off the pitch he barked 'every fucking game' to the fourth official. His disillusionment continued on social media, as he tweeted: "Looking forward to a 12-hour travel day which could be done in six but hey this is MLS."

In the next game, Rooney certainly seemed to have his cards marked – and he was sent off after just 24 minutes of the game against New York Red Bulls, after his tussle with Cristian Cásseres Jr. was seen as more than the 'easing him out' Rooney later claimed it to be. "I think anyone who knows football can see what the intent was," he said. "I'm very disappointed... I need to be careful with what I say."

Rooney's D.C. United career ended with a 5-1 defeat in the MLS Cup first round to Toronto. In real time, he'd been there for around 15 months. His incoming transfer had not been politicised in the same way as Beckham's. You could reason that Beckham's was the transfer that removed that conversation for the likes of Rooney, Lampard, Cole, Henry, Gerrard et al. A move to the MLS didn't need to be justified anymore, even if the North American game was still on a journey to having the sort of respect it wanted. That much was an insular battle. A battle Rooney faced and one he – for a while – embraced. He complained about the standard of refereeing. About the absurdity of some of the scheduling and travel times. About the disparity in pay between domestic and foreign players. He was not able to initiate change – so, while his move *to* America was not politicised, it could be argued that his move back home certainly was.

"He was there to win," says Amarikwa. "To be a good team-mate, a good person. To make a good impact and positive impact. But when you're there and see the limitations you realise it's much more difficult than you thought. Still, Wayne gave it his all. Sometimes that isn't enough. He wasn't there to just go through the motions because if he was, he wouldn't have lasted as long as he did. It's a testament to his character that he didn't want to. That he wanted to compete, win, and make changes."

It could also be argued that Rooney left without making the changes he wanted to see. But Amarikwa sees it differently. He sees the move as a way of forcing those conversations to begin –

and therefore, could ultimately mean Rooney's time in the US will see him as the most influential of all European imports.

"The most influential thing Wayne could do *was* leave," he says. "He came. He was in with the right intention. He was going down every possible path he could to elicit the change, to the point where the only real statement that would catch the attention of the world would be leaving. It brought a focus on to why he was leaving as early as he did when he was playing so well.

"A while after he left he got in touch and asked how things were. 'Bro, you know how it is, MSL.' I had a show where I talk about issues in the game and he volunteered to come on and speak about his experience. He spoke about how owners were taking advantage of players, how and why the system needs to be improved. Someone who had just left because they didn't care wouldn't have done that. Beckham never talked about the pay discrepancy of a guy making $30,000 a year passing him the ball. Zlatan didn't come in trying to help, he just shit on the league. '*I'm a Ferrari, they're Fiats. I am the MLS*'. Fuck you, man.

"Wayne gave our league and our players respect. He saw what was happening and it did affect him because he is such a genuine guy, he couldn't turn a blind eye and let it go. He couldn't pretend it wasn't happening and he spoke out against it. It was a catalyst that set into motion positive changes for the future."

For Ian Harkes, Rooney's spell provided memories that will last a lifetime. He says: "He always had time for everyone. If some of the younger guys were staying behind for extra training, he'd often stay as well and talk to us about finishing. He'd try and help our technique in striking the ball. Sometimes I think back about those times and it just hits me that I was standing there speaking with Wayne Rooney. It was a special time."

Chapter Twenty-Four

BATTERING RAM

I n a role reversal to what is usually expected, it was clear that Wayne Rooney's return to England *from* America was the catalyst for the winding down of his career. Upon his unveiling as a Derby County player, Rooney described it as the 'next transition'.

"I will keep playing until my body says I can't any more," he said. "We've got four young boys and certainly for my oldest it is a crucial time in his schooling. The decision to come and play here in England and develop as a coach with (Derby manager) Phillip Cocu was too good to turn down. Firstly, I'm a player and feel I have a lot of quality to bring to the squad. But, secondly, I want to learn from Phillip for when I take the next step."

Cocu had succeeded Rooney's former England team-mate Frank Lampard at Pride Park. The new Derby player was asked if his eventual plan was to move into management.

"It's great to see my ex-team-mates going into management," he said. "I have always had the ambition to do it. Coaching is what I want to do long-term but my main focus will be on playing and learning. In the next 18 months I will try to learn good habits."

However, there was also a bad habit that was connected to his signing. There was a great deal of controversy when Rooney held up his shirt, with the number 32, a number he'd never worn in his career. Derby owner Mel Morris explained how it was a result of a record-breaking sponsorship deal with Derby's shirt sponsor, gambling company 32Red.

There were plenty who were cynical about the deal, with Professor Jim Orford (a psychologist who studied gambling) telling the BBC: "It's obvious what it is there for. It won't say 32Red, it will just be 32, but it clearly is meant to be a link to 32Red and people will start to associate the number 32 with gambling and gambling on 32Red. It is a loophole in the law...They are trying to just slip it in and get around the regulations."

A spokesman for the betting company insisted it 'wouldn't matter what number' he wore. "As Wayne Rooney said himself during his press conference, the squad number means nothing. The number is a separate issue to the logo," they said. "Other players also wear the number in the Championship – 32Red don't have a trademark on the number 32."

Whatever the truth, when it was time for Rooney to make his debut, more numbers were mentioned. The first was 34, his age. The physicality of the Championship was always going to be a challenge, especially for a player like Rooney who thrived on being in the thick of the action. He proved himself up for the fight, providing the 174th assist of his career when his free-kick was converted by Jack Marriott in a 2-1 win over Barnsley. The other numbers were not revealed, but Derby's players were said to be furious at the fact that the club had not paid them their wages on time. It was not clear whether Rooney's reported £100,000 salary was one of those affected.

Derby were struggling in the bottom half of the division. Rooney, who had been made captain, had high hopes. "I had no doubts about my body holding up," said Rooney. "I have played at a high level in the US. As long as I am fit I will be okay. This is a new chapter in my career and I want to help Derby get promotion."

Cocu was pleased with his contribution, praising his "great vision". Rooney had played at the top of a midfield diamond, but played in a much deeper role in the FA Cup game at Crystal Palace – he was outstanding as the Rams upset their Premier League opponents with a 1-0 win. The scorer, Chris Martin, spoke glowingly of the impact Rooney had made. "The Rooney effect has really paid off so far," said Martin. "We have seen that quality, leadership and experience in training. It has been everything we expected and maybe a bit more. His talking, his experience, helping the young lads and everybody, organising and quality on the ball... it has brought a real lift to the place."

In the league, Rooney netted his first two goals for the club at the end of January. The first was a deflected effort against Luton in a 3-2 defeat, but the second was definitely more memorable – a sublime free-kick in a 4-0 win over Stoke.

The cup run took them to Northampton, then back to Pride Park as the Cobblers forced a replay. Rooney created a goal and scored one as the replay was won comfortably – setting up an emotional fixture against Manchester United in the fifth round. "It is a big game," he said beforehand. "They will be favourites. I love the club, but for this 90 minutes I want us to win and to try to go through."

He was again warmly applauded by the United fans, who by

now were following a very different team to the one he'd left behind. They were now coached by Rooney's former team-mate, Ole Gunnar Solskjaer, and claimed a 3-0 win through goals by on-loan signing Odion Ighalo and Luke Shaw.

Though there was no way of knowing it at the time – for a multitude of different reasons – this was Wayne Rooney's last professional match in front of a crowd. Maybe he would have wanted it this way.

The first reason was the Covid-19 pandemic. The outbreak shook the world, causing unprecedented disruption to the life of almost everyone on the planet. Elite sport was postponed. Major events and competitions were cancelled. The pursuit of trophies and promotion took a backseat as the whole of humanity faced a crisis the likes of which it had never endured before. When it was finally deemed permissible for the football season to resume in June, there was a swell of positivity despite the fact that no crowds would be allowed due to concerns of the spread of the virus.

Derby were hoping for a late push for the play-offs. It seemed on the cards when the first two games after the restart were won, first at Millwall and then at home to Reading. At Preston on July 1st, Rooney served up a real treat. Derby were awarded a free-kick 20 yards from goal. It was ideally placed to be struck at the near post, but Rooney caught the goalkeeper out, curling the ball magnificently into the far corner to give his team a 1-0 win.

Cocu was keen to suggest that the inspirational form of the former England captain might take Derby into a position they could have only dreamed of before his arrival. "It won't be easy to end up in the top six," he said. "But the moment we reach the play-offs, we will see how we can use the experience of myself, the staff and Wayne Rooney. He is a great asset for our team. He was a key player who can make the difference at the top of the Premier

League or national team. There are only a few of those players, so we are extremely pleased.

"In my first thoughts, we were talking about playing him as a striker or a number 10. But sometimes you see a certain balance in a team and the qualities of a player suit something else. It was maybe a surprise that he ended up playing like a holding mid-fielder. He does it so well with his vision and passing game. He is really important in that position. Sometimes later in your career you can get another position and surprise yourself."

Cocu was not so happy with how the next few games went. Derby drew at home to Nottingham Forest and lost consecutive games against West Brom, Brentford and at Cardiff, where Rooney was caught in possession for one of the Bluebirds' goals. "There's been too many mistakes – and that's why we are not in the play-offs," he moaned.

Those mid-season ambitions had disintegrated and the form had been so poor that there were concerns about how the new season would go. Supporters were right to be worried, as Derby were in a relegation fight from the first game.

Rooney played 11 more times for the Rams – 10 in the league and one in the League Cup. It was unfamiliar territory. Nine of those games were lost. Only one was won. That came at Carrow Road in early October. Cocu was planning to bring Rooney off at the next break in play late in the game; but that stoppage came as his team were awarded a free-kick in the 87th minute. Rooney stayed on to take the kick – and it was a wonderful effort, over the wall and past the goalkeeper. Cocu breathed a sigh of relief – but, as the poor results returned and piled up, he found himself with nowhere to go. After a defeat to Barnsley on November 7th, the Dutchman was dismissed.

It was immediately reported that Rooney would be the 'senior figure' in an interim coaching set-up which included coaches Liam Rosenior, Shay Given and Justin Walker. With Derby delaying the appointment of a new permanent manager while they were in the process of a takeover, it was speculated that Rooney would be the first name they would consider for the role.

On November 19th, two days before the game against Bristol City, he admitted he would want the job. "I am ambitious and I want to go into management," he said. "I don't know how long this situation is going to last but I wouldn't be an ambitious person if I said I didn't want the job."

Rooney played the full 90 minutes in his deep midfield role at Ashton Gate as Bristol won late on, and then again at Middlesbrough on November 25th, where the hosts won 3-0 amid a poor Derby display.

Derby's next game was against Wycombe Wanderers. Rooney announced before the game that he was not going to play, explaining he didn't think it was possible to play and manage the team in the long-term. It was suggested to him that the match at the Riverside could be his last ever professional game. "That possibility is there," he admitted. "I will speak to the new owners once it is finalised and see where we go from there."

Rosenior had stressed that the capitulation at Middlesbrough had to be treated as a 'watershed moment'. Rooney, with his concentration now solely on management, had a run of fixtures to try and generate some positive momentum. It started well – Derby drew four and won two of their six games before Christmas. Those 10 points were transformative, pulling Derby level with Nottingham Forest, who were in 21st – separated either side of the relegation zone by one goal in Forest's favour.

On Boxing Day, Derby fell to a cruel 96th-minute defeat to Preston, but made up for that in the last game of 2020 with a thrilling 4-0 win at Birmingham. For the first time in the season, Derby were out of the relegation zone and looking up. "I felt that performance has been coming for a few weeks," Rooney beamed. "It was nice to relax and try to enjoy it. We are starting to see a team who believe in themselves, results are getting better and you can see confidence growing."

Success comes with a cost: maybe not for Wayne Rooney, whose performance as manager earned him the permanent role at Derby that he'd openly coveted, but for the sport of football, which lost one of its playing legends on January 15th, 2021 as Rooney simultaneously confirmed his retirement.

With 883 senior appearances, 366 goals, a bagful of trophies and a multitude of records, Wayne Rooney had ensured nobody would ever forget his name, as he closed the chapter on one of the all-time great football careers.

Chapter Twenty-Five

EMOTION

F ew players in history have been as evocative as Wayne Rooney. That much can be ascertained from the visceral reactions from the supporters of Everton and Manchester United in 2004 and 2010. The connection between player and fanbase was as strong as it could be, because the fans saw themselves in him. They saw him play on the pitch as he would on the streets; kids saw him do extraordinary things and make them moments to aspire towards, and adults saw a breath of fresh air, a boy playing with a liberation that reminded them of their own youth.

There were different versions of Wayne Rooney. The free spirit that probably existed up until 2007. The selfless team player who still benefited from his own sacrifice for the next two years or so. The out-and-out scorer of 2009/10. He was, unquestionably, world class in all of these roles.

From 2010, he was able to fit seamlessly into the role of nine or

10, however the team needed him. There was always a percentage of observers – this writer included – who occasionally missed the earlier incarnation of Rooney, who excelled with a team built around him before he was so consciously aware of professional discipline and responsibilities. If ever there is an argument about fulfilled potential – projected as it always is against Messi and Ronaldo – it often comes back to this period of Wayne's career. You have to frame the argument another way – is what was lost outweighed by what was gained? The answer is emphatically yes, because the trophy count and personal accolades speak for themselves.

When it comes to the issue of his individual accomplishments, time will help to develop a greater appreciation. Frustratingly, that might not happen at international level. The number of international games has increased over the years, making it easier to win caps. The number of, with all due respect, weaker nations included in qualifying groups has also increased, which makes it theoretically easier to score goals. None of this takes away from Harry Kane, who, as of November 2021, has 48 goals in 67 caps – it is not set in stone that he can register another six goals to surpass Rooney, but it is not unreasonable to project that it will happen. One would hope that it won't diminish the perspective of Rooney's remarkable achievement.

Perhaps that perception will be associated with his place as the last of the 'Golden Generation' which ultimately failed to deliver at a major international tournament. Maybe time will be more generous there, with some reassessment to take into account the injuries he went into tournaments with and the quality of players around him. Perhaps Kane is a perfect example – he scored six goals at the 2018 World Cup, but few would genuinely assert that his impact at that tournament was comparable with the explosion Rooney made in 2004.

At club level, there can be little doubt that he will be remembered as one of the all-time greats. As his youth team pal Scott Brown puts it: "They should have statues outside Old Trafford. I would say he's the best player the country has ever had. He did brilliantly for England, and became the leading goalscorer. He became the leading goalscorer for the biggest club in the country and won everything. He did it on the major stage."

Brown has a point, although the subject of statues at Old Trafford is a complicated business. At time of writing there are a few on the grounds of the stadium – statues of legendary managers Sir Matt Busby and Sir Alex Ferguson. A 'Holy Trinity' statue of George Best, Bobby Charlton and Denis Law. Law has another statue high up in the stairwell at the top of the Stretford End. There were years spent lobbying to get a statue in honour of Jimmy Murphy, Busby's legendary coach. Where would you go from there? Eric Cantona? Ronaldo? Another trinity statue of Neville, Scholes and Giggs? At Arsenal, their all-time leading scorer Thierry Henry has a statue. In 2021, Manchester City announced that Sergio Aguero, who had scored more goals for them than any other player, would get a statue outside the Etihad Stadium. At the very least, Rooney's feats make him most worthy of conversation either outside Old Trafford or Wembley, and should one be commissioned, nobody could say it wasn't earned.

In almost every season in his career, Rooney scored a goal that was so good it would be another player's best ever. The frequency of that magnificence was much too strong for those goals to be flukes. The accounts of training ground attempts at the bewildering – and the memory of those that almost came off, such as the halfway line effort against Manchester City in 2009 – emphasise that these were products of imagination and intent. You simply cannot overstate just how talented a footballer has to be for them

Having been appointed permanent manager of Derby County in January 2021, Rooney announced his retirement from playing, bringing an end to an illustrious and record-breaking 19-year senior career

to be able to score a goal from the halfway line three times in his career. How confident they are in their own ability to do it. How at ease they are with the biggest stage in football that – with the scores level late into the toughest game of the season – he could throw his body into the air to try and score an overhead kick.

Rooney's career was pure Roy Race, though even *Roy of the Rovers* creator Frank Pepper would have found it stretching the boundaries of credibility to suggest one player could score three times from the middle of the pitch in top-level games. It's all the more absurd because all of those long-range goals came after the youthful opportunism was replaced by maturity.

It says much about the career Rooney had that those goals would probably not be the first which spring to mind when thinking about his best ever. Everton fans might be inclined to think of the Arsenal 'announcement' goal. D.C. United supporters might think of another Rooney moment that wasn't even a goal as their favourite. Manchester United fans could think of the goal against City in 2011. Considering Ferguson endorsed it as the greatest ever Old Trafford goal, you can consider it gold standard.

To conclude this book, I will leave with my own personal favourite. The overhead kick is difficult to ignore. But the best ever and your favourite moment are often two different things because even in the subjective world of football, you can differentiate between the two. I was lucky enough to have very different views of two of Rooney's best ever goals at Old Trafford. For the goal against City, I was in K Stand. The suspended motion description is the one I often return to when I'm talking about that goal with friends. I think about it now as one of the most jaw-dropping things I've ever seen, and I'm old enough to have seen Bryan Robson rampaging through the pitch dragging the famous Manchester United as if they were a one-man team; old enough to have seen Eric Cantona look as though he was two-foot taller than everyone else on the pitch. Old enough to have seen the Class of 92 mature and Ole Gunnar Solsk-jaer's right-footed stab in 1999.

So too is one of my best friends, Dan, who was at the end of the row – I can still remember turning to search for his face, to see he wore the same incredulous expression as me. Football is as much about the people you see at the game as it is about what happens on the pitch and that goal always reminds me of this.

Almost as vivid is the goal against Newcastle, for which I was in the North Stand. I can still visualise Rooney striking the ball, his body positioned *in the air* as though mid-gallop, the thrash of the ball so powerful that it might still be travelling now if the net hadn't been in the way. But it's that feeling of something bigger than just a goal which sticks with me, and it's why my favourite memory of Rooney is his Manchester United debut. For those of us old enough to wish Paul Gascoigne had signed for the club after thrilling for England and for his club, this was our moment, really. All of the goals were taken with such devastating composure, even if none would feature in his top five or even top 10 in terms of quality. It was enough to take your breath away.

Manchester United have been blessed with many great players, enough for there to be a debate over who is the best of all time. Rooney is now a part of that conversation. Old Trafford has been blessed with many memorable occasions – be it a goal, a game, a landmark, or outstanding performance. Not everything can be historically significant, and so it is even rarer to know that you are observing something of that nature as it unfolds. I can remember walking down the Warwick Road on the evening of September 28th, 2004, and remarking to my brother that we had just witnessed history, and wondering if we had seen the start of one of the greatest careers of all-time. We had.

Acknowledgements

A debt of gratitude is owed to the following people who helped to make this book what it is. Scott Brown, Phil Marsh, Lee Lawrence, Nick Chadwick, Mark Roberts, Rene Meulensteen, Roy Carroll, Fabio & Rafael Da Silva, Ian Harkes, Quincy Amarikwa, and more, for giving your time to speak so openly.

Thanks, as always, to Barney Chilton, Eifion Evans, Barry Shmeizer, Mark Foster (twice!), Stanley Chow, Matthew Smallwood, Bob Bolton, Alan Monger, Justin Eagleton, Roy Cavanagh, Rory Tompkins, Tony Park, Steve Hobin and Rose Cook-Monk. Thanks to Calum Best. To Sammy McIlroy, Paul Parker, Gordon Hill.

Thanks to Paddy Barclay, Danny Taylor, Adam Crafton, and David McDonnell.

Thanks to Dan, Kim and Alex. Dan, your support on this journey, which is connected to this book in a way that only we know, is so precious to me. Thank you.

A big debt of gratitude as always to Dave Murphy, Caroline and the kids. Thanks to Steve and Gem. Oyvind Enger. To Phil, Mikiel and Charlotte Gatt. To Charlie Baker and family. To Gruff, Hayley and Elfyn Roberts. Thank you to Mike Pieri.

I want to thank Nick Walters for your valuable guidance. Thanks to Paul Dove for your enduring support of my work, to Claire Brown for being the best at what you do, and to all the team at Reach Sport.

To my family. To Steven Marrable, whose support, as always, means so much. To my nephews, Freddy, Noah and Logan.

To my wonderful wife – your support of me and faith and belief in the best of me is everything.